PRIORITIES FOR LIVING
Series

REAL LIFE, REAL PEOPLE

➤*Drawing comfort and inspiration from the experiences of Bible personalities*

THOMAS NELSON PUBLISHERS
Nashville • Atlanta • London • Vancouver

Acknowledgments appear on page iv.

Contents

Acknowledgments iv

Foreword v

Introduction: Real Life Stories vi

Chapter 1: Heroes with Human Faces 1

Chapter 2: The Troubled Path of the Prodigal 17

Chapter 3: Keeping in Step with God 31

Chapter 4: Encounters with the Living God 46

Chapter 5: The Healer's Transforming Touch 62

Chapter 6: The Darkness of Despair, the Light of Hope 79

Chapter 7: Little People Who Made a Big Difference 89

Chapter 8: Making Our Footsteps Firm 100

Chapter 9: Those Who Found True Prosperity 113

Chapter 10: Temporary Hardships, Lasting Rewards 126

Chapter 11: Ambassadors of God's Kingdom 137

Chapter 12: Spiritual Living in a Material World 151

Chapter 13: So Great a Cloud of Witnesses 162

Leader's Guide 171

◆ *Acknowledgments* ◆

Narrative and questions written by Timothy J. Richards.

◆ Foreword ◆

The *Priorities for Living* series has been created to offer you friendly companions for discovering the relevance of God's Word and for applying it to everyday life. The series addresses a variety of issues that believers face in today's world. It contains a wide selection of articles and relevant Scripture from *The Word In Life Study Bible*, which allow these workbooks to be used as independent tools for individual or group study. Each workbook in the series is based on a theme that has been developed in *The Word In Life Study Bible*.

It has been said that Scripture was not written merely to be read, but to change lives. James urges us to be "doers of the word, and not hearers only" (James 1:22). The purpose of God's Word is to help us become more like Jesus Christ by making the Word of God part of our lives. *The Word In Life Study Bible* was created to help us discover how to relate God's Word to the world we live in.

Applying biblical truth today is not always easy—especially since the Bible was written thousands of years ago. Many wonder how the Bible can be connected to today's complex society. However, as you explore the pages of this book, you will discover how surprisingly relevant God's Word is to your daily life and how you can make a difference in your world.

REAL LIFE STORIES

Nothing possesses the power to move or inspire like a true-life story. There's something particularly fascinating and meaningful about actual people caught up in the rush of events. In part, it's the thrill of vicarious experience, as we imagine what we ourselves might do in the same circumstances. But in addition it's the knowledge that we are witnesses to things that really happened to human beings like us. And through our common humanity, we share in their actions and experiences. If it happened to them, it could happen to us. If they acted in a particular way, we could, too. And that's why even great fiction can't live up to the real thing.

The Bible is full of such real-life stories. Believers who are tempted to think of the Bible as nothing but a book of theology should keep this in mind. The message of Scripture is delivered against a panorama of real lives and real people.

There's a very important reason for this: the spiritual truths the Bible presents are not meant to be mere theory—they are to be put into practice and lived out in our lives. When we look at the people who lived through the events of the Bible, both great and small, we see biblical truths not only explained but portrayed. In this way, the men and women of the Bible reveal to us what it means to live by the Word of God.

Who Are These People?

Some Christians may wonder how much they can really learn from the people of the Bible. After all, they were unique individuals, especially chosen by God. What can ordinary people gain by examining their lives? And besides, they lived thousands of years ago. What can someone who lives in the modern world learn from them?

But take a closer look and you'll see that the men and women of the Bible were people just like us. God didn't go looking for superhumans to whom to reveal Himself. He did not choose His disciples on the basis of their great leadership abilities or stature in society. On the contrary, "God has chosen the weak things of the world to put to shame the things which are mighty" (1 Cor. 1:27). The believers of the past possessed all the flaws and frailties we do. When we seek to emulate them, we don't have to worry that we are trying to live up to some impossible standard.

And though life in the modern world is quite different than life in ancient times, the fundamental challenges to living a life of faith remain the same. They include remaining faithful to God's will; overcoming the challenges to faith—such as fear, discouragement, suffering, and self-doubts; and incorporating our beliefs into every aspect of our lives—our work, our wealth, our relationships and our ministry in the world.

We are all on the same road—toward perfection in Christ. The believers of old are our guides on the road ahead, there to provide direction for those who follow. By observing the struggles they faced and the successes they achieved, our own walk becomes a little easier and our destination more sure.

How To Use This Book

The Word In Life workbook you hold in your hands is designed to help you understand and apply God's Word in your daily life. Intended for individual use, this workbook may also be *used as a guide for group study. A Leader's Guide has been included in the back of the book for this purpose. In either case, you will benefit from having your own workbook to record your personal and private responses.*

Each chapter treats a specific theme of relevance to the modern believer. The lessons are completely self-contained, with a mix of articles, passages from Scripture, and illustrative stories that explore the topic under investigation.

Questions in the workbook encourage you to personalize each issue, and find practical application for what you learn in your life. The workbook is a tool for opening your heart to Scripture and exposing areas of your life in need of improvement. But you are the one who does the real work! Give your responses thoughtful consideration, and you'll find your attitudes and beliefs challenged and clarified. As new understanding emerges, you'll begin to see the rich possibilities for experiencing a vibrant life in Christ, just like the believers of old!

HEROES WITH HUMAN FACES

Karen opened the door to her apartment, nearly dropping her purse. Her head was still spinning from the events of the previous hour.

Her roommate, Anne, stifled a laugh when she saw her friend's dazed expression.

"Are you all right?" asked Anne. "You look like you've just seen a ghost."

Karen took a deep breath. "I think I just did."

"What happened?" Anne asked, with a look of concern.

"Do you remember when Eric called me a couple of weeks ago?"

Anne nodded. Karen had told her that Eric was an old flame.

"He called me today, and we went out for a cup of coffee after I got off work. And . . ." Karen paused, "you're not going to believe this."

"What?"

"He asked me to *marry him!*" Karen burst out.

"You're kidding!" gasped Anne. "Right out of the blue?"

"Right out of the blue!" Karen rolled her eyes upward. "I think I need to sit down," she said as she collapsed onto the sofa beside Anne.

After a minute or two, Anne grew serious. She felt responsible for Karen, for she had been instrumental in bringing her friend to the Lord following her divorce.

"What did you tell him?" Anne asked.

I was so surprised. I just told him I would have to think about it."

"Is he a Christian?"

"I don't think so but he's a real nice guy. He has a good job, and he says he's ready to settle down. Maybe this is another chance for Jamie to have a full-time father. And I'm not getting any younger either. What do you think I ought to do?"

Anne smiled sympathetically. "I know it's been hard for you being a single mother. But you really need to turn to God to see what is the right thing for you."

Anne picked up her Bible and together they read through the scriptural teaching on marriage. In addition to 1 Corinthians 7, the words of 2 Corinthians 6:14 made an immediate impression on Karen: "Do not be unequally yoked together with unbelievers. For what fellowship has righteousness with lawlessness?"

Three weeks passed, while Karen struggled to make a decision on the matter. She saw

Eric several times during those weeks. She was struck by how open and sincere he was, and he was always gentle and attentive with Jamie, who seemed taken with him. As a potential mate, Eric seemed almost ideal—except he wasn't a Christian. In fact, every time she mentioned Christ, he quickly changed the subject.

Anne continued to encourage Karen to rely on God, and follow His will for her. But doubts troubled her. Did God expect her to be alone the rest of her life? How would she manage to earn a decent living and raise Jamie all alone?

She remembered with chagrin what her cousin Margaret had said to her. *At your age, you might not get another chance, Karen. Divorcees with children aren't exactly in great demand.*

It would be so easy to take the chance that had been offered to her. Was she strong enough to live the life God wanted for her?

One night after dinner with Eric, Karen realized that she had to make a decision. She began to pray.

"Dear God, I know you don't really want me to marry Eric, but I'm afraid. Life has been so hard since my divorce. And now I'm starting to have feelings for Eric. If I'm not supposed to marry him, I need to stop seeing him. I want to obey you, but I don't know if I'm strong enough to do the right thing. Please help me to put my trust in you, Lord. Help me to make the right decision. In your name, Amen."

◆ ◆ ◆ ◆ ◆ ◆ ◆ ◆ ◆

At times, life seems full of difficult choices. If you've ever had to face a tough decision like Karen's, you know what a test it can be to your faith. In our lives as followers of Christ, we will all face such challenges, and be called upon to rely on God's Word and obey His will for us. At such times, it can seem more than any ordinary human being can bear.

Fortunately, we can turn to Scriptures to see others whose faith has been tested by difficult circumstances. Their firm faith can encourage us to rely on God and follow His will for our lives when tough choices have to be made.

Here is a woman who was confronted with a dilemma similar in some ways to the situation Karen found herself in. The situation demanded faithful submission to God's will, but to submit likely meant a life as a single mother, lonely and destitute. Let's see what she chose to do.

THE MAIDSERVANT OF THE LORD

When Gabriel appeared to Mary of Nazareth (Luke 1:26–38), she was perhaps no more than 15 years old. His startling announcement—that she would soon bear the very Son of the Highest—meant the end of a normal life. Mary's name would forever be on the lips of gossips and rumor-mongers. Joseph, her husband-to-be, could decide to end their betrothal through a public, humiliating divorce. Even if he "put her away secretly" (Matt. 1:19), she would still have to return in shame to her father's home or else survive on her own by whatever means she could.

Faced with these ruinous prospects that she had neither caused nor sought, Mary would have had plenty of reason to balk at Gabriel's message. Instead she accepted her assignment: "Let it be to me according to your word" (Luke 1:38). Her response was submissive obedience to the clearly revealed will of God. It was her duty as one of God's people.

Preparations and Follow Through

After Gabriel's departure, Mary took practical action by visiting her relative, Elizabeth, during the third trimester before John's birth (Luke 1:39–56). She might well have helped Elizabeth prepare items for the coming baby, even as she herself produced or acquired what she would need in her new home with Joseph. We can imagine that Mary learned much from this older, righteous woman as she listened to her and observed her marriage to Zacharias.

Once Jesus was born and the family set up housekeeping in Nazareth (Luke 2:39–40), Mary apparently settled into a fairly routine life as a homemaker (Mark 1:29–31). As she carried out responsibilities such as drawing water, baking bread, and spinning wool, she would have tied her Baby on her back or carried Him in a sling over her shoulder.

Luke was careful to record the family's obedience to Jewish law in having Jesus circumcised (Luke 2:21), in regard to Mary's purification (2:22), and in the presentation of Jesus and a sacrifice at the temple (2:22–24). Assuming that such observance carried over into the home, Mary probably provided Jesus' earliest instruction in the ways and values of the Hebrews.

continued

continued

Empty Nest

The New Testament mentions little of Mary's life after Jesus' birth. She is not listed among the earliest followers; indeed, Jesus seemed to treat her with some remoteness (Luke 8:19–21; 11:27–28). Nevertheless, she stood at the cross (John 19:25–27) and was among the first believers in Acts who awaited the Holy Spirit (Acts 1:14). ◆

Luke 1:26–33

26Now in the sixth month the angel Gabriel was sent by God to a city of Galilee named Nazareth, 27to a virgin betrothed to a man whose name was Joseph, of the house of David. The virgin's name *was* Mary. 28And having come in, the angel said to her, "Rejoice, highly favored *one*, the Lord is with you; blessed *are* you among women!"

29But when she saw *him*, she was troubled at his saying, and considered what manner of greeting this was. 30Then the angel said to her, "Do not be afraid, Mary, for you have found favor with God. 31And behold, you will conceive in your womb and bring forth a Son, and shall call His name Jesus. 32He will be great, and will be called the Son of the Highest; and the Lord God will give Him the throne of His father David. 33And He will reign over the house of Jacob forever, and of His kingdom there will be no end."

1. In what ways are Mary's and Karen's situation similar?

_____

_____

2a. Though afraid, with her response, "Let it be to me according to your word" (Luke 1:38), Mary indicated her willingness to trust God and submit to His will for her. Suppose at this very moment, the archangel Gabriel appeared to you. What might he say to you that would invoke the same kind of awe, fear, and elation that Mary must have felt?

_____

_____

2b. How would you respond to the angel's message?

_____

_____

3. Write down one of your greatest concerns for the future:

_____

Luke 1:46–55

⁴⁶And Mary said:

"My soul magnifies the Lord,
⁴⁷ And my spirit has rejoiced in God my
Savior.
⁴⁸ For He has regarded the lowly state of
His maidservant;
For behold, henceforth all generations
will call me blessed.
⁴⁹ For He who is mighty has done great
things for me,
And holy *is* His name.
⁵⁰ And His mercy *is* on those who fear Him
From generation to generation.

⁵¹ He has shown strength with His arm;
He has scattered *the* proud in the
imagination of their hearts.
⁵² He has put down the mighty from *their*
thrones,
And exalted *the* lowly.
⁵³ He has filled *the* hungry with good
things,
And *the* rich He has sent away empty.
⁵⁴ He has helped His servant Israel,
In remembrance of *His* mercy,
⁵⁵ As He spoke to our fathers,
To Abraham and to his seed forever."

A Song to Remember

1. How did Mary's faith in God expressed so beautifully in Luke 1:46–55 affect her perception of her future?

_____

2. Describe the impact Mary believed her selection by God to bear the Messiah would have on her life:

_____

3a. As stated in Luke 1:46–55, describe the characteristics of those God blesses:

_____

3b. What are the characteristics of those God opposes?

_____

4. How might it change Karen's outlook if, like Mary, she saw her future through the eyes of faith?

_____

Whenever events make our future uncertain, we can look for encouragement to the beautiful example of Mary's simple, submissive faith in God. Through her words, "Behold the maidservant of the Lord" (Luke 1:38), she made it known that she was willing to risk everything to obey the word of her Lord.

◆ A Command Beyond Comprehension ◆

The invitation could not have come at a better time. Recently out of seminary, Melvin Peters was anxious to find a full-time position in the ministry. Then he got a call offering him a ministerial position at a church in Wheaton, Illlinois. It was an answer to his prayers.

In the weeks that followed, Melvin was given further confirmation that God was calling him to serve in Wheaton. Through phone conversations and a weekend flight to visit the church, he had developed a real friendship with the pastor. He had a good chemistry with the rest of the church staff as well, and they shared a common vision for the direction of the church's ministry in the community.

His wife, Shirley, was also convinced that this was the right thing for the family. In the past few months, Shirley had developed a strong desire to move closer to her family. And Shirley's parents lived in Chicago, only a half hour's drive from Wheaton. Melvin felt that God's will for him was clear. He accepted the job, and they began preparations for the move.

However, it soon became apparent that their arrival in Wheaton would not be a triumphal entry. Problems emerged unexpectedly. Their arrangements for living quarters in Wheaton had suddenly fallen through. Fortunately, the minister of music invited the Peters to stay with his family until they found a place of their own.

Worse yet, Melvin was left financially strapped by the cost of relocation. The Peters arrived in Wheaton penniless. And recent inhabitants of balmy southern California, they found themselves without winter clothes for their two children. As if in spite, their arrival in Illinois was greeted by a cold snap.

Melvin Peters was at a loss to understand the disastrous turn of events. He had responded faithfully to the Lord's urging, but where was God's provision? He couldn't help wondering, *What in the world are You up to, Lord?*

Even so, he steeled his resolve. "God will provide," he whispered to himself. ◆

◆ ◆ ◆ ◆ ◆ ◆ ◆ ◆ ◆ ◆

Melvin Peters' experience was certainly confusing. His faithful obedience to God's will seemed to result in unexpected troubles rather than the blessings he anticipated.

When circumstances arise that defy our logical explanation, it may be that God intends to use them to test our faith. Such tests are not intended to destroy our trust in God, but to reveal the depth and quality of our faith.

We have seen how Mary's faith was tested when the word of God came to her. Mary's wholehearted response to God will stand forever as an example of faith tried and proven true.

Two thousand years earlier, there lived another whose faith was tested by God. This man was called upon by God not to receive a child but to surrender the life of his son. His name was Abraham. ◆

KILL MY OWN SON?

I t seems incredible that God would tell Abraham to "Take now your son, your only son Isaac, whom you love," and offer him up as a sacrifice (Gen. 22:2). What sort of God would ask such a thing? What sort of God would test a man's faith with such a weighty request?

It was a severe test of Abraham's faith. Perhaps most of us would have failed the test. We might even have rejected God as cruel and bloodthirsty. But Abraham believed God. Though the sacrifice of Isaac seemed to go against God's promise of an heir, Abraham believed that God would still fulfill His Word, even if it required Him to raise Isaac from the dead (Rom. 4:17).

The request was also a harsh lesson that all of life comes from and belongs to God (Gen. 2:7; Job 27:3; 33:4). In essence, life is merely on loan to us, both as parents and children. God can ask for its return at any time. So in that respect, the request to slay Isaac was similar to the difficult period that Abraham and Sarah endured as they waited for the birth of this very son (Gen. 18:1–15; 21:1–7). Their lives and the lives of any children they might have were in the hands of God.

Let there be no mistake: God abhors human sacrifice, as many Old Testament passages make clear (see Lev. 18:21; 20:2; Deut. 12:31; Ps. 106:35–38; Ezek. 20:30–31). So when Abraham was about to slay His son, God stopped him short of the actual sacrifice and provided an alternative in Isaac's place. It proved to Abraham that his faith was well-placed: God is the God of mercy.

He is also the God of wisdom. He sometimes makes what to us may seem like strange requests. But if like Abraham we will believe and obey, He will reward our faith with His goodness and righteousness. ◆

Genesis 22:1–14

Now it came to pass after these things that God tested Abraham, and said to him, "Abraham!"

And he said, "Here I am."

²Then He said, "Take now your son, your only *son* Isaac, whom you love, and go to the land of Moriah, and offer him there as a burnt offering on one of the mountains of which I shall tell you."

³So Abraham rose early in the morning and saddled his donkey, and took two of his young men with him, and Isaac his son; and he split the wood for the burnt offering, and arose and went to the place of which God had told him. ⁴Then on the third day Abraham lifted his eyes and saw the place afar off. ⁵And Abraham said to his young men, "Stay here with the donkey; the lad and I will go yonder and worship, and we will come back to you."

⁶So Abraham took the wood of the burnt offering and laid *it* on Isaac his son; and he took the fire in his hand, and a knife, and the two of them went together. ⁷But Isaac spoke to Abraham his father and said, "My father!"

And he said, "Here I am, my son."

Then he said, "Look, the fire and the wood, but where *is* the lamb for a burnt offering?"

⁸And Abraham said, "My son, God will provide for Himself the lamb for a burnt offering." So the two of them went together.

⁹Then they came to the place of which God

continued

continued

had told him. And Abraham built an altar there and placed the wood in order; and he bound Isaac his son and laid him on the altar, upon the wood. ¹⁰And Abraham stretched out his hand and took the knife to slay his son.

¹¹But the Angel of the LORD called to him from heaven and said, "Abraham, Abraham!"

So he said, "Here I am."

¹²And He said, "Do not lay your hand on the lad, or do anything to him; for now I know that you fear God, since you have not withheld your son, your only *son*, from Me."

¹³Then Abraham lifted his eyes and looked, and there behind *him was* a ram caught in a thicket by its horns. So Abraham went and took the ram, and offered it up for a burnt offering instead of his son. ¹⁴And Abraham called the name of the place, The-LORD-Will-Provide; as it is said *to* this day, "In the Mount of the LORD it shall be provided."

We may be tempted to see Abraham's faithful response to God as unreasoning. After all, who could make sense of the contradictory nature of God's command to sacrifice Isaac, the child of blessing, through whom God had promised to raise a nation? But Hebrews 11:19 lets us in on Abraham's reasoning process, and tells us Abraham offered up Isaac, "concluding that God was able to raise *him* up, even from the dead." Abraham's faith was founded on his trust in God, and his unwavering belief that God would keep His promises.

1. What evidence can you find in the account of Genesis 22:1–14 which suggests Abraham still believed that, whatever happened, God would not take Isaac from him?

_____

_____

2. What did the angel of the Lord mean when he declared, "Now I know that you fear God" (Gen. 22:12)?

_____

_____

3. Write down the name of an individual that you trust implicitly. _____
   Suppose this individual gave you as a gift your heart's desire. Then without reason, he or she demanded the return of the gift. How would this affect your relationship?

_____

4. Abraham had exhibited his faith in God many times before. Why do you think God chose to test Abraham's faith in this way?

_____

_____

Then and Now

Abraham was among the wealthiest of people in his time, yet nothing was more precious to him than his son Isaac. God knew that Abraham would lightly surrender his wealth, so He tested Abraham by commanding him to sacrifice his "only son" (Gen. 22:2). Does God's test of Abraham seem unnecessarily cruel to you?

If so, what a difference it makes to see things from our point in history! For ultimately, God did not require that Abraham sacrifice Isaac as He had commanded. But Abraham's test did foreshadow the price God Himself paid on our behalf (see John 3:16). Although Abraham did not know it, God's test was not an indication of His cruelty, but a sign for the ages of the great depth of His love for us.

1a. If Abraham had known what we now know, how might this have changed his feelings about God's command?

_____

1b. How would this knowledge have changed his actions?

_____

2. What does this say to those of us who would demand that God tell us "why" before we are willing to trust and obey?

_____

Rest assured, God knows what your future holds—in fact, He has not only seen the movie, He's the director! At just the right moment, God provided a ram for Abraham, to take Isaac's place on the altar. God also provided the winter clothes for Melvin Peters' family, donated to them by members of their new church. God has promised to provide for each of us as well. Though events may unfold in ways that are incomprehensible to us at the time, we know that our Lord is One in whom we can place our complete trust. This gives us the confidence we need to act in obedience to His Word, no matter what the circumstance.

——◆ What Makes You So Good? ◆——

Jimmy grimaced as he watched the coach talk over the next play on the sidelines with Willie Scardino, the star running back for the junior high Schraeder Raiders football team. He couldn't help but envy Willie. Last season, Jimmy had started as halfback, but when Willie moved into the school district this year, Jimmy had found himself in serious competition for the starting slot. No matter how hard he tried, he couldn't out-perform his rival. Willie was faster, stronger, rarely fumbled, and seemed to have an instinct for avoiding tackles. In four games, Willie had rushed for more yards than Jimmy did for the previous year's entire football season. As a consequence, Jimmy spent most of his game time where he was now—on the bench.

It hurt his pride to think that someone else was so much better than he was, and he missed the respect and attention he used to get from his classmates. But most of all, he longed for the admiration of

Coach Anderson, who had once been an all-star running back for the Florida Gators. The coach's oldest son, a fullback for a small northern college, had broken school records at Schraeder years earlier. Jimmy wondered despairingly how he could ever hope to impress someone like the coach while he sat on the bench.

By the fourth quarter, the Raiders led the Rams by two touchdowns, and the coach signaled to Jimmy.

"You're in, Jimmy," Coach Anderson told him.

This is my big chance! thought Jimmy. *I'll show the coach what I can do. I'll score a touchdown!*

But on his first run, Jimmy fumbled the ball and the opposing team recovered. Humiliated, Jimmy mentally kicked himself all the way back to the bench.

The coach came over and patted Jimmy on the back.

"That's okay, Jimmy. We've got this game all wrapped up." But Jimmy hardly heard the coach's words.

After the game was over and the rest of the team had left, Jimmy sat alone in the locker room. Stepping out of the supply room, Coach Anderson saw the despondent youth and walked over to him.

"C'mon, Jimmy," he said, "you're not still upset about the fumble, are you? Don't worry, you'll do better next time."

Jimmy swallowed, struggling to hold back tears.

"I know I must be an awful big disappointment to you," said the boy in a broken voice. "I'll probably never be able to run as fast or score as many touchdowns as Willie does. Maybe I shouldn't even play for the team anymore . . ."

His voice trailed off.

"Jimmy, it doesn't matter who else is on the team roster, or how good they are. I'm proud of you because you put your heart into it and give it your best. You'll always be my favorite Schraeder Raider." Coach Anderson sat down beside Jimmy and put an arm around the boy's slumped shoulders, "You're my son." ◆

◆ ◆ ◆ ◆ ◆ ◆ ◆ ◆ ◆

As believers, we sometimes make the same mistake with God that Jimmy made with Coach Anderson. Once saved by faith, the idea somehow becomes instilled into our minds that we must earn God's favor through spiritual accomplishments. Perhaps we see others whose good deeds appear greater than our own, or maybe we look back at the great works for God accomplished by the saints of biblical times. By comparing ourselves to others, gradually we slip into thinking we must live without error or carry out some great accomplishment before God will be pleased with us.

Perhaps you've struggled with the idea of trying to please God. But if you've come to see your relationship with God in this way, you have left out the most important thing—you are a child of God! Through faith in Christ, you have entered a special relationship with the Almighty. It is not your accomplishments on His behalf, but this relationship that determines your standing with God. As a consequence, you can approach God with assurance, knowing He will receive you not with harsh criticism but with the love and acceptance of a heavenly Father for His dear child. ◆

DAVID

If Abraham (Rom. 4:1) was honored as the patriarch of Israel, David (v. 6) was honored as the king of Israel. He was not the nation's first king, but He was God's choice for king (1 Sam. 16:1–13).

If anyone might have a claim on being right with God and meriting His favor, then, it was David. After all, he was said to be a man after God's own heart (1 Sam. 13:14; Acts 13:22). Furthermore, God established a covenant with him, promising that his heirs would have a right to the throne of Israel forever (2 Sam. 7:12; 22:51). He was even a direct ancestor of Jesus Christ (Matt. 1:6; Luke 3:31).

But David relied on none of these advantages or works (see Rom. 4:5) when it came to his standing before God. Instead, he threw himself on God's mercy, trusting in His gracious character to forgive his sin and establish his "righteousness" (v. 6), or right standing in relation to God. Psalm 32, from which Romans 4:7–8 quotes, celebrates this delivery from sin that God brings about.

Do you rely on your own good works to establish your relationship with God? Romans 4 says you can never be good enough. That's why God offers an alternative—trusting in Jesus' righteousness to cover your sin and make it possible for you to know God.

 Romans 4:1–6

What then shall we say that Abraham our father has found according to the flesh? ²For if Abraham was justified by works, he has *something* to boast about, but not before God. ³For what does the Scripture say? "Abraham believed God, and it was accounted to him for righteousness." ⁴Now to him who works, the wages are not counted as grace but as debt.

⁵But to him who does not work but believes on Him who justifies the ungodly, his faith is accounted for righteousness, ⁶just as David also describes the blessedness of the man to whom God imputes righteousness apart from works:

1. This passage mentions both Abraham and David, two individuals who possessed very special relationships with God. According to Romans 4:1–6, what is the role of faith in their relationships with God?

2a. Suppose you are God's accountant of the "right" way to follow Him. Give your rating of the "righteousness" (Rom. 1:17) of each of the following items in the ledger of a believer's life. In column 1, write a percentage value to up to 100%, or complete righteousness, attributed to the believer as a consequence of the activity described.

FAITH AND GOOD WORKS

	RIGHTEOUSNESS	
	1	2
Jim Smith places his faith in Christ for the forgiveness of his sins.		
Jim Smith gives his testimony and is baptized before his church.		
Jim Smith gives a million dollars to the poor.		
Jim Smith serves as a missionary, bringing others to Christ.		

2b. Now go back and do the same in column 2, except calculate the percentage according to how God would account righteousness in the believer's life.

 1 Samuel 17:31–54

³¹Now when the words which David spoke were heard, they reported *them* to Saul; and he sent for him. ³²Then David said to Saul, "Let no man's heart fail because of him; your servant will go and fight with this Philistine."

³³And Saul said to David, "You are not able to go against this Philistine to fight with him; for you *are* a youth, and he a man of war from his youth."

³⁴But David said to Saul, "Your servant used to keep his father's sheep, and when a lion or a bear came and took a lamb out of the flock, ³⁵I went out after it and struck it, and delivered *the lamb* from its mouth; and when it arose against me, I caught *it* by its beard, and struck and killed it. ³⁶Your servant has killed both lion and bear; and this uncircumcised Philistine will be like one of them, seeing he has defied the armies of the living God." ³⁷Moreover David said, "The LORD, who delivered me from the paw of the lion and from the paw of the bear, He will deliver me from the hand of this Philistine."

And Saul said to David, "Go, and the LORD be with you!"

³⁸So Saul clothed David with his armor, and he put a bronze helmet on his head; he also clothed him with a coat of mail. ³⁹David fastened his sword to his armor and tried to walk, for he had not tested *them*. And David said to Saul, "I cannot walk with these, for I have not tested *them*." So David took them off.

⁴⁰Then he took his staff in his hand; and he chose for himself five smooth stones from the brook, and put them in a shepherd's bag, in a pouch which he had, and his sling was in his hand. And he drew near to the Philistine. ⁴¹So the Philistine came, and began drawing near to David, and the man who bore the shield *went* before him. ⁴²And when the Philistine looked about and saw David, he disdained him; for he was *only* a youth, ruddy and good-looking. ⁴³So the Philistine said to David, "*Am* I a dog, that you come to me with sticks?" And the Philistine cursed David by his gods. ⁴⁴And the Philistine said to David, "Come to me, and I will give your flesh to the birds of the air and the beasts of the field!"

⁴⁵Then David said to the Philistine, "You come to me with a sword, with a spear, and with a javelin. But I come to you in the name of the LORD of hosts, the God of the armies of Israel, whom you have defied. ⁴⁶This day the LORD will deliver you into my hand, and I will strike you and take your head from you. And this day I will give the carcasses of the camp of the Philistines to the birds of the air and the wild beasts of the earth, that all the earth may know that there is a God in Israel. ⁴⁷Then all this assembly shall know that the LORD does not save with sword and spear; for the battle *is* the LORD's, and He will give you into our hands."

⁴⁸So it was, when the Philistine arose and came and drew near to meet David, that David hurried and ran toward the army to meet the Philistine. ⁴⁹Then David put his hand in his bag and took out a stone; and he slung *it* and struck the Philistine in his forehead, so that the stone sank into his forehead, and he fell on his face to the earth. ⁵⁰So David prevailed over the Philistine with a sling and a stone, and struck the Philistine and killed him. But *there was* no sword in the hand of David. ⁵¹Therefore David ran and stood over the Philistine, took his sword and drew it out of its sheath and killed him, and cut off his head with it.

And when the Philistines saw that their champion was dead, they fled. ⁵²Now the men of Israel and Judah arose and shouted, and pursued the Philistines as far as the entrance of the valley and to the gates of Ekron. And the wounded of the Philistines fell along the road to Shaaraim, even as far as Gath and Ekron. ⁵³Then the children of Israel returned from chasing the Philistines, and they plundered their tents. ⁵⁴And David took the head of the Philistine and brought it to Jerusalem, but he put his armor in his tent.

1. Read the account of David's battle with Goliath in 1 Samuel 17:31–54. This is the first of David's many great accomplishments recorded in the Bible. What in the story shows that David trusted in God's power rather than his own skill and abilities for victory?

2. Did you ever face a "Goliath," a task that seemed beyond your power? What happened?

3. How can David's defeat of Goliath be an example to us in our efforts to accomplish things in God's name?

──◆ Heroes for Hire ◆──

What does it take for someone to be a "hero of the faith?" What would you look for if you were trying to find such an individual? What would be the attributes of your hero if you needed to hire one? Go ahead and write out your want ad in the box below. Be sure to include the basic qualifications and experience required by the position. Also include those characteristics that would be a "plus" if possessed by the applicant. Finally, include characteristics that would definitely disqualify the individual for employment.

WANTED: HERO OF THE FAITH

List the names of people you know, or know of, that might be hired if they responded to your want ad:

What if you were among the respondents—how well do you think the job interview would go?

WHO ARE THESE PEOPLE?

Hebrews 11 is the Bible's "Hall of Faith," its review of Old Testament believers, called "the elders," who "obtained a good testimony" by exhibiting trust in God's promises (vv. 2, 39). *Their faith is worth our praise and their example is worth following.*

See if you can identify some of the "spiritual giants" mentioned in this chapter from the descriptions that follow (answers are given at the end of this chapter):

EXAMPLES OF FAITH

(1) After deceiving his elderly father in order to trick his brother out of an inheritance, this man gets caught in the vicious intrigue of his wife's family. Struggling to break free and eager to build his own wealth, he resorts to lying. Later he loses most of what he has during a severe famine and dies as a refugee in a foreign land.

(2) The beautiful wife of a wealthy rancher, this woman joins her husband in a lie out of fear that his trading partner will kill him in order to marry her. Later, she resorts to using a surrogate to provide her husband with an heir. The union causes great trouble in the family and among its descendants.

However, long after the time when she would be expected to conceive, she bears a son who becomes a sign of God's commitment to honoring His promises.

(3) While doing farm chores one day, this man is called by God to lead an uprising against his people's enemies. Unsure about the veracity of the message, he requests a sign from heaven, not once but twice. Later, after paring his "army" down to a small band of men, he uses stealth, surprise, and good timing to thoroughly rout the opposition.

(4) This wealthy man leaves a prosperous city for a land that he has never visited. Once there, however, his wealth multiplies beyond all expectation, and he and his nephew negotiate a major subdivision of the real estate. God gives him a new name.

(5) Raised in the family herding business, this man has jealous brothers who sell him to foreign slave traders. Eventually he winds up as a top-level manager, only to be imprisoned on false charges of sexual misconduct. But a fortunate opportunity distinguishes him before

the king, and he ends up in a highly responsible position from which he manages large-scale grain storage and distribution.

(6) A handsome body builder with a penchant for charming women, this man is called by God to lead his people but proves unreliable because of weak character. Nevertheless, he wreaks havoc among the nation's enemies. After his foreign-born wife betrays him, he is made into an object of curiosity and scorn before a final prayer leads to a burst of God's power and vengeance on his enemies.

(7) The younger son of displaced parents, this man continues their legacy of working the land. He also takes a special interest in matters of faith and holiness. However, a disagreement with his jealous brother leads to his murder and the anguished grief of his mother.

(8) A manufacturer of dyed linen, this woman escapes the destruction of an invading army by housing two of its soldiers in stalks of flax. Later, she bears a son and through him becomes an ancestor of some of history's most important leaders.

Hebrews 11:1—40

Now faith is the substance of things hoped for, the evidence of things not seen. ²For by it the elders obtained a *good* testimony.

³By faith we understand that the worlds were framed by the word of God, so that the things which are seen were not made of things which are visible.

⁴By faith Abel offered to God a more excellent sacrifice than Cain, through which he obtained witness that he was righteous, God testifying of his gifts; and through it he being dead still speaks.

⁵By faith Enoch was taken away so that he did not see death, "and was not found, because God had taken him"; for before he was taken he had this testimony, that he pleased God. ⁶But without faith *it is* impossible to please *Him,* for he who comes to God must believe that He is, and *that* He is a rewarder of those who diligently seek Him.

⁷By faith Noah, being divinely warned of things not yet seen, moved with godly fear, prepared an ark for the saving of his household, by which he condemned the world and became heir of the righteousness which is according to faith.

⁸By faith Abraham obeyed when he was called to go out to the place which he would receive as an inheritance. And he went out, not knowing where he was going. ⁹By faith he dwelt in the land of promise as *in* a foreign country, dwelling in tents with Isaac and Jacob, the heirs with him of the same promise; ¹⁰for he waited for the city which has foundations, whose builder and maker *is* God.

¹¹By faith Sarah herself also received strength to conceive seed, and she bore a child when she was past the age, because she judged Him faithful who had promised. ¹²Therefore from one man, and him as good as dead, were born *as many* as the stars of the sky in multitude—innumerable as the sand which is by the seashore.

¹³These all died in faith, not having received the promises, but having seen them afar off were assured of them, embraced *them* and confessed that they were strangers and pilgrims on the earth. ¹⁴For those who say such things declare plainly that they seek a homeland. ¹⁵And truly if they had called to mind that *country* from which they had come out, they would have had opportunity to return. ¹⁶But now they desire a better, that is, a heavenly *country.* Therefore God is not ashamed to be called their God, for He has prepared a city for them.

¹⁷By faith Abraham, when he was tested, offered up Isaac, and he who had received the promises offered up his only begotten *son,* ¹⁸of whom it was said, "In Isaac your seed shall be called," ¹⁹concluding that God *was* able to raise *him* up, even from the dead, from which he also received him in a figurative sense.

²⁰By faith Isaac blessed Jacob and Esau concerning things to come.

²¹By faith Jacob, when he was dying, blessed each of the sons of Joseph, and worshiped, *leaning* on the top of his staff.

²²By faith Joseph, when he was dying, made mention of the departure of the children of Israel, and gave instructions concerning his bones.

²³By faith Moses, when he was born, was hidden three months by his parents, because they saw *he was* a beautiful child; and they were not afraid of the king's command.

²⁴By faith Moses, when he became of age, refused to be called the son of Pharaoh's daughter, ²⁵choosing rather to suffer affliction with the people of God than to enjoy the passing pleasures of sin, ²⁶esteeming the reproach of Christ greater riches than the treasures in Egypt; for he looked to the reward.

²⁷By faith he forsook Egypt, not fearing the wrath of the king; for he endured as seeing Him who is invisible.

²⁸By faith he kept the Passover and the sprinkling of blood, lest he who destroyed the firstborn should touch them. ²⁹By faith they passed through

continued

continued

the Red Sea as by dry *land, whereas* the Egyptians, attempting *to do* so, were drowned.

30By faith the walls of Jericho fell down after they were encircled for seven days. 31By faith the harlot Rahab did not perish with those who did not believe, when she had received the spies with peace.

32And what more shall I say? For the time would fail me to tell of Gideon and Barak and Samson and Jephthah, also *of* David and Samuel and the prophets: 33who through faith subdued kingdoms, worked righteousness, obtained promises, stopped the mouths of lions, 34quenched the violence of fire, escaped the edge of the sword, out of weakness were made strong, became valiant in battle, turned to flight the

armies of the aliens. 35Women received their dead raised to life again.

Others were tortured, not accepting deliverance, that they might obtain a better resurrection. 36Still others had trial of mockings and scourgings, yes, and of chains and imprisonment. 37They were stoned, they were sawn in two, were tempted, were slain with the sword. They wandered about in sheepskins and goatskins, being destitute, afflicted, tormented— 38of whom the world was not worthy. They wandered in deserts and mountains, *in* dens and caves of the earth.

39And all these, having obtained a good testimony through faith, did not receive the promise, 40God having provided something better for us, that they should not be made perfect apart from us.

1a. Hebrews 11 provides some surprises among those found to be faithful, including a murderer (Moses), an adulterer (David), a prostitute (Rahab), and others whose lives seem undistinguished or marred by human failings. List those that based on your want ad you might have eliminated as job applicants for the position as hero of the faith, and the reason for their rejection.

1b. Which might you have hired?

2a. Hebrews 11:1 provides a brief definition of faith. Given your understanding of the nature of faith, what would you add to this definition?

2b. Hebrews 11 is a testimony to the power of faith in the believer's life. The author begins the account of each individual's accomplishments with the phrase: "by faith." Describe something that faith has enabled you to accomplish.

Taking Hold of the Promise

1. God doesn't guarantee us "good times," as is shown by the suffering that many of the Old Testament faithful underwent (see Heb. 11:32–38). But God is "a rewarder of those who diligently seek Him" (Heb. 11:6). Name one thing granted to you by God as a reward for your faith. _____

2. What are some of the ways recounted in Hebrews 11 that God rewarded the faithful?

_____

3. These men and women from every station in life were empowered to live lives of faith by looking forward to the reward God had promised them. What is the promise in Hebrews 11:39 that the saints of olden times "did not receive," but was reserved for us?

_____

———◆ You Can Be a Hero ◆———

The heroes of the Bible have achieved legendary status in the minds of many Christians, so much so that it is tempting to think of them as near-perfect beings, whose great deeds are beyond the ordinary believer. But a close look at their lives reveals a wonderful secret: they're human—just like us! *These men and women shared our flaws and frailties; they knew fear, doubt, temptation, hope, and sorrow. In every way, they bore human faces.*

Yet one thing set these ordinary people apart: their extraordinary faith. In faith, they willingly responded to the voice of God. We too can respond to God's voice in our lives, and like the heroes of old, having faith in who God is will enable us to trust and obey His will for us. By relying fully on the Lord's strength, we too can accomplish great things in His name! As we live our lives by faith, great too will be our reward from our heavenly Father, both in this life and in eternity.

As Christians, we can claim all this as ours, but faith demands one thing of us: a choice. We can choose to respond to God and submit our wills to Him—or we can choose to reject His will for us, and rebel against Him. This is a danger not only for those unbelievers who live in a state of rebellion against God, but also for believers. At times, we too may turn away from God.

Prodigal believers walk a perilous road, and their decision to serve themselves rather than God can exact a terrible toll. Nonetheless, there is hope for those who stray from God.

In the next chapter, we'll explore the lives of those who chose to turn from God to follow their own ways. In them, we may see a reflection of our own rebellious tendencies, and in God's dealing with them, we will once again discover how deep is the grace of God, who remains faithful to us even when we are faithless to Him. ◆

Answers to quiz at "Who Are These People?" (Heb. 11:2)	
(1) Jacob (Heb. 11:21; Gen. 25–35, 43–50)	(5) Joseph (Heb. 11:22; Gen. 37–48)
(2) Sarah (Heb. 11:11; Gen. 13–17, 20–22)	(6) Samson (Heb. 11:32; Judg. 13–17)
(3) Gideon (Heb. 11:32; Judg. 6–8)	(7) Abel (Heb. 11:4; Gen. 4)
(4) Abraham (Heb. 11:8; Gen. 11–26)	(8) Rahab (Heb. 11:31; Josh. 2, 6)

THE TROUBLED PATH OF THE PRODIGAL

The history of Old Testament Israel is a sad one, for though no other nation was so blessed by God, the people of Israel were rebellious. To them was given the promised land, in fulfillment of God's promise to Abraham, the Hebrew patriarch (Gen. 12:7). Through the prophet Moses, God had also given Israel the Law, the moral and religious code intended to shape Hebrew society, and make Israel a great and holy nation. And though they had done nothing to deserve His special favor, God made the Israelites His chosen people, promising to bless them if they would only follow the statutes of the Law He had given them.

They did not, but instead repeatedly turned away from Yahweh, the God of Israel, and gave themselves over to idolatry. Throughout the centuries, God sent His prophets to each succeeding generation to remind them of His great love for them and urge them to turn back to Him. Though there were times of national revival during which the Israelites repented and renewed their covenant with God, these periods were few and brief. Unable to remain faithful to God, the Israelites, first in the Northern Kingdom in 722 B.C. and then in Judah in 586 B.C., were taken into exile and painful servitude in foreign nations. Given so much, Israel ultimately rejected God, squandered God's gifts, and lost everything.

◆ ◆ ◆ ◆ ◆ ◆ ◆ ◆ ◆

A History Lesson

History taught Israel a harsh lesson. The willful rebellion of the Israelites did not bring them the freedom of self-determination, but instead brought God's judgment upon them. Rebelliousness also robbed them of the blessings God had prepared for them.

Israel's history provides a lesson to modern Christians as well. The writer of Hebrews warns believers: "Today, if you will hear His voice, do not harden your hearts as [Israel did] in the rebellion" (Heb. 3:7, 8). Christians too can be guilty of the sin of rebellion, for only those that have a personal relationship with God can violate it.

When we turn our hearts away from God, we not only take the chance of missing out on the good things God has waiting for us, but we expose ourselves to the possibility of judgment. But we can guard ourselves from rebelling against God. Hebrews 3:12–13 advises us to: "Beware, brethren, lest there be in any of you an evil heart of unbelief in departing from the living God; but exhort one another daily, while it is called 'Today,' lest any of you be hardened through the deceitfulness of sin."

PRODIGAL WIFE, PRODIGAL PEOPLE

Perhaps you are familiar with Jesus' story of the prodigal son (Luke 15:11–32). Hosea describes the real-life stories of Gomer, his prodigal wife, and of Israel, the Lord's prodigal people.

Hosea's marriage was extraordinary in that he was called to marry "a wife of harlotry" (Hos. 1:2). Gomer's exact background is unknown, but it may be that she had been unfaithful to a previous husband, or she may have been a known prostitute. It may also be that she was one of the temple prostitutes believed to have been part of the idolatrous rites then being practiced in Israel.

Whatever Gomer's background, she was a powerful symbol of Israel's spiritual adultery against the Lord (Hos. 2:2). The nation had departed almost entirely from worship as prescribed in the Law. Instead, the people had adopted the religions of the cultures around them, particularly the Canaanites, Phoenicians, and Moabites. Canaanite religion was essentially a fertility cult in which ritual sexual intercourse with prostitutes is believed to have played a major role.

God utterly rejected these Canaanite practices, calling them what they were— "harlotries." The Lord, not the Canaanite god Baal, was Ruler over the land and Israel's faithful Lover and forgotten Provider of bounty (See Hos. 2:8).

Like Israel, Gomer left her loving husband and returned to her life of harlotry. Apparently she ended up in the slave market, where Hosea redeemed her for fifteen shekels and some barley (Hos. 3:2). This was a fairly minor cost in terms of value, merely the common price of a slave (see Ex. 21:32). But it was a great sacrifice of love on Hosea's part. The prophet was mirroring the love of God for His prodigal people and symbolizing the reconciliation that would someday take place (Hos. 3:4–5).

Spiritual adultery is still a danger for God's people today. The New Testament likens the relationship between believers and Christ to marriage (Eph. 5:25–33). When Christians turn away from Christ and adopt beliefs, values, practices, and rituals that are unworthy of Him, they commit the same sort of "harlotries" as ancient Israel committed against the Lord (2 Cor. 11:2–4). ◆

Hosea 3:1–5

Then the LORD said to me, "Go again, love a woman *who is* loved by a lover and is committing adultery, just like the love of the LORD for the children of Israel, who look to other gods and love *the* raisin cakes *of the pagans*."

[2]So I bought her for myself for fifteen *shekels* of silver, and one and one-half homers of barley. [3]And I said to her, "You shall stay with me many days; you shall not play the harlot, nor shall you

continued

> *continued*
> have a man—so, too, *will* I *be* toward you."
>
> ⁴For the children of Israel shall abide many days without king or prince, without sacrifice or sacred pillar, without ephod or teraphim. ⁵After-ward the children of Israel shall return and seek the Lord their God and David their king. They shall fear the Lord and His goodness in the latter days.

An Unfaithful Nation and a Forgiving God

1. Hosea wrote during the reign of Jeroboam II. Israel experienced great prosperity under Jeroboam, but though superficially religious, the nation was spiritually bankrupt. What parallels exist between ancient Israel of Hosea's time and our modern nation?

_____

2. What signs of spiritual idolatry can be found in modern America?

_____

3a. In the Book of Hosea, Gomer is used as a representation of the spiritual adulteries of the nation of Israel. In what ways does Gomer also represent unbelievers?

_____

3b. How does Gomer represent the believer who has drifted away from God?

_____

4a. How do you think Hosea felt when Gomer deserted him for her foreign lovers?

_____

4b. Describe how God must feel when we as believers turn away from Him:

_____

◆ Don't Look Back ◆

"C'mon, it'll be like old times. You never have any fun anymore," coaxed Jesse, "not since you *became a Christian*."

Steve hesitated. Jesse was an old drinking buddy, back from his partying days before he had been saved. "I don't know, Jesse. I've kind of given up that kind of thing."

"Hey, it's just a party, man. You don't have to drink if you don't want to. Kathy and Peter will be at the party, too, so come on over if you feel like it."

"Okay. I'll think about it."

Steve thanked his friend for the invitation and said goodby. It was tempting to see the old gang again, but he knew it would be better not to go. Before he'd turned his life over to Christ, he'd had a drinking problem.

Besides, though it must have seemed to his old friends that he used to have a good time, only Steve knew how empty and dissatisfying his old lifestyle had been. He had something to live for now— other than the weekend.

"That was the beginning of my slide back into my old way of life," explained Steve. He stood before a group of people at the Second Chances meeting for recovering alcoholics. "I ended up going to that party, and when offered a drink, thought to myself, 'What could it hurt? Besides, I've been good

for quite some time. A little fun won't kill me.'"

"I started going to more parties, and because I was feeling guilty, I stopped going to church. The funny thing is, the farther I turned away from God, the less guilty I felt, and the more I blamed Him for what was happening in my life. 'God just wants to spoil my fun,' I'd tell myself, or 'If God really cares about how I live, why doesn't he just change me?'"

"Soon I stopped making excuses for my behavior altogether. I no longer cared what God thought."

Steve told the group about his marriage to a non-Christian woman, after she'd gotten pregnant. He was drinking all

the time during their marriage, which ended in divorce after three years. He went through several jobs in the next several years, and eventually his alcoholism reached the point that he became unemployable. He found himself out of money and out of work, and his old friends were nowhere to be found. It was at that point that he broke down and asked God to forgive him.

"Then I made some calls and found out about this program. I've been on the wagon ever since. But sometimes I look back at the last ten years of my life, and wonder what might have been if I had only remained faithful to God." ◆

 Genesis 19:15–22

15When the morning dawned, the angels urged Lot to hurry, saying, "Arise, take your wife and your two daughters who are here, lest you be consumed in the punishment of the city." 16And while he lingered, the men took hold of his hand, his wife's hand, and the hands of his two daughters, the LORD being merciful to him, and they brought him out and set him outside the city. 17So it came to pass, when they had brought them outside, that he said, "Escape for your life! Do not look behind you nor stay anywhere in the plain. Escape to the mountains, lest you be destroyed." 18Then Lot said to them, "Please, no, my

lords! 19Indeed now, your servant has found favor in your sight, and you have increased your mercy which you have shown me by saving my life; but I cannot escape to the mountains, lest some evil overtake me and I die. 20See now, this city is near enough to flee to, and it is a little one; please let me escape there (is it not a little one?) and my soul shall live."

21And he said to him, "See, I have favored you concerning this thing also, in that I will not overthrow this city for which you have spoken. 22Hurry, escape there. For I cannot do anything until you arrive there."

Lot's wife serves as an example to believers that long to go back to the sinful lifestyle they have left behind. Though she knew the God of Abraham and Lot, her attachment to the wicked city of Sodom was far more important to her than God. Given a chance to avoid the destruction of Sodom, she did not follow Lot all the way to Zoar, but turned back, perhaps to watch and see if the city would actually be destroyed as promised (Gen. 19:26). Her unbelief led to her death, as she was caught up in the destruction of the cities of the plain.

——◆ Reaching the Rebellious Heart ◆——

"Resistance is futile!"

Anyone who enjoys watching old movies will have heard these words before. The typical scenario goes as follows:

The bad guys have our hero surrounded. There seems to be no hope of escape, and he faces overwhelming numbers. Then the leader of his foes utters those fateful words: "Give yourself up! Resistance is futile!"

A look of desperation crosses the face of our hero.

But then something happens! A diversion distracts his enemies, unexpected help arrives in the nick of time, or some clever trick by the hero catches his foes unprepared.

Suddenly, the tables have turned!

In old movies, the hero always wins and the villains always eat their words. But when we struggle against God, the story goes a little differently. Resisting God's will never leads to personal victory. Scripture makes plain God's absolute sovereignty over the world. Thus, when God tells us resistance is futile, we can be sure it's true! No matter how we fight against God, His purposes will inevitably be achieved. Unfortunately, our resistance may cause much unnecessary grief. How much better to surrender our wills to God, and accept His lordship over our lives! ◆

A great example of the futility of resisting God is Jonah, a prophet of God. According to 2 Kings 14:25, he lived during the reign of Jeroboam II, king of Israel (793–753 B.C.). Jonah was commissioned by God to go to Nineveh, the capital of the Assyrian Empire.

Jonah had different plans. He rebelled against God's instructions and instead took a ship headed for Tarshish, which was probably Tarsesus, on the southern coast of Spain, and almost certainly the farthest destination known to Jonah in the opposite direction from Nineveh! The story might have ended there with Jonah basking in the sun of southern Spain had it not been for the fact that the prophet was contending with the Almighty God.

Jonah 1:1–17

Now the word of the LORD came to Jonah the son of Amittai, saying, ²"Arise, go to Nineveh, that great city, and cry out against it; for their wickedness has come up before Me." ³But Jonah arose to flee to Tarshish from the presence of the LORD. He went down to Joppa, and found a ship going to Tarshish; so he paid the fare, and went down into it, to go with them to Tarshish from the presence of the LORD.

⁴But the LORD sent out a great wind on the sea, and there was a mighty tempest on the sea, so that the ship was about to be broken up.

⁵Then the mariners were afraid; and every

continued

continued

man cried out to his god, and threw the cargo that *was* in the ship into the sea, to lighten the load. But Jonah had gone down into the lowest parts of the ship, had lain down, and was fast asleep.

⁶So the captain came to him, and said to him, "What do you mean, sleeper? Arise, call on your God; perhaps your God will consider us, so that we may not perish."

⁷And they said to one another, "Come, let us cast lots, that we may know for whose cause this trouble *has come* upon us." So they cast lots, and the lot fell on Jonah. ⁸Then they said to him, "Please tell us! For whose cause *is* this trouble upon us? What *is* your occupation? And where do you come from? What *is* your country? And of what people are you?"

⁹So he said to them, "I *am* a Hebrew; and I fear the LORD, the God of heaven, who made the sea and the dry *land*."

¹⁰Then the men were exceedingly afraid, and said to him, "Why have you done this?" For the men knew that he fled from the presence of the LORD, because he had told them. ¹¹Then they said to him, "What shall we do to you that the sea may be calm for us?"—for the sea was growing more tempestuous.

¹²And he said to them, "Pick me up and throw me into the sea; then the sea will become calm for you. For I know that this great tempest *is* because of me."

¹³Nevertheless the men rowed hard to return to land, but they could not, for the sea continued to grow more tempestuous against them. ¹⁴Therefore they cried out to the LORD and said, "We pray, O LORD, please do not let us perish for this man's life, and do not charge us with innocent blood; for You, O LORD, have done as it pleased You." ¹⁵So they picked up Jonah and threw him into the sea, and the sea ceased from its raging. ¹⁶Then the men feared the LORD exceedingly, and offered a sacrifice to the LORD and took vows.

¹⁷Now the LORD had prepared a great fish to swallow Jonah. And Jonah was in the belly of the fish three days and three nights.

1. Who did Jonah bring trouble on by fleeing from the Lord?

_____

2. What in Jonah 1:1–17 indicates Jonah's firm belief in the power and sovereignty of his God?

_____

_____

3. Jonah slept through the violent storm. Why do you suppose Jonah showed so little concern for the danger to his life or the lives of the others on the ship?

_____

    After being swallowed by the great fish, Jonah repented of his disobedience, and called upon God's grace for deliverance. The Lord responded, and the fish "vomited Jonah onto dry land" (Jon. 2:10).

    Once again Jonah received the call to go to Nineveh, and having learned the futility of defying God, he obeyed. Yet in his heart, Jonah remained opposed to God's will.

Jonah 3:1–4:11

Now the word of the LORD came to Jonah the second time, saying, 2"Arise, go to Nineveh, that great city, and preach to it the message that I tell you." 3So Jonah arose and went to Nineveh, according to the word of the LORD. Now Nineveh was an exceedingly great city, a three-day journey *in extent.* 4And Jonah began to enter the city on the first day's walk. Then he cried out and said, "Yet forty days, and Nineveh shall be overthrown!"

5So the people of Nineveh believed God, proclaimed a fast, and put on sackcloth, from the greatest to the least of them. 6Then word came to the king of Nineveh; and he arose from his throne and laid aside his robe, covered *himself* with sackcloth and sat in ashes. 7And he caused *it* to be proclaimed and published throughout Nineveh by the decree of the king and his nobles, saying,

Let neither man nor beast, herd nor flock, taste anything; do not let them eat, or drink water. 8But let man and beast be covered with sackcloth, and cry mightily to God; yes, let every one turn from his evil way and from the violence that is in his hands. 9Who can tell *if* God will turn and relent, and turn away from His fierce anger, so that we may not perish?

10Then God saw their works, that they turned from their evil way; and God relented from the disaster that He had said He would bring upon them, and He did not do it.

CHAPTER 4

1But it displeased Jonah exceedingly, and he became angry. 2So he prayed to the LORD, and said, "Ah, LORD, was not this what I said when I was still in my country? Therefore I fled previously to Tarshish; for I know that You *are* a gracious and merciful God, slow to anger and abundant in lovingkindness, One who relents from doing harm. 3Therefore now, O LORD, please take my life from me, for *it is* better for me to die than to live!"

4Then the LORD said, "*Is it* right for you to be angry?"

5So Jonah went out of the city and sat on the east side of the city. There he made himself a shelter and sat under it in the shade, till he might see what would become of the city. 6And the LORD God prepared a plant and made it come up over Jonah, that it might be shade for his head to deliver him from his misery. So Jonah was very grateful for the plant. 7But as morning dawned the next day God prepared a worm, and it *so* damaged the plant that it withered. 8And it happened, when the sun arose, that God prepared a vehement east wind; and the sun beat on Jonah's head, so that he grew faint. Then he wished death for himself, and said, "*It is* better for me to die than to live."

9Then God said to Jonah, "*Is it* right for you to be angry about the plant?"

And he said, "*It is* right for me to be angry, even to death!"

10But the LORD said, "You have had pity on the plant for which you have not labored, nor made it grow, which came up in a night and perished in a night. 11And should I not pity Nineveh, that great city, in which are more than one hundred and twenty thousand persons who cannot discern between their right hand and their left—and much livestock?"

Jonah was fervently patriotic, and hoped that God's judgment would fall on the Assyrians, who were his nation's enemies. Jonah was probably a contemporary of Amos and Hosea, who prophesied against Israel. In both of their prophecies, Assyria would be the instrument of God's judgment on his unrepentant people. Jonah may have known this, which would have only added to his bitterness over the assignment God had given him. His nationalistic fervor put him at odds with God, who desired to show mercy to the people of Nineveh.

1. It is amazing to see how childish the behavior of this prophet of God is as he is portrayed in Scripture (at least until we remember how childish we can become when displeased with God!). What in your opinion is the most effective way for a parent to respond to a willful and disobedient child? a) through discipline, b) through gifts and gentle coaxing, c) through a combination of the two.

2a. How does God respond with severity to Jonah's disobedience?

2b. How does God respond with mercy when dealing with the difficult prophet?

Though a prophet of God, Jonah exhibited the characteristics that are at the heart of a rebellious spirit: pride and selfishness. When questioned by the sailors, Jonah proudly announced to the sailors his nationality and the greatness of his God. Yet his pride in God and country seem to have become a matter of selfish pride for this prophet. Jonah's self-centeredness is shown by his willingness to deny the Ninevites the same mercy from God that he himself received in the belly of the great fish.

Whether the surface motivation for turning away from God is lust or greed, patriotism or dedication to an ideal, at the bottom of it lies self-centered pride. Pride tells us that we know better than God what is right for us and others. Selfishness insists that we get our own way, regardless of what God desires for us. Only humility before God and faithful response to His will are certain defenses against a spirit of rebellion establishing a foothold in our hearts.

◆ ◆ ◆ ◆ ◆ ◆ ◆ ◆ ◆

——◆ Coming Home ◆——

Blanka felt an inner urging to call her cousin, Rosa. Though once very close, Blanka hadn't spoken to Rosa in two years—not since her marriage and move out of state. Blanka could not imagine the reason for the inner impulse, for she would certainly have known if anything significant had happened to Rosa. Her relatives made sure to keep in touch with each other during family problems or illnesses. Blanka picked up the phone and called Rosa.

Rosa was pleased to hear from Blanka, and they shared with each other the happenings in their lives since they had last spoken. Then Blanka asked Rosa if she was having any trouble of any kind.

"No, everything's fine with us," Rosa responded, then hesitated. "Uncle Roberto had a second heart attack just a couple of days ago. He's in the hospital right now."

"He is?" Blanka remembered him clearly. He was an angry old man, always yelling and cursing. "Is he going to be all right?"

"They don't really know for sure. The doctor said his heart attack was much worse than the first one."

Blanka asked her cousin if anyone had talked to her uncle about the Lord. Rosa sighed and explained that

Roberto had never shown anything but scorn for religion. Even so, Blanka asked for the phone number of the hospital and called Uncle Roberto.

"Yah," he answered gruffly. Blanka told him she had spoken to Rosa and had heard about his condition. She wanted to let him know she would be praying for his recovery.

At first, Uncle Roberto remained silent. But Blanka continued on, and talked with him about the salvation offered in Christ. Slowly, her uncle began to respond. He told her that he believed he would not live long and was afraid. Then Blanka described to him the comfort that could be his in Christ.

Blanka found herself praying with her uncle as he accepted the Lord from his hospital bed. Afterward, she thanked God and excitedly called Rosa to tell her the news.

Uncle Roberto died that very week. At the funeral, her relatives described the change they had seen in the angry old man during his last few days. He seemed to have found peace, and had even smiled at them during their visits.

They realized that something miraculous had happened. A lost hope had come home to the Lord. ◆

ARE YOU BROKENHEARTED OR HARDHEARTED?

Job was a broken man (Job 17:1). He not only lost his family, possessions, and health, he was stripped of whatever pride he might have had. Yet, because he was brought low, he was able to reaffirm his faith and dependence on God (Job 19:25–27).

The Bible tells us that God is opposed to the proud, but gives grace to the humble (Prov. 3:34; James 4:6). It also provides numerous illustrations of people who at times fit into one category or the other.

Contrasts of the Heart

THE HARDHEARTED	THE BROKENHEARTED
Pharaoh Defied God by steadfastly refusing to let His chosen people leave Egypt, which brought ten plagues on Egypt and great loss of life (Ex. 7–14).	**Nebuchadnezzar** Spent perhaps seven years living as a wild beast until he acknowledged the preeminence and sovereignty of God (Dan. 4). *continued*

continued

THE HARDHEARTED	THE BROKENHEARTED
The Israelites at Kadesh Barnea Rebelled against God's promises to help them take the promised land, for which they spent forty years dying in the wilderness (Num. 13–14).	**Joshua and Caleb** Demonstrated a "different spirit" by keeping faith in the Lord, for which they were rewarded with entry into Canaan (Num. 13:30; 14:6–9, 24, 30, 36–38).
Saul Repeatedly disobeyed, disregarded, and dishonored God, for which he was stripped of his kingdom and eventually lost his life (1 Chr. 10:13–14).	**David** Confessed his sins of adultery and murder, fasted, and prayed after being confronted by Nathan the prophet, after which God pardoned him (2 Sam. 12:1–25; Ps. 51).
Jesus' Disciples Were unable to understand the significance of the feeding of the 5,000 because of their hardness of heart—a blindness that continued on a similar occasion not long after (Mark 6:33–52; 8:1–21).	**The Hemorrhaging Woman** Recognized Jesus' ability to heal and touched Him, believing that that was all she needed to do (Mark 5:25–34).
People Who Insisted on Divorce Told by Jesus that the Law permitted divorce in Israel as an accommodation to the people's hardness of heart (Mark 10:2–12).	**The Woman Caught in Adultery** Told by Jesus that she was forgiven and urged to sin no more (John 8:1–11).
Jesus' Disciples Rebuked for their unwillingness to believe the report of the women about His resurrection because of their "hardness of heart" (Mark 16:14).	**Mary Magdalene** Heartbroken over the loss of her Lord, but rewarded with the first encounter with the risen Christ (John 20:1, 11–18).
The Jewish Council Rebuked by Stephen for being "stiff-necked and uncircumcised in heart and ears" in regard to God, as evidenced by their mistreatment of Jesus and His followers (Acts 7:51–53).	**Cornelius** Was devoted to God, as evidenced by fasting and praying, in response to which God sent Peter to tell him about the gospel (Acts 10).

Which side are you on? Do you stubbornly resist God? If so, be forewarned that hardheartedness can become a chronic condition, leading to spiritual bankruptcy (1 Cor. 10:1–13; Heb. 3:7—4:11). On the other hand, developing a tender heart toward God can only lead to greater intimacy with God. Trials and difficult times may break us down, but in the end God uses them to build us up—if we let Him (James 1:2–8). ◆

Job 17:1

"My spirit is broken, my days are extinguished, the grave *is ready* for me."

A Lost Hope Becomes a Broken Spirit

1. Look at the list of hardhearted people above. Describe the characteristics of those that are hardhearted toward God.

2. What is the attitude toward God of the brokenhearted listed above?

 Luke 15:11–30

¹¹Then He said: "A certain man had two sons. ¹²And the younger of them said to *his* father, 'Father, give me the portion of goods that falls *to me.*' So he divided to them *his* livelihood. ¹³And not many days after, the younger son gathered all together, journeyed to a far country, and there wasted his possessions with prodigal living. ¹⁴But when he had spent all, there arose a severe famine in that land, and he began to be in want. ¹⁵Then he went and joined himself to a citizen of that country, and he sent him into his fields to feed swine. ¹⁶And he would gladly have filled his stomach with the pods that the swine ate, and no one gave him *anything.*

¹⁷"But when he came to himself, he said, 'How many of my father's hired servants have bread enough and to spare, and I perish with hunger! ¹⁸I will arise and go to my father, and will say to him, "Father, I have sinned against heaven and before you, ¹⁹and I am no longer worthy to be called your son. Make me like one of your hired servants." '

²⁰"And he arose and came to his father. But when he was still a great way off, his father saw him and had compassion, and ran and fell on his neck and kissed him. ²¹And the son said to him, 'Father, I have sinned against heaven and in your sight, and am no longer worthy to be called your son.'

²²"But the father said to his servants, 'Bring out the best robe and put *it* on him, and put a ring on his hand and sandals on *his* feet. ²³And bring the fatted calf here and kill *it,* and let us eat and be merry; ²⁴for this my son was dead and is alive again; he was lost and is found.' And they began to be merry.

²⁵"Now his older son was in the field. And as he came and drew near to the house, he heard music and dancing. ²⁶So he called one of the servants and asked what these things meant. ²⁷And he said to him, 'Your brother has come, and because he has received him safe and sound, your father has killed the fatted calf.'

²⁸"But he was angry and would not go in. Therefore his father came out and pleaded with him. ²⁹So he answered and said to *his* father, 'Lo, these many years I have been serving you; I never transgressed your commandment at any time; and yet you never gave me a young goat, that I might make merry with my friends. ³⁰But as soon as this son of yours came, who has devoured your livelihood with harlots, you killed the fatted calf for him.' "

1. Read the parable of the prodigal son. What finally drove him to return to his father?

_____

_____

2. What in the parable shows that upon his return the prodigal now possesses a broken spirit?

_____

_____

3. Was there a time in your own life when you were prodigal? What happened to return you to dependence on God?

_____

_____

We can turn away from God and reject Him if we choose, but our faithlessness will never cause God to reject us. No matter what we do, our heavenly Father will always love us and long for our return when we stray. We may suffer when we rebel against God, but this

continued

——◆ The Great Emancipator ◆——

Lincoln detested slavery. He first made public his condemnation of the institution back in his days in the Illinois legislature in 1837, when he pronounced slavery a social, economic, and moral ill.

But it was not until March of 1862, with civil war raging between the Union and Confederacy, that Abraham Lincoln took his first steps toward abolishing slavery in the United States. Caught between strident voices on both sides of the issue, Lincoln presented Congress with a joint resolution calling for a gradual abolition of slavery. The resolution offered federal compensation to the states for the difficulties that such a dramatic change in the social fabric would produce. The time was right, and the president's resolution passed.

Yet putting the plan into effect stalled. Democratic opposition was strong, and states bordering the South utterly rejected the plan as impractical. While the war continued with much loss of life, Lincoln was under constant pressure to maintain a Union that threatened to come apart at the seams. Political realities stayed his hand, but Lincoln made a promise to God that with further progress in the war effort, he would issue a proclamation freeing the four million slaves in the United States.

When General Lee, commander of the Confederate army, withdrew across the Potomac, Lincoln called together his cabinet and showed them a manuscript he had written. The substance of the document lay in the first sentence of the third paragraph:

"that on the first day of January in the year of our Lord, one thousand eight hundred and sixty-three, all persons held as slaves within any State . . . shall be then, thenceforward, and forever free . . ."

On New Year's Day, Abraham Lincoln signed the Emancipation Proclamation, and with the stroke of his pen struck a fatal blow to the South and its entrenched system of human bondage.

An assassin's bullet claimed Lincoln as the last life to be lost in the dreadful Civil War, but it could not stop the revolution that made "liberty for all" a reality for the first time in the United States of America. ◆

REAL FREEDOM

One of the greatest motivating factors for people throughout the world today is the quest for freedom, for self-determination. Armies fight for it. Nations vote for it. Individuals work for it.

But here in Romans 6, Scripture teaches that, ultimately, no one is ever totally "free." In the end, everyone serves either God or sin. In fact, Paul uses the word "slaves" to describe the relationship (vv. 16–20). We are either slaves of righteousness or slaves of sin.

What does that imply for our understanding of the nature of freedom? Is complete autonomy possible? Is there such a thing as self-rule or political self-determination? Yes, in a limited sense. But here, as elsewhere, Scripture describes real freedom as a change of masters: being set free from slavery to sin in order to become slaves to righteousness instead.

All of us are enslaved to sin from the moment of conception. Our only hope is Christ, who is able to emancipate us from that bondage (Rom. 7:24–25). Then, having saved us, He enables us through His Holy Spirit to do what we could not do in and of ourselves—live in obedience to God's law (8:3–4). Therein lies true freedom.

 Romans 6:15–22

15What then? Shall we sin because we are not under law but under grace? Certainly not! 16Do you not know that to whom you present yourselves slaves to obey, you are that one's slaves whom you obey, whether of sin *leading* to death, or of obedience *leading* to righteousness? 17But God be thanked that *though* you were slaves of sin, yet you obeyed from the heart that form of doctrine to which you were delivered. 18And having been set free from sin, you became slaves of righteousness. 19I speak in human *terms* because of the weakness of your flesh. For just as you presented your members *as* slaves of uncleanness, and of lawlessness *leading* to *more* lawlessness, so now present your members *as* slaves *of* righteousness for holiness.

20For when you were slaves of sin, you were free in regard to righteousness. 21What fruit did you have then in the things of which you are now ashamed? For the end of those things *is* death. 22But now having been set free from sin, and having become slaves of God, you have your fruit to holiness, and the end, everlasting life.

continued

isn't simply a punitive response. Through our need, God is reaching out to us, reminding us of our dependence upon Him. We should never let pride or fear keep us from repentance. When we do come back to God, He will be waiting for us with open arms.

Like Peter, who was miraculously freed from prison (Acts 12), we who have accepted Christ are free from sin through His redemptive blood. How sad it is that we sometimes forget what God's grace has done for us and long for the old shackles we've left behind! When we choose to reject God's will for us, it is as though we have rejected the paradise God has prepared for us and crawled back into our cage of sin, locking the door behind us.

Rebellion against God and His ways is as old as the Fall, and arises from a will that, as the serpent in the garden said, seeks to "be like God" (Gen. 3:5). As a result of the Fall, a will that desires to be its own god and remain unconstrained by law has become second nature to human beings. Humanity became slaves to this sinful nature, but God's grace has emancipated those who place their trust in Him.

Now that we are free, how should we live? In Galatians 5:13, the apostle Paul tells us: "For you, brethren, have been called to liberty; only do not use liberty as an opportunity for the flesh, but through love serve one another." God's liberation frees us from the pull of petty self-ishness, hatred, and ambition, which seeks to control and dominate others. And freed from our bondage to sin, God has opened the door for us to serve others out of love and to experience peace and joy regardless of our circumstances. Through submission to God's will, we can discover true freedom—the freedom to be what we were meant to be.

♦ ♦ ♦ ♦ ♦ ♦ ♦ ♦ ♦

Hebrews 3:12–13 warns us not to become "hardened through the deceitfulness of sin." Our sin nature whispers to us of the promise of freedom—freedom from God's standards, free-dom from society's norms, freedom to do anything we please. But sin doesn't deliver on its promises!

——♦ From Enslaved to Saved ♦——

God's grace has set us free from the slavery we once knew as unbelievers. By faith, we were saved and have found liberation in a new life in Christ. And as we continue to live by faith, we come to more fully know the true freedom that is ours when God is Lord of our lives.

But like those that rebelled against God in the Bible, we too may turn away from our God. We remain free to repudiate God and seek to live for ourselves. In doing so, we return to the life of slavery to our sinful natures that we had earlier discarded.

Thanks be to God for His boundless forgiveness! Even though we reject Him at times, He does not give up on us. When we turn back to Him with penitent hearts, God will joyfully take us back, no questions asked!

For some, open rebellion against God is not a great temptation, but these individuals still may struggle with learning to differentiate God's will from their own. The Bible shows us some of these people, who tried to serve God, but often erred or ended up serving their own interests. Self-deception is always a danger. An examination of their lives in the next chapter will help us to discover how we can learn to silence the voices of our own desires so that we can better hear the voice of our God.

KEEPING IN STEP WITH GOD

To my way of thinking, there are far more sophisticated formulations of morality than rule-based ethical systems," said Professor Randall. "Many modern ethicists believe society has become too complex for such outmoded systems of morality, such as the Ten Commandments. Rather than blind obedience to a moral standard, an individual should use reasoning based on specific circumstances to determine what he or she ought to do. According to this ethical model, if the goal or intention is good, then the action is a moral one, even if it fails to conform to the prevailing standard of moral behavior."

Janet feverishly took notes in Professor Randall's philosophy course, Ethics and Values.

The student sitting next to her held up his hand. "But if something is wrong, isn't it always wrong?"

"Well, Jim, let's think about that. "Now, suppose someone whose wife is dying steals the medication she needs because he is too poor to afford the life-saving drug. A rule-based ethic would say what he did was wrong because stealing is always wrong, but situational ethics would find it a moral decision, given the situation and the man's goal to save his wife's life. So, Jim, do you think the man's theft was moral or immoral?"

The young man shrugged.

"Okay, let's get an example from the class. Does anyone have a moral dilemma that we can solve by applying situational ethics?"

Janet raised her hand. "It's kind of dumb," she said apologetically.

"Perfect! Just what we're looking for," said the professor.

"Well, my mother wants me to come home for Thanksgiving but I'd rather spend the weekend with my friend and her family. I don't want to hurt my mother's feelings, but what choice do I have?"

"Excellent!" The professor looked around the room. "Do we have any suggestions based on Janet's situation that would make things work out for everyone's good?"

"Tell her you're sick," called out a student.

"She'd just worry about me," pointed out Janet.

"Tell her you promised to work at a mission preparing Thanksgiving meals for the homeless," suggested another. This brought a chorus of laughs from his classmates.

"I think we have a winner," said Professor Randall. "Good to see you contributing to the class instead of disrupting it for a change, Patrick. What do you think, Janet?"

"I don't really feel that comfortable with the idea of lying to my mom just to make things easier," she said. "I was brought up believing lying was wrong."

"Okay," said the professor, "but look at it this way. You'll make your mother proud instead of hurting her feelings, and you get to have fun for the weekend. A little white lie, and the goods of happiness and social harmony are achieved. Now what could be wrong about that?"

"I suppose," she said, feeling a little confused. It did sound like the ideal solution, but why did she feel guilty just at the idea of lying to her mother? Was it really right?

◆ ◆ ◆ ◆ ◆ ◆ ◆ ◆ ◆

1. What good ends does the professor say will be achieved through a "little white lie"?

_____

_____

2. Do you think the solution the class gave to Janet's problem is a good one?

_____

_____

3. Do you think that there could be a case in which it would be all right to use questionable means to achieve a worthy goal?

_____

_____

4. Explain how the complexity of modern life does or does not make it more difficult than it was in the past to strictly adhere to the moral principles found in the Bible?

_____

_____

What If

Suppose Janet takes her professor's advice. Do you think something might happen that would throw a monkey wrench into her carefully laid plans?

What if Janet's friend, Crystal, is invited by her grandparents to take a trip to Bermuda for the weekend—by herself. It just so happens that Crystal took Professor Randall's Ethics and Values class last semester. So she decides to tell Janet that her parents changed their plans at the last minute, and are flying her up to Maine to visit her sick uncle.

All of Janet's other friends have left school for the holiday, and Janet is too ashamed to go home and admit to her mother that she lied. Janet ends up eating Thanksgiving dinner by herself at the fast food restaurant near campus.

As Professor Randall intimated, life is complex. In fact, it is so complex that a person would have to be omniscient to know what the consequences of his or her actions would be. That is why situational ethics, which is founded on the presumption that the ends justify the means, is an inadequate method for guiding a believer's actions. Paul makes explicit his rejection of situational ethics by his condemnation of those who do "evil that good may come" (Rom. 3:8), and also declares, "Do not be deceived, God is not mocked; for whatever a man sows, that he will also reap" (Gal. 6:7).

Only God knows what is best for us. When we use immoral means to accomplish our goals—even when the goals themselves are noble—we are in essense mocking God's sovereignty in our lives. We are sending a message to God that we don't trust Him to work things out to our satisfaction, and we don't need to follow the rules God has given to us in His Word. When we are tempted by circumstances to take things into our own hands, we need to remember God's promise that "all things work together for good to those who love God, to those who are the called according to His purpose" (Rom. 8:28). Our duty is not to manipulate the tide of events on God's behalf, but to obey God's laws for our lives. And God has so constructed our world that His laws will lead to good.

HELPING GOD OUT

Do you resort to scheming when faced with trouble? Do you ever try to "help God out" in solving thorny problems?

Jacob had a tendency to do that, as his experience with Laban shows. Laban must have been a difficult father-in-law at best. He constantly found new ways to cheat his son-in-law, whether it involved switching sisters on Jacob's wedding night (Gen. 29:14–30) or manipulation in the family business (30:25–36).

At times Jacob responded as a principled man. But at other times he resorted to treating Laban in kind, using his own style of deception and scheming.

Eventually God told Jacob to return to his homeland with the promise, "I will be with you" (Gen. 31:3). But instead of trusting God and making a clean break with Laban, Jacob began complaining to his wives (31:4–16), with the result that the family stole away, taking some of Laban's property with them (31:17–21). Pursued and caught by Laban, Jacob grew angry and attempted to justify himself (31:36–42).

Much of this could have been avoided if Jacob had simply trusted and acted upon God's promise to be with him. Instead, he further complicated his troubled family by causing Laban's daughters to turn on their father in deceit and treachery.

Are you like Jacob when you find yourself frustrated? Do you create ways to avoid God's clearly revealed will, just because it may be hard to carry out? Do you run from conflict and hide from facing up to problems, or do you deal with them out in the open? ◆

 Genesis 31:1–21

Now *Jacob* heard the words of Laban's sons, saying, "Jacob has taken away all that was our father's, and from what was our father's he has acquired all this wealth." ²And Jacob saw the countenance of Laban, and indeed it *was* not *favorable* toward him as before. ³Then the LORD said to Jacob, "Return to the land of your fathers and to your family, and I will be with you."

⁴So Jacob sent and called Rachel and Leah to the field, to his flock, ⁵and said to them, "I see your father's countenance, that it *is* not *favorable* toward me as before; but the God of my father has been with me. ⁶And you know that with all my might I have served your father. ⁷Yet your father has deceived me and changed my wages ten times,

continued

continued

but God did not allow him to hurt me. ⁸If he said thus: 'The speckled shall be your wages,' then all the flocks bore speckled. And if he said thus: 'The streaked shall be your wages,' then all the flocks bore streaked. ⁹So God has taken away the livestock of your father and given *them* to me.

¹⁰"And it happened, at the time when the flocks conceived, that I lifted my eyes and saw in a dream, and behold, the rams which leaped upon the flocks *were* streaked, speckled, and gray-spotted. ¹¹Then the Angel of God spoke to me in a dream, saying, 'Jacob.' And I said, 'Here I am.' ¹²And He said, 'Lift your eyes now and see, all the rams which leap on the flocks *are* streaked, speckled, and gray-spotted; for I have seen all that Laban is doing to you. ¹³I *am* the God of Bethel, where you anointed the pillar *and* where you made a vow to Me. Now arise, get out of this land, and return to the land of your family.' "

¹⁴Then Rachel and Leah answered and said to him, "Is there still any portion or inheritance for us in our father's house? ¹⁵Are we not considered strangers by him? For he has sold us, and also completely consumed our money. ¹⁶For all these riches which God has taken from our father are *really* ours and our children's; now then, whatever God has said to you, do it."

¹⁷Then Jacob rose and set his sons and his wives on camels. ¹⁸And he carried away all his livestock and all his possessions which he had gained, his acquired livestock which he had gained in Padan Aram, to go to his father Isaac in the land of Canaan. ¹⁹Now Laban had gone to shear his sheep, and Rachel had stolen the household idols that were her father's. ²⁰And Jacob stole away, unknown to Laban the Syrian, in that he did not tell him that he intended to flee. ²¹So he fled with all that he had. He arose and crossed the river, and headed toward the mountains of Gilead.

Jacob's pattern of dealing with difficult situations was established long before the event recorded in Genesis 31. Earlier, Jacob and his mother, Rebekah, conspired to trick Isaac into giving Esau's blessing to Jacob (Gen. 27). In his old age, Isaac had lost his sight. He could still tell his sons apart, though. He knew Esau by the smell of his clothes and the thick hair on his hands and neck! So at Rebekah's suggestion, Jacob brought Isaac his favorite meal, dressed in Esau's clothes and draped with goatskins on his hands and neck (obviously, Esau was very hairy!). The plot was successful, and Jacob received the blessing Isaac meant for Esau.

Perhaps Rebekah and Jacob told themselves they were fulfilling God's will with their act of deceit. After all, prior to the birth of her twin sons, Rebekah had been informed by God that the older, Esau, would serve Jacob, the younger twin, contrary to the customs governing inheritance in those times (Gen. 25:22–23). But though their ends may have agreed with God's promise, the manipulative means used by Jacob and Rebekah had unforeseen consequences. Jacob had probably imagined that as a result of the blessing, he would receive his father's wealth as his inheritance, and Esau would willingly submit to serving him. Instead, an enraged Esau determined to kill Jacob once Isaac passed away. Jacob was forced to flee to Paddan Aram. He spent the next twenty years in arduous servitude to his uncle Laban. On numerous occasions, Laban used Jacob's own methods against him, tricking him into marrying Leah rather than Rachel, and repeatedly changing his wages to squeeze more labor out of his nephew (Gen. 29:21–25; 31:41). All of this resulted because Jacob was unwilling to wait on God, and allow the Lord to accomplish His promises in His own time and way.

◆ ◆ ◆ ◆ ◆ ◆ ◆ ◆ ◆

1. When Jacob received a word from God to return to Canaan, the Lord told Jacob, "I will be with you." What in Jacob's attitude and behavior reveals a failure to trust that God would be with him?

_____

2. What do you think would have happened if Jacob had told Laban he was leaving, instead of stealing away in secret?

_____

3. What if Jacob and Rebekah had not sought to manipulate events, but had waited on God to make good on His promise. Describe how Jacob's life might have been changed:

_____

──◆ Plans for the Future ◆──

By the time they reach their eighteenth birthday, some people have their whole lives planned out. Others prefer the "fly by the seat of their pants" approach to life. Which type of individual do you see yourself as—someone who:

a) plans for tomorrow   b) lives in the moment

Which approach to life do you think is more appropriate to the believer, and why?

_____

_____

Do you have a life plan for yourself? If so, it should be easy for you to fill out the schedule below. If not, try to come up with at least one goal that you would like to accomplish within the time frame indicated. Put an asterisk before the goal that is most important to you:

WITHIN 5 YEARS:

_____

WITHIN 10 YEARS:

_____

WITHIN 20 YEARS:

_____

1. Do you think your life plan corresponds to God's plan for you?_____

2. What would you do if the time elapsed, and you had failed to attain your most important goal? Would you most likely:
    a. Wait patiently for God to fulfill your goal in good time.
    b. Desperately focus all of your energies on achieving your goal as quickly as possible.
    c. Become frustrated and angry with God.
    d. Find a different goal or make a radical change in your life plans.
    e. Passively ignore the problem and follow the path of least resistence.

3. Suppose a blunder by the angelic postal service mistakenly delivered to your address a sealed envelope containing God's plans for your life. Would you open it?_____

4. Let's imagine that you did. You discover that God's plan for you requires you to wait an additional fifteen years to accomplish your most important goal in life—but you see an opportunity to achieve your goal on your own initiative. To act would cause you to diverge from God's plan. Which do you think you would do?
    a) Take the shortcut to your goal, or   b) wait it out

◆ ◆ ◆ ◆ ◆ ◆ ◆ ◆ ◆ ◆

The Shortcut

A cold winter wind rattled the station wagon's windows as Larry Radcliff and his two sons drove homeward. In the back seat, Timmy shivered. "Hey, Dad," he whined, "when are we gonna get home? I'm freezing back here."

"Now don't grump, Tee. It won't be long," Larry responded. "I've got the heat on for you."

"It feels just fine to me," said Paul.

"Yah, but you get to sit in the front seat. "I can't feel it back here. The cold air is coming in the windows."

"Okay, okay. I'm going as fast as I can in this snow," said his father, as the station wagon sloughed through the foot of slush on Main Street.

Usually, the trip from the supermarket to their house

was only about ten minutes, but the winter conditions made things frustratingly slow, especially for young Timmy. To make matters worse, about a half mile from their turn, traffic slowed to a crawl, and then stopped. A car had slid on the icy street and turned sideways across both lanes. They waited for a few minutes, until Larry announced a change in plans.

"Boys, we're going to take a shortcut," he said.

"Hurray," cheered Timmy, "I thought we'd never get out of here."

They turned off on a dirt road. It was a seldom-used road but it wound its way back to their neighborhood. Soon they came to a fifty-foot stretch of road that had become submerged by overflow from a pond and frozen over. Larry

asked Paul, who went bike riding with his friends on the back roads, if he thought it was very deep.

"It was always pretty deep after a rain," Paul said. "There's almost always some water on the road here. We usually go around it."

Larry had Paul walk out a little way onto the ice to test it and see if it was frozen solid. Paul stamped on the ice a few times, and ran back to the car.

"Seems to be frozen solid."

It wasn't until the car was halfway across that the ice gave way. The car lurched, tilted crazily, and dropped a foot and a half. After that, it wouldn't budge. Timmy looked around in panic. "What do we do now?"

"It looks like we walk," said Larry. "We're going to

have to come back tomorrow and dig the car out.

Larry, Paul, and Timmy climbed out of the windows, and trudged the last quarter of a mile back to the house. By the time they arrived, Timmy's teeth were chattering.

As he stepped through the door, Timmy commented sar-castically, "That must have been the longest shortcut ever." ◆

◆ ◆ ◆ ◆ ◆ ◆ ◆ ◆ ◆

"GOD PROMISED TO . . ."

God has no problem committing Himself to people (Heb. 6:13). He has utter confidence that He can fulfill what He has promised. But His promises usually are not carried out for us immediately. God is not a vending ma-chine dispensing treats at the press of a but-ton. Nor should we expect to be able to call Him up and tell Him to send us what we need by overnight express. Like Abraham, we must receive His promises in faith, with great pa-tience (Heb. 6:12–13).

Actually, trusting in others and waiting for them to deliver is hardly foreign to us. Most of us face that every day in the work-place. We accept contracts for products and services weeks, months, or even years in ad-vance of actual delivery.

Are you asking God to deliver on your time schedule? God wants to make you *grow* rather than just *give* to you. He cultivates faith and perseverance by doing His work in our lives in His way and in His time.

Hebrews 6:11–15

¹¹And we desire that each one of you show the same diligence to the full assurance of hope until the end, ¹²that you do not become sluggish, but imitate those who through faith and patience in-herit the promises.

¹³For when God made a promise to Abraham, because He could swear by no one greater, He swore by Himself, ¹⁴saying, "Surely blessing I will bless you, and multiplying I will multiply you." ¹⁵And so, after he had patiently endured, he ob-tained the promise.

Abraham had to wait a long time to receive his promised son—certainly longer than he could have imagined! When Abraham first arrived in Canaan, God promised him that his seed would take possession of the land. Abraham and his wife, Sarah, had no children, and Abra-ham was about 75 years old. Even so, Abraham believed God's promise and trusted that the Lord would provide a male heir. Yet it was not until Abraham was over 100 years of age that Isaac was born. As believers, we too are to patiently endure as Abraham did while waiting for God to fulfil His promise.

1. Does being patient mean that we should simply sit and wait for God to deliver? What does the writer of Hebrews 6:12 mean by his expression that believers should "not become sluggish?"

2. Describe something in your life that you have been impatient to receive.

_____

3. Is there anything that would make the wait easier for you to endure?

_____

Abraham was commended for his great patience, but even he suffered lapses while waiting on God. At such times, Abraham made plans that diverged from what God had planned for him. Although God had assured Abraham of offspring, while sojourning in foreign lands, Abraham feared he would be killed for his wife, and told the inhabitants of these nations that Sarah was his sister. This was a half-truth, since she was his half-sister. However, it betrayed a lack of trust on Abraham's part for doubting that God would preserve his life long enough for the promised heir to be born. Only God's intervention prevented Abraham from losing his wife, who would become the mother of Isaac. Later, the childless Abraham made a favored servant, Eliezer of Damascus, heir to his wealth, but God reassured Abraham that his own flesh and blood would become his heir.

Perhaps Abraham's weakest moment came when he took Sarah's advice to make Hagar his second wife and have a child by her. There was nothing illicit in this relationship. Sarah's suggestion accorded with the legal customs of the time. It was, however, an attempt at a short-cut solution. Perhaps Abraham thought God needed a little help in carrying out His promise, or maybe he rationalized that God intended the promise to be realized in this way. In any case, Abraham's decision indicated a failure to rely on God to accomplish what He had promised. His reliance on human efforts ultimately brought much grief and conflict to all those concerned.

Receiving the promise was a long and painful process for Abraham, but in the end, he learned to trust God fully. When called upon to sacrifice Isaac, his promised son, Abraham did not even hesitate—in fact, he even got an early start (Gen. 22:3)! Abraham had learned that short cuts and alternative routes that depart from God's chosen path turn into long and arduous detours. The wise course of action is always guided by a firm faith that God is carefully superintending our life journey and will bring us safely to our destination.

 Genesis 16:1–6

Now Sarai, Abram's wife, had borne him no *children*. And she had an Egyptian maidservant whose name was Hagar. ²So Sarai said to Abram, "See now, the LORD has restrained me from bearing *children*. Please, go in to my maid; perhaps I shall obtain children by her." And Abram heeded the voice of Sarai. ³Then Sarai, Abram's wife, took Hagar her maid, the Egyptian, and gave her to her husband Abram to be his wife, after Abram had dwelt ten years in the land of Canaan. ⁴So he went in to Hagar, and she conceived. And when she saw that she had conceived, her mistress became despised in her eyes.

⁵Then Sarai said to Abram, "My wrong *be* upon you! I gave my maid into your embrace; and when she saw that she had conceived, I became despised in her eyes. The LORD judge between you and me."

⁶So Abram said to Sarai, "Indeed your maid *is* in your hand; do to her as you please." And when Sarai dealt harshly with her, she fled from her presence.

——◆ Let Christ Set the Pace ◆——

In full sprint, the runners ran toward the ribbon, the crowd cheering in excitement. Hank held the lead at the turn, but one after another of the runners pulled in front of him on their final kick. At the ribbon, Hank crossed fifth in a field of eight and slipped to his knees, exhausted. From the sidelines, his track coach watched with disapproval.

In the locker room, Hank's coach, Ivan, admonished him.

"Hank, everyone knows you have the talent to make it to the nationals, but you lack discipline," growled Ivan. "How many times must I tell you before you'll get it into your head that you must keep your pace? Instead, every time a runner challenges you for the lead, you speed up, and by the end of the race you have lost the energy you need for the kick. Your attitude is all wrong! What good is it to be in the lead if you end up losing the race?"

"Hey, is it really necessary to yell?" snapped Hank in annoyance.

"Apparently it is!" the coach snapped back. "You don't seem to be paying attention, so maybe if I yell a little louder, you'll hear me!"

They eyed each other angrily for a moment, and Ivan threw up his hands in despair.

"Okay, tomorrow we adjust your training program. If you hope to have a chance of running the ten thousand meter in the NCAA championships by year's end, be at the track tomorrow at 7 o'clock."

Hank showed up the next morning and was surprised to see two figures out on the track.

"This is Aaron Beck," Ivan told him. "Aaron, Hank Wallace. Now down to business."

The coach instructed Hank to allow Aaron to set the pace, and he would follow, matching Aaron's stride step for step. Hank immediately started to complain, but the coach wouldn't hear it.

"Just do it," he said.

As they ran their laps, Aaron deliberately set a slow pace. Lap after lap, they seemed to crawl around the track. Hank found it almost

unbearable, but somehow managed to restrain himself. On the final two laps, the coach gave a signal to Aaron, who opened up the pace.

As they came toward the final bend, the coach yelled, "Now, kick!"

They sprinted, and Hank felt himself flying effortlessly past Aaron. When he passed the line, he was hardly winded. He was even more astonished when the coach announced his time. Yes, it was slow, but not nearly as slow as it had felt to Hank.

Over the next few weeks, Aaron set the pace for Hank. It wasn't too long before Hank surpassed his personal best. The program had worked, and Hank had become a more disciplined and better runner as a result. A few months later, Hank ran in his first NCAA championship race. ◆

◆ ◆ ◆ ◆ ◆ ◆ ◆ ◆ ◆

The author of Hebrews describes the Christian life in terms of a footrace, and exhorts us to "run with endurance the race that is set before us, looking unto Jesus, the author and finisher of our faith" (Heb. 12:1–2). Just as Aaron was for Hank, Christ is to be our pacesetter. As we lead our lives, we need to avoid the tendency to run ahead of God. Instead, we should keep in step with our Lord. We can do this by adopting God's values and focusing on His desire for us rather than blindly running after what we want. This may require a big "attitude adjustment" on our part. When we make a habit of turning to God for direction, over time our values will come to conform to His own. By keeping our eyes on Christ, we will develop the discipline we need to follow His will in everything we do.

LIVING WITHIN YOUR LIMITS

*A*re you impulsive? Are you quick to step forward with a plan of action? As the exchange between Peter and the Lord in Matt 16:22–23 shows, there were times when Peter liked to take charge quickly and set the agenda for himself and others. But just as often he found himself in over his head:

- When Jesus came walking on water to a storm-tossed boat that held His terrified disciples, Peter demanded that He show that it was He by bidding Peter also to walk on water. After a few steps, Peter noticed the wind and the waves and promptly sank, requiring Jesus to rescue him again (Matt. 14:22–32).
- He overstated his commitment to Christ, claiming that "even if I have to die with You, I will not deny You!" (Matt. 26:35). Yet only a few hours later he denied having any association with the Lord (26:69–75).

- He took charge of defending Jesus against Roman soldiers when they came to arrest Him— even though he had failed to "watch and pray" with Christ as had been requested (Matt. 26:36–46; John 18:1–11).
- He refused to allow Jesus to wash his feet at the Last Supper, then called on Him to wash his hands and his head as well (John 13:5–11).

Eventually Peter's leadership skills were captured in a more controlled spirit and he became a significant figure in the early church. Despite many false starts as a result of Peter's impetuous nature, Jesus enlisted this impulsive but loyal follower to "feed My sheep" (John 21:17).

Have your personality and skills become more mature and thoughtful? Or are you still in the raw stage, ready to jump at the first idea that occurs to you? ◆

 Matthew 16:21–23

21From that time Jesus began to show to His disciples that He must go to Jerusalem, and suffer many things from the elders and chief priests and scribes, and be killed, and be raised the third day.

22Then Peter took Him aside and began to rebuke Him, saying, "Far be it from You, Lord; this shall not happen to You!"

23But He turned and said to Peter, "Get behind Me, Satan! You are an offense to Me, for you are not mindful of the things of God, but the things of men."

---

1. What did Christ mean when he told Peter he was "not mindful of the things of God, but the things of men" (Matt 16:23)?

---

2. Several instances are described in the article above in which Peter failed to keep in step with the Lord. What characteristics does Peter seem to share with the runner, Hank, that causes him to run ahead of God?

---

3. Like Peter, when we act impulsively, we are usually directed by our passions and ingrained attitudes. These are often contrary to the values of God. Describe a time when impulsiveness caused you to act in a way you later regretted.

_____

_____

——◆ Look to God Before You Leap ◆——

In the winter of 1951, Francis Schaeffer suffered a crisis of faith.

For twenty years, he had been a leader of the separatist movement, established to defend the historical truth and divine inspiration of the Bible against the influence of liberal theology in the United States. Wherever he heard the voices of theological compromise within the church, Francis Schaeffer spoke out. He worked tirelessly to preserve the purity of the faith, convinced he was doing what God wanted him to do.

But after almost two decades of strife and division among believers, he felt an inner emptiness. He moved his family to Switzerland, ostensibly to strengthen the international base of the separatist movement. Instead, it became a time of soul-searching for him. The cause had seemed so right—why had it failed to receive God's blessing?

At a conference in Geneva, Schaeffer saw people that shared with him a recognition of the dangers posed by liberal theology. Yet they were filled with peace and joy rather than the anger and pride that grew out of religious dispute. He came to the realization that his dedication to holiness reflected Christ's truth, but failed to mirror His unifying love.

Francis Schaeffer came away from that conference a changed man. Although he held firm to his beliefs, he gave up his bitter theological battles. In 1955, he began the L'Abri Fellowship, a youth ministry dedicated to fighting for the souls of the lost and not against Christians of differing belief. ◆

◆ ◆ ◆ ◆ ◆ ◆ ◆ ◆ ◆

1a. From the age of 18, Francis Schaeffer had dedicated his life to serving God. He spent two decades pursuing a cause that he came to realize was out of step with God. In Geneva, he found believers that exhibited an inner life different from his own. Before the life-changing experiences of 1951, what characterized the inner life of Francis Schaeffer?

_____

_____

1b. What inner qualities did the believers in Geneva possess that Francis Schaeffer longed for?

_____

_____

2a. As Schaeffer strove for the purity of the body of Christ, he overlooked the impurity of his own heart. Only self-introspection at a moment of disillusionment opened his eyes. Conflict and quarrels broke out among believers in the early church as well. James indicates that conflict arises out of impure desires and motives (James 4:1–3).

What spiritual motive directed Francis Schaeffer in his cause?

_____

2b. What unspiritual motive(s) might have been behind this spiritual motive?

_____

3. Describe an occasion in which you did something for spiritual reasons that you came to realize was also motivated by more selfish desires.

_____

So often we do things from mixed motives, usually without even realizing it. Self-deception is an ingrained characteristic of our fallen natures. According to Scripture, "the heart is deceitful above all things" (Jer. 17:9). Thus, even long-time believers need to continually examine their motives, to remain in harmony with God's holy character.

◆ ◆ ◆ ◆ ◆ ◆ ◆ ◆ ◆

THE TRAGIC DEATH OF KING JOSIAH

The *"dead" for whom Jeremiah was rhetorically told not to weep (Jer. 22:10) may have been King Josiah, Judah's boy-king who grew up to lead nationwide reforms (see Jer. 11:1–8).*

Josiah died in battle against Pharaoh Necho of Egypt. Necho was advancing north to help the Assyrians defend themselves against the Babylonians when Josiah brought his army against him. Josiah may have seen Necho's trespass through Canaan as a challenge to Judah's sovereignty.

Whatever Josiah's reasoning, the Egyptian king warned him against attacking. He insisted that God had summoned him to aid the struggling Assyrians. But Josiah ignored Necho's advice and joined the battle. As a result, he was mortally wounded by Egyptian archers (2 Chr. 35:20–24).

This was a grievous loss for Judah. In the first place, it brought to an end the spiritual vitality that had been revived under Josiah. Moreover, it signaled the beginning of the end for the nation. Even before Josiah was born, God had promised that judgment was coming (2 Kin. 21:10–15). He reaffirmed that intention when Josiah asked for a word from the Lord, though He promised to delay the end until after Josiah's death (2 Kin. 22:15–20).

continued

continued

Now the final days of the kingdom were at hand. Ironically, Josiah's attack on the Egyptians had delayed them from arriving in time to help the Assyrians, and as a result Babylonia became master of the Middle East. In about 598 B.C., Nebuchadnezzar captured Jerusalem and deported most of its leadership. In about 586 B.C., he returned to destroy the city and carry off the survivors into exile. ◆

2 Chronicles 35:20–24

²⁰After all this, when Josiah had prepared the temple, Necho king of Egypt came up to fight against Carchemish by the Euphrates; and Josiah went out against him. ²¹But he sent messengers to him, saying, "What have I to do with you, king of Judah? *I have* not *come* against you this day, but against the house with which I have war; for God commanded me to make haste. Refrain *from meddling with* God, who *is* with me, lest He destroy you." ²²Nevertheless Josiah would not turn his face from him, but disguised himself so that he might fight with him, and did not heed the words of Necho from the mouth of God. So he came to fight in the Valley of Megiddo.

²³And the archers shot King Jomsiah; and the king said to his servants, "Take me away, for I am severely wounded." ²⁴His servants therefore took him out of that chariot and put him in the second chariot that he had, and they brought him to Jerusalem. So he died, and was buried in *one of* the tombs of his fathers. And all Judah and Jerusalem mourned for Josiah.

King Josiah was the last of the godly kings of Judah. The Chronicler says of him: "he did what was right in the sight of the Lord, and walked in the ways of his father David, he did not turn aside to the right hand or to the left" (2 Chr. 34:2). Yet his reign was tragically cut short.

How could Josiah, who went farther than any other king of Judah or Israel in seeking to purge the sin of idolatry, make such a terrible mistake? How did this man who "walked in the ways of his father David" end up out of step with God?

Perhaps like Francis Schaeffer, Josiah had, after twenty years of success as the righteous leader of Judah, permitted self-righteousness and spiritual pride to lead him astray. In his early years, Josiah had been commended for seeking God's will with humility (2 Chr. 34:19–28), but there is no indication that Josiah inquired of the Lord before going out to confront Pharaoh Necho. Nor did he take seriously Necho's warning that God had sent him to help the Assyrians. Both Egypt and Assyria were his nation's enemies, and thus the enemies of God. The very idea that God may have spoken to Necho but not Josiah might have seemed absurd to the righteous king of Judah. Unfortunately, Necho was telling the truth, and Josiah unknowingly opposed God. It proved to be a fatal misstep for this godly king.

◆ ◆ ◆ ◆ ◆ ◆ ◆ ◆ ◆

The First Step Is to Kneel

As we walk with God, we must guard against becoming overly confident that we have His blessing in our activities. We must also be careful of questionable motives. Cultivating an attitude of humility before God will protect us from the self-deception that arises from spiritual pride. We can keep in step with God through daily submission of our plans and our hearts to Him.

WHO'S IN CHARGE HERE?

All of us have hopes, dreams, and plans, and the Bible never discourages us from looking to the future with bright expectation. However, passages like James 3:13–16 enforce a crucial qualification. As we make our plans, whether in business, in relationships, or in our personal lives, we must do so with a perspective on who is ultimately in charge—God! In other words, we need to plan with an attitude of humility.

Our tendency as humans is to seek control over our circumstances. Certainly the Bible encourages us to take responsibility for our lives (1 Thess. 4:11; 1 Pet. 2:12). But even so, we must ultimately submit to the sovereignty of God. The Old Testament prophet Isaiah likens us to clay in the hands of a potter; the divine Craftsman can do with us as He wishes (Is. 64:8; 1 Cor. 12:15–18).

As a result, we need to submit every intention to God—even our business proposals and plans. He may allow us to proceed according to our desires; or He may decide to alter our plans according to His own purposes. In either case, we need to accept what He decides to bring into our lives, without arguing and complaining (Rom. 9:20–21; Phil. 2:13–14).

The result: tremendous peace! We can feel confident that an infinitely wise, powerful, and good God ultimately controls our lives and our world. Of course, that doesn't mean that life will always go the way we want. Sometimes, from our human perspective, it will seem unfair, maybe even absurd. Nevertheless, God rules the world. Humility demands that we acknowledge and accept what He allows to happen in it.

 James 4:13–16

13Come now, you who say, "Today or tomorrow we will go to such and such a city, spend a year there, buy and sell, and make a profit"; 14whereas you do not know what *will happen* tomorrow. For what *is* your life? It is even a vapor that appears for a little time and then vanishes away. 15Instead you *ought* to say, "If the Lord wills, we shall live and do this or that." 16But now you boast in your arrogance. All such boasting is evil.

1. In whose power are these individuals trusting to carry out their plans?

_____

_____

2. What motives are at the root of their chosen course of action?

_____

_____

3. Do you think that God honors plans that are made in this spirit?

_____

_____

Examining Your Walk with God

1. Which of the individuals who ran ahead of God discussed in this chapter do you think you are most prone to behave like?
   a.   Jacob and Rebekah: used unethical means to achieve God's ends.
   b.   Abraham and Sarah: rather than waiting on God, they attempted to accomplish God's ends through their own efforts.
   c.   Peter: impulsive leader who often failed to let God lead him.
   d.   Josiah: spiritual pride caused him to fall out of step with God.

2. What did you learn from that person's tendency to "run ahead" that will help you to keep in step with God in your daily life?

_____

◆ ◆ ◆ ◆ ◆ ◆ ◆ ◆ ◆

Running ahead never ceases to be a concern for the Christian in his or her walk with God. Each of us must diligently examine our motivations before we act. By cultivating an attitude of patient waiting, and looking to the Lord for guidance, we can give God control over the direction of our lives.

Yet sometimes we come to feel lost and separated from God. At such times, we may long for the Lord to reveal Himself to us. Fortunately, our God is a loving God. Even when we stray, we need not fear permanent separation from God's guiding hand. Our Good Shepherd will search for us like the lamb who strayed, and bring us back into His fold. And when He does, our sense of isolation will give way to the comfort and wonder of His presence.

In history, God drew people to Himself through such personal encounters with His presence. What is it like to encounter God? How can we more fully experience the fellowship of the Lord? In the next chapter we'll look at what it means to encounter the living God.

ENCOUNTERS WITH THE LIVING GOD

Blaise Pascal was a genius. At age 16, he published his first essay on mathematics, and later became the founder of the modern theory of probabilities. Between 1642 and 1654, his studies in physics and mathematics led him to invent the syringe, the hydraulic press, and the first digital calculator. He also became a famous writer and philosopher. He achieved great status in France as a consequence of his intellectual gifts, and was always in great demand at the court of Louis XIV. He spent his days in his studies, at the theatre, and at society parties.

Yet prestige and success left Pascal unsatisfied, and the pleasures of Paris left him feeling separated from fellowship with God. Depression and a deep spiritual dryness set in. He grew to hate the world to which he had grown accustomed. In remorse, and with a sense of being abandoned by God, Pascal told his sister, "I want to quit my occupation with the world."

Then something happened. The night of November twenty-third, 1654, Blaise Pascal experienced a personal encounter with God.

FIRE, wrote Pascal, in the midst of spiritual communion with God. *God of Abraham, God of Isaac, God of Jacob, not of the philosophers and scholars.*

Certitude, certitude, feeling, joy, peace. His separation from the Lord was over, and in praise, Pascal vowed to devote his life to God.

From a young age, Pascal suffered from physical pain and illness. Even when confined to his bed in agony, Pascal kept hidden in his clothes the parchment upon which he had scratched out words during his ecstatic encounter with God. Sickness reasserted itself during the last years of his short life, yet did not keep him from expending all his energies in service to his Lord. He accomplished much before his death at the age of 39. His religious writings have inspired generations after him to draw close to God so that they too can know the intimate oneness with their heavenly Father that Blaise Pascal had found.

* * * * * * * * * *

In the Darkest Night

Blaise Pascal's life reminds us that Christianity is more than a set of doctrinal beliefs. At heart, Christianity is the pathway to personal encounter and restored relationship with the living God. Encounters with God in Bible times were both longed for and unexpected, and in many cases awakened a new knowledge and vital faith in those that experienced God firsthand.

Yet the ancients too suffered separation from God. The entrance of sin into the world created a wall between God and humans. Though humanity longs for God, only God has the power to break through this barrier. Throughout history, God has reached out to human beings, to make Himself known to them, and to draw them to Him. His redemptive plan for humanity is designed to open the way to personal encounter with the Lord for every individual *who believes. The climax of this plan saw God become man, in the body of Jesus Christ, the ultimate revelation of the Deity (Col. 2:9).*

Long before the time of Christ lived a man named Job. He was "blameless and upright," a person who "feared God and shunned evil" (Job 1:1). A blessed man, disaster shattered his life, taking from him his family, health, and prosperity. In dire need, Job yearned for God to make Himself known to him.

WHERE IS GOD?

Distressed and frustrated over his ongoing pain and suffering, Job longed to arrange a meeting with God where he could present his case (Job 23:3–4). But where was God to be found? Job went on a mental journey of the geography surrounding him, looking for God, but to no avail (Job 23:8–9). It could be that the terms "forward," "backward," "left," and "right" indicated the points of the Hebrew compass, not just general directions with reference to Job.

If we assume that compass directions are meant, and that Job lived in or near Edom, as many believe, then "forward" indicated the great Arabian Desert, with its trackless wastes and occasional oases. Job could not find God there.

Turning "backward," Job could envision Egypt on the Nile and the Great (Mediterranean) Sea. But he could not perceive God there.

To Job's "left" was the land of Canaan, beyond that the cedar forests of Lebanon, and far to the north the upper Euphrates River and the Taurus and Ararat mountain ranges. Yet Job could not find God there.

Finally, to Job's "right" was the Gulf of Aqaba and the Red Sea, and far to the south his trading partners, the Sabeans. But Job could not see God there.

Where was God? Job would eventually encounter Him (Job 38—41). But for now he was left sitting in his ashes, struggling to make sense of his suffering.

Job 23:3–9

3 Oh, that I knew where I might find Him,
 That I might come to His seat!
4 I would present *my* case before Him,
 And fill my mouth with arguments.
5 I would know the words *which* He would
  answer me,
 And understand what He would say to
  me.
6 Would He contend with me in His great
  power?
 No! But He would take *note* of me.

7 There the upright could reason with
  Him,
 And I would be delivered forever from
  my Judge.
8 "Look, I go forward, but He is not *there,*
 And backward, but I cannot perceive
  Him;
9 When He works on the left hand, I
  cannot behold *Him;*
 When He turns to the right hand, I
  cannot see *Him.*

1. Why did Job desire an encounter with God?

_____

2. Describe a time when you longed for God to show Himself to you.

_____

3. Was your desire fulfilled? If so, describe how:

_____

4. Like Job, believers today also yearn for personal encounter with God. In what ways do you think modern Christians can experience God's reality and presence in their lives?

_____

AHA!

Have you ever puzzled long and hard over a difficult problem, only to have a sudden flash of insight? "Aha!" you may have exclaimed with a sense of satisfaction and resolution. *Job came to the end of his trials with an "Aha!" experience (Job 42:1–6).*

Job's moment of insight came after God plied him with questions (Job 38—4)—questions to which Job had no answers. God's point was not to humiliate Job through his ignorance, but to reveal Himself as the all-powerful, all-wise God whose ways are unimpeachable. It was when he finally saw God (Job 42:5) that things suddenly began to make sense for Job.

But the "Aha!" that Job experienced was not merely an intellectual satisfaction, as if he had finally entered all the right words on some theological crossword puzzle. Rather, Job felt a sense of wonder after having nothing less than a dazzling encounter with the living God.

This is clear from the language Job used to describe his reaction. After hearing from God, Job realized that he had been uttering "things too wonderful for me, which I did not know" (Job 42:3). The Hebrew word translated "know" implies more than a grasp of information; it suggests intimate knowledge of the sort that comes by personal experience. In effect, Job was admitting that all of his high-sounding talk had been so much blabber; he hadn't really known what he was talking about, certainly not the way God knows.

continued

continued

Likewise, Job had been pontificating on things that were "too wonderful" for him—literally incomprehensible or astonishing, things that only God could understand (see Ps. 139:6). Job thought he was coming to terms with his troubles. Then he saw God, and he realized that he had no idea.

Job's response to this unexpected encounter with God was a sense of utter and absolute humility (Job 42:5–6). The words, "I abhor myself" might be translated, "I reject what I have spoken;" "I cast away my words;" "I despise or disdain them." It's as if Job had written a journal or a book to detail and interpret his experience (Job 19:23–24), or a legal brief to make his case before God (Job 31:35–37). But upon realizing who God was, he threw the book away.

As for Job's repentance (Job 42:6), the word translated "repent" is not the term used for repentance from sin (*shub,* "to turn back or return," see 1 Kin. 8:47; Jer. 5:3), but a word meaning "to be sorry" or "to console oneself" (*nacham*). In other words, Job threw away his pretensions to wisdom and comforted himself "in dust and ashes," a common symbol of mourning or humility. He was satisfied with the humble knowledge that his sufferings were all part of the purpose of God—even if he could not understand those purposes with his finite mind.

Perhaps you are encountering a problem in life that seems to make no sense. Like Job, you may have an "Aha!" experience with God. It is comforting to know that someday all mysteries will find their meaning in Him. Right now such knowledge may be "too wonderful" for us to grasp. ◆

 Job 42:1–10

Then Job answered the Lord and said:

2   "I know that You can do everything,
    And that no purpose *of Yours* can be
      withheld from You.
3   *You asked,* 'Who *is* this who hides
      counsel without knowledge?'
    Therefore I have uttered what I did not
      understand,
    Things too wonderful for me, which I
      did not know.
4   Listen, please, and let me speak;
    You said, 'I will question you, and you
      shall answer Me.'

5   "I have heard of You by the hearing of the
      ear,
    But now my eye sees You.
6   Therefore I abhor *myself,*
    And repent in dust and ashes."

7And so it was, after the Lord had spoken these words to Job, that the Lord said to Eliphaz the Temanite, "My wrath is aroused against you and your two friends, for you have not spoken of Me *what is* right, as My servant Job *has.* 8Now therefore, take for yourselves seven bulls and seven rams, go to My servant Job, and offer up for yourselves a burnt offering; and My servant Job shall pray for you. For I will accept him, lest I deal with you *according to your* folly; because you have not spoken of Me *what is* right, as My servant Job *has.*"

9So Eliphaz the Temanite and Bildad the Shuhite *and* Zophar the Naamathite went and did as the Lord commanded them; for the Lord had accepted Job. 10And the Lord restored Job's losses when he prayed for his friends. Indeed the Lord gave Job twice as much as he had before.

The Thunder Spoke

1. Job 38:1 tells us that God spoke to Job "out of the whirlwind." What must it have been like to encounter the living God in this way?

_____

2. What was Job's response when he saw God with his own eyes?

_____

3a. How was Pascal's encounter with God similar to Job's?

_____

3b. How did their encounters with God differ?

_____

4a. Job 36:26 affirms, "Behold, God *is* great, and we do not know *Him*." Was there ever a time when you felt as Job did when he said, "I have heard of You by the hearing of the ear, but now my eye sees You" (Job 42:5)?

_____

4b. If so, how did this experience change your view of God?

_____

——◆ The Hand of Deliverance ◆——

It was Saturday evening at Our Heritage Church in Phoenix, Arizona. A small group of church members were gathered in a circle in the Sunday school building.

Sally wore thick round-lensed glasses and had long, curly blond hair. She wore blue jeans and a T-shirt, and sat cross-legged on her folding chair. She spoke in a soft voice, describing an event that had happened on her vacation with her husband, Rick, and their four-year-old son, Tommy:

"We went tubing last weekend on the Salt River. Rick had the big inner tube and was carrying Tommy on his lap. Because of the rains last week, the river was high and faster than usual. We could see it was over the banks, so we were trying to stay out in the middle, away from the heavy underbrush.

"It's not too easy steering an inner tube. We had gone a couple of miles downriver when we came to a bend with overhanging trees. Rick tried to paddle away from the trees but he didn't have much luck. The river was running too fast to do anything. I yelled 'watch out' as I saw them go right into the branches of this big cotton-wood."

Sally stopped momentarily to slide her glasses off and dry her eyes. "It was awful. There was a loud snapping of branches and the inner tube flew out. But they were both gone. I started paddling toward the shore, screaming their names. The current was so fast, I just went sailing by. I saw Rick's head come up behind me, looking around for Tommy. I must have been two hundred yards downriver by the time I could climb up on shore. I could hear Rick calling out to Tommy as the current carried him along.

"Rick pulled himself ashore just past me. His back was cut from the branches. 'Where is Tommy?' I yelled, and he told me that the inner tube had flipped over and

pushed them underwater. Tommy was just ripped right out of his arms. Rick told me to run farther down the river in case Tommy was carried past us by the current. He started to run along the shore looking in the branches.

"My glasses were covered with water spots, and I was crying so hard that I had trouble seeing. Tommy doesn't know how to swim. I came to a stretch of the river clear of brush along the shore. All of a sudden, Tommy bobbed up right in front of me, coughing. I dived in and got him out of the river.

"First thing he said was, 'Hi, Mom,' so I knew he was

okay. I was so relieved! We went and found his dad and walked back upstream to the car.

"When we asked him what happened, Tommy told us he sank and bounced along the bottom of the river. I asked him if he was scared, and he told us no, because God said everything was all right.

" 'Is that right, honey?' I bent over to ask Tommy, who shook his head. 'Is that what God said?'

" 'God said, "It's okay, Tommy. I'm here." ' he answered shyly, looking down at the ground. 'So I wasn't scared no more.' " ◆

◆ ◆ ◆ ◆ ◆ ◆ ◆ ◆ ◆

God encounters us in our need. All of unsaved humanity stands in desperate need of the Lord, but only in moments of fear and despair are most people truly aware of their great need. Out of distress, they call out to God. It is at such moments that the Lord often chooses to reveal Himself to individuals.

THE HEMORRHAGING WOMAN

For twelve years the woman in Matthew 9:20–22 had sought a cure for her condition. Perhaps worse than the drain on her physical strength and finances was the stigma of uncleanness. Jews considered women ritually unclean during menstruation, and whoever touched a menstruating woman was made unclean until evening. If a woman experienced bleeding other than at her normal menses, she was considered unclean until the bleeding stopped (Lev. 15:19–27). That meant exclusion from participating in the life and worship of the community.

Scripture is silent on the source of this woman's livelihood. Perhaps she lived off an inheritance, or perhaps she was divorced and her dowry had been returned to her. Whatever her means of support, it was gone. Jesus was her last hope.

So she approached Him, breaking a rule that made it an unclean person's responsibility to keep away from others. In desperation, she reached out and touched Jesus.

Perceiving that power had gone out from Him, Jesus sought her out. Perhaps as she explained her disease the crowd backed away, not wanting to contaminate themselves. But Jesus didn't withdraw. Rather, He drew her to Him with the affectionate term "daughter" and sent her away in peace, healed at last.

Who are the "untouchables" in your world? Who is desperately trying to reach out for help? How can you respond to their needs with Christlikeness?

Mark 5:25–34

²⁵Now a certain woman had a flow of blood for twelve years, ²⁶and had suffered many things from many physicians. She had spent all that she had and was no better, but rather grew worse. ²⁷When she heard about Jesus, she came behind *Him* in the crowd and touched His garment. ²⁸For she said, "If only I may touch His clothes, I shall be made well."

²⁹Immediately the fountain of her blood was dried up, and she felt in *her* body that she was healed of the affliction. ³⁰And Jesus, immediately knowing in Himself that power had gone out of Him, turned around in the crowd and said, "Who touched My clothes?"

³¹But His disciples said to Him, "You see the multitude thronging You, and You say, 'Who touched Me?' "

³²And He looked around to see her who had done this thing. ³³But the woman, fearing and trembling, knowing what had happened to her, came and fell down before Him and told Him the whole truth. ³⁴And He said to her, "Daughter, your faith has made you well. Go in peace, and be healed of your affliction."

1. The Hebrew term for "made well" in Mark 5:28 means "saved" or "delivered." What was responsible for the woman's miraculous deliverance from disease?

_____

_____

2a. When the woman touched the hem of his garment, Christ turned around and asked, "Who touched My clothes?" (Mark 5:30). Do you think Jesus already knew who it was?

_____

_____

2b. If Christ did know, then why might He have asked the question?

_____

_____

3. If you have ever experienced God's deliverance—from an illness, a difficult or dangerous situation, or in some other way—describe the occasion.

_____

_____

──◆ The Letter ◆──

Suppose that you have a new pen pal—someone that has never met you. What would you tell this person so that he or she could get to know the real you? Would you describe how you look, what you like to do, your thoughts and feelings? Perhaps you would include all of these.

Compose a letter to someone who does not know you in the space provided below. Although your letter will necessarily be brief, make it as revealing and as intimate a portrayal as you can. Be honest. If the letter were ever to be delivered, the receiver should be able to say, "I feel as if I really know you!"

To Whom It May Concern,

My name is _____

_____

_____

_____

_____

_____

_____

_____

_____

_____

Let's find out how well the person to whom you are writing knows you now. Circle all of the following that you included in your letter:
  a) a description of yourself.
  b) things that are of value to you.
  c) others who are close to or familiar with you.
  d) things you've said or done in the past.
  e) an idea of your future plans or goals.
  f) your reason for writing—such as a desire to get to know that person.
God included all of the items listed above in His letter to us! Read the following verses and write down what God has revealed to us about Himself.

a) **His character**—*"For the Lord your God is God of gods and Lord of lords, the great God, mighty and awesome, who shows no partiality, nor takes a bribe" (Deut. 10:17–19).*

b) **What He values**—*"He has shown you, O man, what is good; and what does the LORD require of you but to do justly, and to love mercy, and to walk humbly with your God?" (Mic. 6:8).*

c) **One who is close to Him**—*"And He who sent Me is with Me. The Father has not left Me alone, for I always do those things that please Him" (John 8:29).*

FATHERS AND PROPHETS

Who were the "fathers" and "prophets" privileged to hear God's voice "in these last days" (Heb. 1:1)? The writer was referring to some of the Hebrews' most well-known ancestors and others to whom God made astonishing promises and through whom He communicated His Word, now known as the Old Testament. See if you can identify some of these important figures in Israelite history from the descriptions that follow (answers are given at the end of this chapter).

OLD TESTAMENT FIGURES

1	The father of three sons in especially evil times, this man is warned of coming disaster and prepares for it despite his neighbors' ridicule. But when calamity strikes and destroys his opponents, he is vindicated by surviving. However, drunkenness leads him into sin with long-term consequences. Nevertheless, God makes an everlasting promise to him and his descendants.
2	A prisoner of war becomes a government trainee who resists cultural assimilation. Later, his coworkers hatch an evil plot which results in orders for his execution. However, by God's power he emerges unscathed and becomes the king's most trusted advisor. Through him God reveals great and awesome visions concerning history.
3	Born in poverty to a minority couple, this man is raised among the wealthy and powerful. But after committing murder, he flees to a remote land and adopts the life of a shepherd. Years later he stages a dramatic comeback, leading his people on the world's largest known expedition back to their homeland. Through him God reveals a moral code that still impacts civilization today.

continued

d) **What He has done**—*"Lift up your eyes on high, and see who has created these things, who brings out their host by number; He calls them all by name" (Isa. 40:26).*

e) **His plans**—*" 'For I know the thoughts that I think toward you,' says the Lord, 'thoughts of peace and not of evil, to give you a future and a hope.' " (Jer. 29:11).*

f) **His reason for revealing Himself to us**—*Now we have received, not the spirit of the world, but the Spirit who is from God, that we might know the things that have been freely given to us by God (1 Cor. 2:12).*

	continued
4	One of the youngest sons of a family of shepherds develops musical ability and becomes a military prodigy. However, his prowess causes the existing leadership to view him as such a threat that he is marked for death. Nevertheless, he eventually becomes his nation's leader. Through him God causes to be composed a large portion of the Hebrews' songs of worship.
5	Himself the son of a king, he becomes the most powerful militarist, builder, and judge of his day, trading with foreign nations in military arms, construction materials, treasure cities, and wives. However, frustrations beset him and he writes of the hopelessness of life apart from God. Through him God reveals many practical nuggets of wisdom and the beauty of love.
6	Describing himself as nothing but "a herdsman and a tender of sycamore fruit," this man rises from obscurity and announces to a rebellious kingdom that God is sending invaders to punish it for its idol worship, corruption, and oppression of the poor. Through his message and its fulfillment, God shows that He can be counted on to keep His Word.
7	The answer to a barren woman's prayer, this man hears as a child the call of God to be His spokesman. Later he serves as a judge of his people and warns them against the perils of establishing a kingdom. Nevertheless, he presides over the anointing of two kings and records the early history of his nation's kingdom era.
8	A poet of deep emotional strength, this man is so outraged by his nation's sin that he cries out to God for judgment. Then when God reveals His plans, he challenges the justice of the proposal. A man of deep faith, he leaves behind a beautiful poem of praise in response to the mysterious ways of God.

God made Himself known to the people of ancient times through stunning personal encounters. To some, like Noah and Abraham, God spoke directly. To Moses, he first appeared "in a flame of fire from the midst of a bush" (Ex. 3:2). He led the Israelites during the Exodus by a pillar of cloud by day and a pillar of fire at night (Ex. 13:21–22). Other Old Testament figures, such as Isaiah, Joseph, and Daniel, encountered God through dreams and visions. To Jacob, God manifested Himself in physical form (Gen. 32:22–32). Still others witnessed signs and wonders worked by the hand of God. Even enemies of God and Israel beheld the power of God made terrifyingly real. Pharaoh and the Egyptians saw with horror the plagues God brought upon Egypt. Ahab and Jezebel watched in amazement as Elijah called on God, and in response fire fell from heaven (1 Kings 18:36–39).

All of these were witnesses to things beyond the realm of the everyday world. They knew they had come face to face with the divine. Their responses ranged from awe to terror, sudden insight to incomprehension.

Today, we possess the testimony of these witnesses, recorded in the Scriptures. The Bible is the record of God's revelation of Himself through personal encounter with humankind. From its pages, we can hear God's voice speaking to us today.

1a. Whom do you think is able to know God more fully: a) Those who experienced special encounters with God in ancient times; b) Modern believers who possess the Holy Word?

_____

_____

1b. Explain your answer.

_____

_____

2. Do you think someone would get to know you better by spending a day with you or by reading your letter describing yourself?

_____

◆ ◆ ◆ ◆ ◆ ◆ ◆ ◆ ◆

Some people feel that the Bible is a poor substitute for the dramatic experiences witnessed by individuals in Old Testament times. Yet in many ways our encounter with God, available through His Word, is incomparably richer! For the experience of those who encountered God in ancient times was shrouded in mystery and limited by their ignorance. They had not received the full revelation of God, but we have. For the modern believer, the nature of God and the meaning of history have been made plain through the written Word.

And Scripture is no dry and impersonal history lesson. Rather, it is the inspired Word of God (2 Tim. 3:16–17), describing who He is, His plans, and His great love for us. More than that, it is a powerful and living Word (Heb. 4:12). No human document can compare with this divine Word, which is both objective and deeply personal, historical and existential in its nature. Through the Word, we not only know of God, we come to truly know God.

——◆ Christ Shines Through ◆——

A letter from Charles Colson's Prison Fellowship Ministries, here paraphrased, tells the story of one family touched by the ministry:

Mencia was seven, Alex was five, and Ricky was two when their father was arrested on drug charges. Much of their lives had been spent in shelters, grimy hotel rooms, and the streets of Queens, New York. And in their brief lives, they had seen too much. They had silently watched their mother Myra's growing addiction to cocaine, the moments of desperation when she needed a fix. They had seen their father pull his gun on strange men, and the looks of fear and hatred on those strangers' faces. But young Alex and Mencia had never seen the love of God.

Yet Jose Abreu, their father, met an unlikely person in his jail cell. He met the Lord Jesus Christ. Surrounded by prison bars, he accepted Christ into his heart. Jose shared his new faith with his wife, Myra, but sadly, her heart was still devoted to her drug addiction. She did not realize that God would enter her life as well.

On Christmas Eve, a box arrived at the small apartment in which Myra lived with her three children. The box was filled with Christmas presents sent to the Abreus by a prison fellowship ministry, at Jose's request. It was an exciting day for Mencia, Alex, and Ricky—new toys and clothes . . . all from their daddy! For Myra, it was an encounter with the love of God.

"I cannot explain to you or describe to you the joy that my children and I felt when we opened it," Myra recalls. "I thanked God right there. I cried, and I went on my knees. That is when I knew that God loved me, and I accepted the Lord Jesus Christ into my life."

It was the first true Christmas that Myra and her children had ever known. ◆

◆ ◆ ◆ ◆ ◆ ◆ ◆ ◆ ◆

When Christ came into the world, lost humanity witnessed God in the flesh. But how can lost souls encounter Christ today? Through believers, that's how! "For in Him dwells all the fullness of the Godhead bodily; and you are complete in Him, who is the head of all principality and power" (Col. 2:9–10). As Christ is made manifest through us by the power of the Holy Spirit, we can become living conduits for encounter with God. And through us, others, like Jose, Myra and their children, can have a personal experience with the love of God!

ANDREW THE NETWORKER

In addition to working in his family's commercial fishing enterprise, Andrew followed the teaching of John the Baptist and was considered one of his disciples (John 1:35–40). Thus he heard John declare that Jesus was the Lamb of God—a clear reference to Him as the Messiah. Eager to know more about this new Teacher, Andrew pursued Jesus, prompting an invitation to spend an evening with Him. The meeting convinced Andrew that he had indeed met the long-awaited Christ. The text is quite clear that the first thing Andrew

continued

continued

did after coming to this conclusion was to find his
brother, Simon, and tell him the extraordinary news: "We
have found the Messiah!" He then brought his brother to
meet Jesus (John 1:41–42).

Later, after Jesus called both of the brothers to follow
Him as His disciples, Andrew and the others found themselves on one occasion confronted by thousands of people. Jesus asked His disciples where they could buy food
for the crowd to eat, a proposition that staggered them.
But Andrew had made the acquaintance of a boy with a
handful of barley loaves and a couple of fish. He brought
this meager supply to the attention of the Lord, who then
multiplied it to feed the entire crowd of about 5,000 (John
6:4–14).

Shortly before Jesus' arrest, certain Greeks desired to
meet Him. Once again, Andrew acted as a go-between,
carrying their request to his Teacher (John 12:20–22). All
of these incidents suggest that Andrew was a networker, a
man who liked to put people together—and especially to
put them together with Jesus. He serves as a model for
believers today in bringing others to Christ.

Tradition holds that Andrew devoted the later years of
his life to spreading the news about Jesus to Scythia, the
region north of the Black Sea. Some say that he was martyred at Patrae in Achaia by crucifixion on an X-shaped
cross. ◆

1. Like Andrew, Prison Fellowship Ministries uses networking to bring others to Christ. What
   is another networking technique that believers could use to reveal Christ to those who do
   not know Him?

2. How is someone you know a reflection of Christ to others?

3. How can you better reflect Christ in your life as a witness to fellow Christians and unbelievers alike?

——◆ Experiencing God Every Day ◆——

So how was the retreat?" asked Patricia.

Sam sat back with his arms crossed. "You know, maybe I won't go to any more retreats. Instead of getting uplifted, I end up feeling demoralized."

"How come?" Patricia looked surprised. "I've never had that reaction."

"I don't know. Maybe there's something wrong with me." Sam sighed. "I keep hearing about these special religious experiences others have had. But I've never had anything like that happen to me. Is there some reason why God doesn't want to show Himself to me?"

"Well, I'm not sure that every Christian will experience a revelation of God in their lives. I'm not sure I've had the kind of experience you're talking about myself," answered Patricia. "But I do sense God's presence in my life. I don't really need some supernatural encounter because the Lord is with me all the time."

Sam looked unconvinced. "How do you *know* He's with you?"

"It's kind of hard to explain," Patricia replied. "Remember when the Lord appeared to Elijah on Mount Horeb? He looked for God's presence, but God wasn't in the wind or the fire or the earthquake. God appeared as a gentle whisper. That's what God's presence is like in my heart." ◆

◆ ◆ ◆ ◆ ◆ ◆ ◆ ◆ ◆

Like Sam, we may sometimes long for a dramatic revelation of the Lord. But if we look only for some spectacular sign of God's presence, we may very well miss the gentle whisper of His voice within our hearts. We need not wait to encounter God on some mountaintop, for His Spirit lives within us. Through our personal relationship with God, we can experience His loving presence in our lives.

Yet like any relationship, we need to cultivate intimacy with the Lord. As believers, God will always remain with us, but sin can separate us from a sense of communion with God. We need only "Draw near to God and He will draw near to you" (James 4:8). As we walk in His ways and strive to know Him better, we can experience the fullness of fellowship with God (Eph. 3:14–19; 1 John 1:6–7).

SINLESS PERFECTION?

Most followers of Christ would agree that they should pursue the highest moral integrity that they can. But John's statements in 1 John 3:6 appear to raise that standard to the point of sinless perfection. In fact, if the person who sins "has neither seen [Christ] nor known Him," then what hope is there for believers who fail?

Here is a case where the English language fails us. In English the word "sins" appears absolute and final: one sin and you're cut off from God. However, the form of the Greek verb here (hamartanei) conveys a sense of continuous action: "No one who abides in Christ makes a habit of continually sinning." The point is that true believers diminish their old patterns of sin as they grow in Christ, replacing them with new patterns of faith and love.

continued

continued

The situation is similar to losing weight by changing one's eating habits. No one obtains instant health, but over time and by sticking to a disciplined diet, one can make great strides in that direction.

Of course, the fact that we won't obtain sinless perfection in this life does not mean that we should deal lightly with sin. To do so would be an offense to God, as well as destructive to ourselves. Yes, God forgives individual sins, but if we persist in sinful patterns, we keep the power of Christ from operating in our lives. We also risk grave spiritual consequences, such as losing the ability to repent (Heb. 6:1–12).

Do you keep falling into a particular area of sin? John says that the way out of that frustrating predicament is to learn to continually "abide" in Christ. Confess your sins to Him and then concentrate not so much on avoiding sin as on maintaining your relationship with Him. After all, He has come to keep you from sin (1 John 2:1–2). But if you turn away from Him and capitulate to sin's mastery, then, as John has written, you can neither see Him working in your life nor know the joy of His presence. ◆

1. With whom do you identify?   a) Sam   b) Patricia

2. The movie *Chariots of Fire* was based on the true story of Olympic runner Eric Liddell, who experienced the joy of closeness with God while running. When do you feel God's presence most fully (for example: in prayer)?

_____

3. Have you ever had a friendship that suffered due to "lack of maintenance?" If so, give an account of what happened to the relationship.

_____

_____

4. Describe a period when disobedience interfered with your sense of intimacy with God.

_____

_____

5. Deepened relationship with God is the pathway to greater experience of His presence in our lives. What are three habits that you can practice to deepen your relationship with God?

a.

_____

b.

_____

c.

_____

——◆ The God Who Lives in Our Hearts ◆——

In this life, few believers will experience encounters with the Almighty to rival the experiences of those special few whom God chose to reveal Himself to in ancient times. Yet today we have so many ways that we can know and personally experience God's presence! Through prayer, through meditation on His Word, through gathering together in worship, we come to know the joy and inner assurance of close fellowship with the Lord. And at special moments in our lives, God reaches out to touch us, and give us a renewed wonder of His very real presence.

Rarely were those who encountered God left unchanged. Indeed, encounters with the living God are transformational. Souls are healed; lives are changed. We looked at a few such transformational experiences in this chapter. As we'll see in the next chapter, we too can experience God's power of transformation in our own lives.

Answers to quiz at "Fathers and Prophets" (Heb. 1:1)
(1) Noah (Gen. 6–9)
(2) Daniel (Dan. 1–12)
(3) Moses (Exodus, Leviticus, Numbers, Deuteronomy)
(4) David (1 Sam. 16–31, Psalms)
(5) Solomon (2 Sam. 12, 1 Kin. 1–12, Proverbs, Ecclesiastes, Song of Solomon)
(6) Amos (Amos)
(7) Samuel (1 and 2 Samuel)
(8) Habbakuk (Habbakuk)

CHAPTER 5

THE HEALER'S TRANSFORMING TOUCH

After graduating from Bible college, Rick Yeargain became involved in the production of amphetamines. The manufacturing operation brought him significant monetary rewards. It also brought him a five-year jail term on drug charges.

Yeargain's prison sentence proved a turning point in his life. He turned his back on a life of ill-gotten gains, and turned to the Lord in repentance. After his release, Yeargain resolved to use his talents for business in a responsible way.

And that he did. He earned a master's degree in business from George Washington University, and went on to help build an electronics company from a basement project to a flourishing firm with 60 employees. It was a process that took many years, during which his business practices profited from the application of the Christian values of honesty and good stewardship.

At the peak of success, however, Yeargain felt a void in his life. He had accomplished his business goals, but they did not bring him happiness. Though he did not know it, God was not done with the

life-changing process begun in that lonely jail cell.

On a weekend retreat, Rick Yeargain reached another turning point in his life. In a moment of complete surrender, he prayed, "Lord, I want to give you everything." A month later he was on his way to Romania.

It was 1990, a year after the overthrow of dictator Nicolae Ceauşescu, and Romania itself was in the process of transformation from a Marxist regime to a capitalist society. It was no easy transition, as Yeargain would discover, for years of communism had effectively destroyed the will to self-sufficiency among Romanians.

Now living in Romania with his family, Yeargain uses his business expertise to help Romanian believers build successful businesses of their own. Profitech Plastics, a Romanian company that started in 1990 with $200 in the bank now has dozens of employees. It is

just one of the new businesses Yeargain's advice and American seed money have helped to create.

Rick Yeargain's transformation from drug dealer to Christian business advisor in Romania is certainly a work of God. But even now the process is not over. Yeargain's wife, Candace, volunteers at Sectia Distrofici orphanage, which cares for 65 of the thousands of ill or abandoned children in Romania. Rick Yeargain had seen the economic enablement of fellow Christians as his calling in Romania, but the recognition of this terrible problem has drawn the Yeargain family toward relief efforts as well. One consequence of this is a transformation the whole Yeargain family has experienced—the adoption of a little orphan named Ionela.

◆ ◆ ◆ ◆ ◆ ◆ ◆ ◆ ◆

A RICH MAN ENTERS THE KINGDOM

Jesus said it would be hard for the rich to enter the kingdom of heaven (Matt. 19:23). The remark has led some to believe that rich people can't enter the kingdom, and others to feel that Jesus was opposed to wealth and the wealthy. But Matthew's response to Jesus' call (9:9–13) contradicts both of those assumptions.

The incident recorded here contrasts sharply with Jesus' encounter with the rich young ruler (Matt. 19:16–30; Mark 10:17–31; Luke 18:18–30). In many ways, the ruler seemed to make a more likely prospect than Matthew for membership in Jesus' burgeoning movement.

Yet despite the young ruler's apparent edge, it was Matthew who ended up following Jesus. The other "went away sorrowful" (Matt. 19:22). What accounts for the difference? For

one thing, the wealthy young man clearly perceived himself as already righteous (19:17–20). He felt that he was able to meet God's requirements on his own merits (19:16). But no one had to convince Matthew that he needed the Great Physician (9:11–12). As a tax collector, he was among the most despised members of Jewish society.

Yet there was a more fundamental difference between these two men, a difference that depended on Jesus' attitude more

than on theirs. His words to the Pharisees explained the matter clearly: "*I desire mercy and not sacrifice.* For I did not come to call the righteous, but sinners, to repentance" (9:13). In calling Matthew but turning away the rich young ruler, Jesus demonstrated in real-life parables precisely this point: that salvation depends on the mercy of God, not on the merits or sacrifice of people.

In the end, the crucial difference between the rich man who followed and the rich man who rejected was the merciful choice of God. Of course, none of us knows that choice beforehand. Therefore, we as believers need to be equally eager to present the gospel of Christ to everyone, rich or poor, wise or foolish, mighty or weak. ◆

 Matthew 9:9–13

⁹As Jesus passed on from there, He saw a man named Matthew sitting at the tax office. And He said to him, "Follow Me." So he arose and followed Him.

¹⁰Now it happened, as Jesus sat at the table in the house, *that* behold, many tax collectors and sinners came and sat down with Him and His disciples. ¹¹And when the Pharisees saw *it,* they said

to His disciples, "Why does your Teacher eat with tax collectors and sinners?"

¹²When Jesus heard *that,* He said to them, "Those who are well have no need of a physician, but those who are sick. ¹³But go and learn what *this* means: '*I desire mercy and not sacrifice.*' For I did not come to call the righteous, but sinners, to repentance."

Matthew the tax collector would become the author of the Gospel that bears his name. A man of remarkable humility, whenever he refers to himself in his Gospel, it is as "Matthew the tax collector." By so doing, he identifies himself with a despised profession, known for its dishonesty. Perhaps he desired to make clear just how great was the mercy Christ the Physician extended to a sinner in need of His healing touch. This may also explain why he calls himself Matthew, which means "gift of God," when he is referred to elsewhere as Levi—presumably his more familiar name. Matthew wanted his readers to know that the salvation he had received was an unmerited gift from God.

It is fascinating to see the account of Matthew's conversion—described in his own words (Matt. 9:9). Yet only the barest of information is provided: Christ came to him and said, "Follow me," and Matthew responded. In all likelihood, Matthew had been a witness to Christ's teaching in the city. Certainly, Christ knew Matthew's heart when he called him. Even so, there is little evidence of the dramatic transformation that must have taken place in Matthew's life. For in this brief incident, Matthew the tax collector was changed into Matthew the apostle of Jesus Christ.

The Gospels of Mark and Luke both provide accounts of Matthew's calling (in which he is referred to as "Levi") (Luke 5:27). A comparison of these parallel accounts proves quite enlightening. From Mark we learn that the "house" where Christ eats is in fact Matthew's own residence (Mark 2:15). Luke reveals that the dinner was in fact a "great feast" hosted by Matthew, with a huge crowd of guests that were counted among the "tax collectors and sinners" of the city (Luke 5:29–30).

1. In Matthew 19:21, Jesus instructs the rich young ruler to "go, sell what you have and give to the poor," then follow Him. In Luke 5:28, we are told that Levi "left all, rose up, and followed Him." What transformation in Matthew's life following his call by Christ does the account in Luke subtly reveal?

_____

2. Christ referred to Himself as a physician sent to heal the sick (Luke 5:31). Who are the sick?

_____

3. Who did the Pharisees presumably think were the "righteous" to which Jesus referred?

_____

4. Jesus also suggested that the Pharisees needed to learn the verse: "I desire mercy and not sacrifice" (Hos. 6:6). What did he want the Pharisees to understand?

_____

5. Did you ever have a meal with someone that was considered unsavory or held in contempt? If so, did you respond in a Christlike or Pharisee-like manner?

_____

Luke 19:1–10

Then *Jesus* entered and passed through Jericho. ²Now behold, *there was* a man named Zacchaeus who was a chief tax collector, and he was rich. ³And he sought to see who Jesus was, but could not because of the crowd, for he was of short stature. ⁴So he ran ahead and climbed up into a sycamore tree to see Him, for He was going to pass that *way*. ⁵And when Jesus came to the place, He looked up and saw him, and said to him, "Zacchaeus, make haste and come down, for today I must stay at your house." ⁶So he made haste and came down, and received Him joyfully.

⁷But when they saw *it*, they all complained, saying, "He has gone to be a guest with a man who is a sinner."

⁸Then Zacchaeus stood and said to the Lord, "Look, Lord, I give half of my goods to the poor; and if I have taken anything from anyone by false accusation, I restore fourfold."

⁹And Jesus said to him, "Today salvation has come to this house, because he also is a son of Abraham; ¹⁰for the Son of Man has come to seek and to save that which was lost."

1. How was Zacchaeus' view of wealth transformed after he came face to face with Christ?

_____

2. Matthew gave up his occupation, but Zacchaeus may have continued to serve as a tax collector. How has being a Christian affected your work?

_____

MARY, THE RELIABLE WITNESS

The Gospels mention Mary of Magdala by name more than any other female disciple. One reason may be the dramatic turnaround in her life that the Lord brought about by casting out seven demons. She responded by supporting His ministry and joining with several other women who traveled with Him (Luke 8:1–3).

Mary's loyalty proved unwavering right to the end. While the Twelve fled after Jesus' arrest, Mary stood by at His crucifixion (Matt. 27:56; Mark 15:40; John 19:25). She also helped prepare His body for burial (Matt. 27:61; Mark 15:47; Luke 23:55). Perhaps it was to reward her undying devotion that the Lord allowed her to be the first person to meet Him after His resurrection (Mark 16:9–10; John 20:14–18).

Curiously, however, the disciples refused to believe Mary's report of the risen Lord. In fact, they dismissed it as an "idle tale" (Mark 16:11; Luke 24:11). Perhaps their skepticism betrayed long-held doubts about Mary's credibility: after all, hadn't she been possessed by seven demons? Moreover, Jewish culture raised its men to consider the testimony of women as inferior.

Nevertheless, Jesus chose Mary to report the good news of His resurrection to His other followers. Later, He rebuked them for their unwillingness to believe her (Mark 16:14). Thanks to Him, she was a changed person. Moreover, she was a reliable witness, having proven her trustworthiness through her perseverance and steadfastness in the face of danger and doubt.

One Woman's Testimony

Prior to becoming a follower of Christ, Mary of Magdala was possessed by seven demons. The number seven in Scripture is often used to indicate completion. Evidently, Mary's life before her miraculous healing was completely under the domination of demonic powers.

Mary was but one of many that Jesus freed from demonic control. Christ's time on earth was a period of greatly increased demonic activity. The many examples in the Gospels provide a picture of demonic possession. These evil spirits afflicted their human victims, causing disease and physical impairment (Matt. 12:22; Mark 9:25), madness (Mark 5:5), and violent fits (Mark 1:26; Luke 9:39–42). We can only imagine the human torment that Mary Magdalene must have experienced while under spiritual oppression.

Mary's life changed dramatically after Jesus healed her. Yet there were many lives transformed by Christ during His ministry as He healed the sick and cast out demons. These changed individuals responded with joy, but few apparently became His loyal followers, as Mary did. Indeed, even an expression of gratitude was sometimes lacking—of the ten lepers Christ healed in Samaria (Luke 17:11–19), only one bothered to return to thank Him!

Mary's response sets her apart. She devoted herself entirely to Christ, traveling with Him and serving His needs. Even after the apostles fled at Christ's arrest, she remained steadfast, witnessing the crucifixion, and accompanying His body as it was taken to the tomb. After the Sabbath, Mary returned to the tomb, "while it was still dark" (John 20:1). As a consequence, she became an eyewitness to a transformation even greater than the one she had experienced.

John 20:11–18

¹¹But Mary stood outside by the tomb weeping, and as she wept she stooped down *and looked* into the tomb. ¹²And she saw two angels in white sitting, one at the head and the other at the feet, where the body of Jesus had lain. ¹³Then they said to her, "Woman, why are you weeping?"

She said to them, "Because they have taken away my Lord, and I do not know where they have laid Him."

¹⁴Now when she had said this, she turned around and saw Jesus standing *there,* and did not know that it was Jesus. ¹⁵Jesus said to her, "Woman, why are you weeping? Whom are you seeking?"

She, supposing Him to be the gardener, said to Him, "Sir, if You have carried Him away, tell me where You have laid Him, and I will take Him away."

¹⁶Jesus said to her, "Mary!"

She turned and said to Him, "Rabboni!" (which is to say, Teacher).

¹⁷Jesus said to her, "Do not cling to Me, for I have not yet ascended to My Father; but go to My brethren and say to them, 'I am ascending to My Father and your Father, and *to* My God and your God.'"

What a dramatic moment! Only John's Gospel gives us such a vivid look at what it must have been like to see the risen Christ. As Mary stood weeping beside the tomb, she did not even recognize her Lord at first. But when He called her by name, she turned, and in an instant her sorrow was changed to joy (see John 20:16).

Women Find Their Proper Place

Mary Magdalene was only the first to see the risen Christ, for immediately afterward, the Lord appeared to a group of women who had also followed Him. He gave to these women the same instruction: go and tell the others the good news that He has risen from the dead (see John 20:17).

To you or me, this might not seem particularly strange, but it must have come as quite a shock to first-century Jews who later heard the gospel story. For women were not considered trustworthy witnesses. In fact, a woman's testimony was not acceptable in a Jewish court of law. And in the Jewish spiritual world, women were clearly second-class citizens. The great temple in Jerusalem excluded women from the inner courts. Women were rarely permitted to study the Law. In fact, the very presence of women among Jesus' followers was no doubt considered scandalous by many traditional Jews of the time.

So you see, what Christ had done was a truly revolutionary act! He had chosen women to be the first witnesses to the greatest event in history!

In so doing, Christ had issued a complete repudiation of the traditional view of women in Palestine. Through his commission to "go and tell," the Lord had declared that women were trustworthy witnesses. And in making His initial resurrection appearances to these women, He made it known that they were equal citizens in His kingdom.

1. Jesus gave little credence to many of the gender-related customs and taboos of the day. Suppose Christ's ministry had been in modern times—what current sexual stereotypes might the Lord disregard?

_____

_____

2a. What is a common perception about women that conflicts with the biblical view of women?

_____

_____

2b. What is a commonly held perception about men that conflicts with the Bible's view?

_____

_____

◆ A World without Boundaries ◆

Christ clearly shook up His disciples' attitudes about men and women. The early church reflected the changed attitude toward women. Women gathered with the disciples (Acts 1:14;

2:1), shared the gospel message with others (Acts 8:3–4; 9:2), and participated in church meetings (Acts 12:1–17; 1 Cor. 11:2–16). The changes in male-female relationships led to some tension and conflict (1 Cor. 11:1–16; 14:34–35), but clearly a whole new world had opened to women believers to become involved in spiritual worship and to exercise their gifts in the service of God.

Yet an even greater change awaited the early church.

ETHNIC WALLS BREAK DOWN

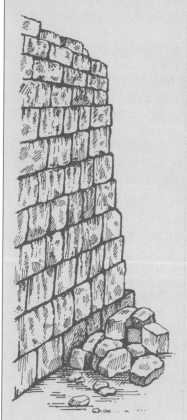

A major breakthrough in race relations is described in Acts 10. For years a virtual wall between Jews and Gentiles had hampered the apostles in sharing Jesus with the Gentile world. But when Peter met Cornelius—an officer of Rome's occupation troops in Palestine—two conversions took place: Cornelius, his family, and his friends came to faith; and Peter came to realize that God wants Gentiles in the church.

God easily could have used Philip the evangelist (see Acts 8:5) to bring the gospel to Cornelius. After all, he lived in Caesarea and had already shown his willingness to share the gospel across ethnic lines. But no, God called Peter to bring His message to the Roman centurion. Apparently He wanted to break down barriers against Gentiles in Peter's heart.

How Peter Saw Cornelius

- *Living in Caesarea,* Roman military capital of Palestine (Acts 10:1).
- *A centurion,* commander of 100 occupying Roman troops (10:1).
- *Of the Italian Regiment,* all men from Italy (10:1).
- *Gentile* (10:1).
- *Unclean,* like the unclean animals of the Old Testament dietary laws (10:11–16).
- *Unlawful for a Jew to visit,* as he was from another nation (10:28).
- *Uncircumcised,* therefore not right to eat with (11:3).

In Peter's mind, these factors disqualified Cornelius from serving him dinner, let alone coming to faith. But Peter was following a "Jewish gospel."

God's intention had been that Hebrews would treat their Gentile neighbors cordially (Num. 35:15; Deut. 10:19; Ezek. 47:2). Of course, He also charged His people to exclude heathen practices,

continued

continued

particularly idolatry (Lev. 18:24—19:4; Deut. 12:29–31). Intermarriage was condemned, though sometimes allowed (compare Ex. 34:16; Deut. 7:3; Ezra 9:12; 10:2–44; Neh. 10:30). But the main concern was moral purity.

Through rabbinic tradition strict separation became the rule. By Peter's day, four hundred years of Greek and Roman oppression had only hardened Jewish resolve to avoid as much contact as possible with foreigners.

Peter and the other Jewish believers brought these attitudes with them into the church, which made it almost impossible for them to reach out to Gentiles.

How God Saw Cornelius

- *Devout* (Acts 10:2).
- *A God-fearer,* along with his household (10:2).
- *Generous to the poor* (10:2).
- *A man of prayer* whose prayers and alms were received by God (10:2, 4).
- *Obedient to God's angel* (10:7–8).
- *Cleansed by God,* so not unclean (10:15).
- *Crucial for Peter to visit* (10:5, 19–20).

God's view of Cornelius was a contrast to Peter's. Because of Christ, God was ready to throw the doors of faith wide open to Gentiles: "What God has cleansed you must not call common," He sternly declared to Peter (Acts 10:9–16). Because of Christ, the centurion could be "cleansed" from sin and be acceptable to God.

But Peter was confused. Should he break with his culture and visit this Gentile, violating traditional codes handed down as if carrying the force of God's law? He had at least two days to sort out his thoughts as he walked to Caesarea to meet Cornelius. His emotional struggle can be seen in his first words to the assembled group:

"You know how unlawful it is for a Jewish man to keep company with or go to one of another nation" (v. 28).

But God broke down the wall in Peter's heart by pouring out the Holy Spirit on these Gentile believers (vv. 44–45).

Peter's New Perspective

- "In truth I perceive that *God shows no partiality*" (Acts 10:34, italics added).
- "But *in every nation* whoever fears Him . . . is accepted by Him" (10:35, italics added).
- "Jesus Christ . . . is Lord of *all*" (10:36, italics added).
- "*Whoever believes* in Him will receive remission of sins" (10:43, italics added).
- "Can *anyone* forbid water, that *these* should not be baptized who have received the Holy Spirit *just as we have?*" (10:47, italics added).
- "God gave *them* the *same gift* as He gave us when we believed" (11:17, italics added).
- "*Who was I* that I could withstand God?" (11:17, italics added).

Breaking Down Barriers Today

Attitudes of prejudice and legalism trouble the church today just as they did the early church. Believers sometimes mingle cultural biases with biblical mandates, creating wrenching controversies over numerous sensitive issues. Certainly issues need to be addressed, particularly when essentials of the faith are at stake. But one of those biblical essentials is that believers eagerly seek out *all* people, look at them from God's perspective, love them for the gospel's sake, and rejoice over those that respond in faith. Can the church ever afford to wall itself off through fear or prejudice? Doing so would be to turn away from God's compassionate heart. ◆

Acts 10:9–44

9The next day, as they went on their journey and drew near the city, Peter went up on the housetop to pray, about the sixth hour. 10Then he became very hungry and wanted to eat; but while they made ready, he fell into a trance 11and saw heaven opened and an object like a great sheet bound at the four corners, descending to him and let down to the earth. 12In it were all kinds of four-footed animals of the earth, wild beasts, creeping things, and birds of the air. 13And a voice came to him, "Rise, Peter; kill and eat."

14But Peter said, "Not so, Lord! For I have never eaten anything common or unclean."

15And a voice *spoke* to him again the second time, "What God has cleansed you must not call common." 16This was done three times. And the object was taken up into heaven again.

17Now while Peter wondered within himself what this vision which he had seen meant, behold, the men who had been sent from Cornelius had made inquiry for Simon's house, and stood before the gate. 18And they called and asked whether Simon, whose surname was Peter,.was lodging there.

19While Peter thought about the vision, the Spirit said to him, "Behold, three men are seeking you. 20Arise therefore, go down and go with them, doubting nothing; for I have sent them."

21Then Peter went down to the men who had been sent to him from Cornelius, and said, "Yes, I am he whom you seek. For what reason have you come?"

22And they said, "Cornelius *the* centurion, a just man, one who fears God and has a good reputation among all the nation of the Jews, was divinely instructed by a holy angel to summon you to his house, and to hear words from you." 23Then he invited them in and lodged *them*.

On the next day Peter went away with them, and some brethren from Joppa accompanied him.

24And the following day they entered Caesarea. Now Cornelius was waiting for them, and had called together his relatives and close friends.

25As Peter was coming in, Cornelius met him and fell down at his feet and worshiped *him*. 26But Peter lifted him up, saying, "Stand up; I myself am also a man." 27And as he talked with him, he went in and found many who had come together. 28Then he said to them, "You know how unlawful it is for a Jewish man to keep company with or go to one of another nation. But God has shown me that I should not call any man common or unclean. 29Therefore I came without objection as soon as I was sent for. I ask, then, for what reason have you sent for me?"

30So Cornelius said, "Four days ago I was fasting until this hour; and at the ninth hour I prayed in my house, and behold, a man stood before me in bright clothing, 31and said, 'Cornelius, your prayer has been heard, and your alms are remembered in the sight of God. 32Send therefore to Joppa and call Simon here, whose surname is Peter. He is lodging in the house of Simon, a tanner, by the sea. When he comes, he will speak to you.' 33So I sent to you immediately, and you have done well to come. Now therefore, we are all present before God, to hear all the things commanded you by God."

34Then Peter opened *his* mouth and said: "In truth I perceive that God shows no partiality. 35But in every nation whoever fears Him and works righteousness is accepted by Him. 36The word which *God* sent to the children of Israel, preaching peace through Jesus Christ—He is Lord of all— 37that word you know, which was proclaimed throughout all Judea, and began from Galilee after the baptism which John preached: 38how God anointed Jesus of Nazareth with the Holy Spirit and with power, who went about doing good and healing all who were oppressed by the devil, for God was with Him. 39And we are witnesses of all things which He did both in the land of the Jews and in Jerusalem, whom they killed by hanging on a tree. 40Him God raised up on the third day, and showed Him openly, 41not

continued

> *continued*
> to all the people, but to witnesses chosen before by God, *even* to us who ate and drank with Him after He arose from the dead. ⁴²And He commanded us to preach to the people, and to testify that it is He who was ordained by God *to be* Judge of the living and the dead. ⁴³To Him all the prophets witness that, through His name, whoever believes in Him will receive remission of sins."
>
> ⁴⁴While Peter was still speaking these words, the Holy Spirit fell upon all those who heard the word.

Even before this event, Peter had been made aware that God intended for Gentiles to be among His people. Peter had been present at the Great Commission, when Christ had commanded the disciples to "Go into all the world and preach the gospel" (Mark 16:15). He had witnessed as Samaritans, despised by Jews as a hybrid people corrupted by intermarriage with Gentiles, received the Holy Spirit by his own hand (Acts 8:14–17). Yet generations of Jewish hostility to the Gentiles made the acceptance of Gentile believers almost unthinkable. Peter may not have realized himself how deeply embedded in his own heart were the attitudes and prejudices derived from his strict Jewish upbringing.

Only a vision from God opened Peter's eyes. And through that vision, and his subsequent experiences in the house of Cornelius, Peter finally came to realize that the ancient wall of separation between Jew and Gentile had fallen with Christ's sacrifice and resurrection. With the shock of insight, Peter understood that Jesus Christ truly is "Lord of all!"

1. Peter saw Cornelius in terms of the group to which he belonged—the Gentiles. In contrast, on what did God base his judgment of Cornelius?

2. Peter was leader of the church in Jerusalem. However, Philip the evangelist had already shown a willingness to preach to the non-Jew, and he even resided in Caesarea. In addition, Paul—who would become God's chosen apostle to the Gentiles—had already been converted. Why did God choose Peter for the first mission to convert Gentiles?

3. Which barriers between people are harder to overcome: a) cultural and language barriers; or b) barriers that exist in our hearts and minds?

4. The Middle East in modern times is still a hotbed of conflict and ethnic hatred. What change would end the hostilities in this part of the world?

Divisions in the Church

Prior to the events of Acts 10, Peter considered Gentiles to be ungodly, and as a Jew he would not think of associating with them. Even after this experience, Peter struggled with his prejudices. *In Jerusalem, Paul confronted Peter on his unwillingness to eat with Gentile believers (Gal. 2:11–21). Peter admitted his error, but though he knew better, he still felt discomfort as a result of the old distinctions with which he grew up.*

A spirit of unity and unconditional acceptance should distinguish our relationship with fellow believers. Yet barriers of all kinds threaten to divide Christians. Below is a list of characteristics that may create divisions between believers. Circle those characteristics that would make you uncomfortable or cause you not to associate with one who professes to be a believer.

gambles	a Roman Catholic	divorced
drinks alcohol	a charismatic	remarried
smokes	a "Bible-thumping" fundamentalist	cross-racial couple
a liberal Democrat	a soldier	dresses immodestly
a conservative Republican	a pacifist	drives a luxury car

1. Which characteristic in another would make you most uncomfortable?

_____

2. Could you associate with such a Christian without compromising your convictions? _____

——◆ Before and After ◆——

The conversion of Cornelius and his household opened the door to missions directed toward converting the Gentiles. Conditions in the first century A.D. for such missionary work were ideal in many ways: The Roman Empire had united much of the world under a common law. Greek had become an international language, simplifying communications with peoples of many lands. Rome had built a system of paved roads across the empire, and sea trade was very active, making travel in those times relatively easy. Finally, the dispersion of Jews throughout the Gentile nations ensured that there were Jews and God-fearing Gentiles in all the major cities who were familiar with Old Testament Scripture and prophecy. God had providentially prepared a ready seedbed for the gospel message.

But who would God choose to lead the missionary work among the Gentiles? The man the Lord chose turned out to be an even more unlikely candidate than Peter!

SAUL OF TARSUS

Few backgrounds could have better prepared Saul to be the chief persecutor of the early church. He was born at Tarsus—"no mean city," as he liked to describe it (Acts 21:39)—a major Roman city on the coast of southeast

continued

PAUL, THE APOSTLE TO THE GENTILES

Ironically, Paul's background not only prepared him to be the early church's chief opponent, but also to become its leading spokesperson. Devout, energetic, outspoken,

continued

Saul continued

Asia Minor. Tarsus was a center for the tent-making industry, and perhaps that influenced Saul to choose that craft as an occupation. Teachers of the Law, which Saul eventually became, were not paid for their services and had to earn a living in other ways.

However, Saul said that he was "brought up" in Jerusalem "at the feet of Gamaliel," the most illustrious rabbi of the day (Acts 22:3) and a highly respected member of the Jewish council (Acts 5:34; see Acts 6:12). In making that statement, Saul was describing a process of technical training in the Law that prepared him to become one of the Pharisees, the religious elite of Judaism. For many Jewish youth, the rigorous course of study began at age 14 and continued to the age of 40.

Apparently Saul was an apt pupil. He claimed to have outstripped his peers in enthusiasm for ancestral traditions and in his zeal for the Law (Phil. 3:4–6). Probably through Gamaliel, he had opportunity to observe the council and come to know many of its principals and some of its inner workings.

So it was that he chanced to be present when the conflict between the council and the early church came to a head in the stoning of Stephen (Acts 7:57—8:1). He had likely watched earlier encounters between the council and members of the Way, such as those with Peter and John (Acts 4:5–18; 5:17–40). But apparently the incident with Stephen galvanized his commitment to traditional Judaism and set him off on a mission to seek out and destroy as many believers as he could (8:1–3).

Paul continued

stubborn, and exacting, Paul became far more troublesome to the Jews than he had ever been to the Christians, not in terms of violence, but ideology. Indeed, he lived with a price on his head as his former colleagues among the Jews sought to destroy him (Acts 9:23–25, 29; 23:12–15; 2 Cor. 11:26, 32–33).

Perhaps the chief irony of Paul's life was his calling to be the apostle to the Gentiles (Acts 9:15; Gal. 1:16; 2:7–9). Paul had been a Pharisee, the very title meaning "to separate." Some Pharisees even refused to eat with non-Pharisees for fear of being contaminated by food not rendered ritually clean. They also separated from women, from lepers, from Samaritans, and especially from Gentiles (or "foreigners").

So for Paul to take the gospel to the Gentiles was a reversal of his life and a thorough repudiation of his background as a Pharisee. Perhaps three people proved invaluable in helping him make this dramatic change: Barnabas, who like Paul was a Hellenistic Jew and came from a Levite background—he embraced Paul and mentored him in the faith when no one else would come near him (see Acts 4:36–37); and Priscilla and Aquila, fellow tentmakers—they joined Paul in business in Corinth and probably discussed the faith and its implications with Paul much as they did with Apollos (Acts 18:1–3, 24–28; see Rom. 16:3–5).

Paul eventually became Christianity's leading evangelist and theologian. But even as his status in the church rose, his perspective on himself changed. At first he saw himself as an important Christian leader, but then as "the least of the apostles" (1 Cor. 15:9). Later he realized that he was capable of "nothing good" (Rom. 7:18) and was "less than the the least of all the saints" (Eph. 3:8). Finally he described himself as the "chief" of sinners (1 Tim. 1:15)—and threw himself on God's mercy and grace.

The fearsome Pharisee of Pharisees became the fearless apostle to the Gentiles whose credo was, "To live is Christ, and to die is gain" (Phil. 1:21).

Acts 9:1–9

Then Saul, still breathing threats and murder against the disciples of the Lord, went to the high priest ²and asked letters from him to the synagogues of Damascus, so that if he found any who were of the Way, whether men or women, he might bring them bound to Jerusalem.

³As he journeyed he came near Damascus, and suddenly a light shone around him from heaven. ⁴Then he fell to the ground, and heard a voice saying to him, "Saul, Saul, why are you persecuting Me?"

⁵And he said, "Who are You, Lord?"

Then the Lord said, "I am Jesus, whom you are persecuting. It *is* hard for you to kick against the goads."

⁶So he, trembling and astonished, said, "Lord, what do You want me to do?"

Then the Lord *said* to him, "Arise and go into the city, and you will be told what you must do."

⁷And the men who journeyed with him stood speechless, hearing a voice but seeing no one. ⁸Then Saul arose from the ground, and when his eyes were opened he saw no one. But they led him by the hand and brought *him* into Damascus. ⁹And he was three days without sight, and neither ate nor drank.

New Directions

Paul describes himself as he was before his conversion as "a blasphemer, a persecutor, and an insolent man" (1 Tim. 1:13). He stood by approvingly as Stephen was stoned to death, and thereafter began his crusade against the church. The persecution he led was so great that the members of the early church scattered in an effort to escape him.

When Paul set out on the road to Damascus, his directions were clear: go to the synagogue in Damascus and take prisoner any Christians he found. But on the way, he received new directions from Jesus Christ! Paul's experience is the prime example of conversion, *a term that implies a "new direction" in one's attitude and behavior. Indeed, it's hard to imagine how his conversion could have resulted in a more radical change in the course of his life!*

A stunning change within Paul's own being must have occurred to have such a dramatic impact on his life. Based on what you know of Paul before and after his conversion experience, describe the transformation in each of the following facets of Paul's character.

	BEFORE	AFTER
His emotional nature:	_____	_____
His ambitions:	_____	_____
His spirituality	_____	_____
His attitude toward others:	_____	_____

1. Describe how Paul's view of himself continued to change as he grew spiritually during the remainder of his life:

_____

2. Has greater change in your own life and character come as a consequence of:
  a) conversion, or   b) long-term growth as a believer?

3. There were many reversals in Paul's personality as a consequence of his conversion. His attitude toward others changed from self-righteous intolerance to unconditional acceptance. Describe a reversal in your personality that has resulted from your faith in Christ.

4. In 2 Corinthians 5:17, Paul states: "If anyone *is* in Christ, *he is* a new creation; old things have passed away; behold, all things have become new." What does it mean to you to be "a new creation?"

◆ A Lifelong Journey ◆

Janice carried her tray from the buffet to a nearby table and sat down. Soon she was joined by her friends, Jack, Peggy, and Diane. As a matter of habit, the four friends met for lunch after attending Sunday church service. As they ate, they began talking about the week's events. Janice, however, did not seem to be her usual talkative self.

"You seem awfully quiet today, Janice," Peggy remarked. "Is everything okay?"

"Oh, I suppose," mumbled Janice, picking at her food.

"C'mon," Jack coaxed, "spill it."

Janice looked at her friends questioningly. "You guys have known me since I became a Christian. Do you think I've changed?"

"What do you mean?" asked Peggy.

"A couple of months ago, my nephew became a Christian, too. Everyone keeps talking about how much he's changed. Today, when Pastor

Smith was talking about becoming more Christlike, it just struck me how little I've changed since becoming a Christian. I feel like I'm the same person I always was."

"Who else would you be?" Jack teased.

Janice shrugged. "I just expected I'd see more change in myself. I've been a Christian for five years, and I don't know if I've really grown much. I'll certainly never be like Christ!"

"Don't you think you're being a little hard on yourself?" asked Peggy. "Maturing as a Christian takes time."

"Besides, I think you've changed a lot," added Diane. "I remember a time when all you talked about was clothes or a new car. You think more about how you ought to spend your money now."

"Yeah," agreed Peggy enthusiastically, "and you used to be one of the quiet ones during Bible study, but nowadays you share lots of insights."

"Last Wednesday, your prayer for my grandmother re-

ally meant a lot to me," said Diane. "Maybe you've been looking for the wrong kind of change."

"Maybe you're right. I was just thinking I should be—you know—*more spiritual*. But the pastor did say that confidence in the faith is a sign of maturity."

Janice went back to her meal, but between mouthfuls, a look of surprise dawned on her face.

"All living things grow, don't they? If our faith is alive, we'll grow, too, don't you think?"

"Now there's an insight! Sounds to me like you're practically super-spiritual right now, Janice," said Jack, with a grin. "If you become any more spiritual, you won't want to spend any time with us mere mortals!"

"Oh, I'll always have time for you guys," said Janice, laughing.

"Now, Jack," Diane shook her head with mock-disapproval, "growing as a Christian doesn't mean turning into some spiritual giant. I think being Christlike just means expressing His values in our normal lives."

"I stand corrected," said Jack, "and now that that's taken care of, I'll race you to the desert tray—in a Christlike way, of course!"

Jack started off as his friends got to their feet.

"I think it's Jack's maturity we really have to worry about," whispered Peggy to Janice with a wink. ◆

• • • • • • • • •

Scripture assures us that each of us is in a continuing process of transformation into the very image of Christ. Christlikeness is the ultimate goal of our walk (Eph. 4:23–24; Col. 3:10).

It is tempting to think that we should see some special sign of our spiritual growth. We imagine that, like bodybuilders who can see the results of their training, we too should be able to look in a mirror and see our spiritual muscles bulging! Perhaps we think of the apostle Paul's example, and look for a miraculous transformation such as he experienced. But even Paul took pains to point out he had not attained some kind of spiritual perfection (Phil. 3:12–14).

The truth is we have undergone a miraculous transformation! When we accepted the Lord as our Savior, something wonderful happened. A reorientation of our inner being took place. As any growth process, our change is often imperceptible to us. Yet over time, as we spiritually mature, we will come to exhibit more and more of Christ's holy character. First John 3:2 describes the nature of our lifelong journey as Christians: "Beloved, now we are children of God; and it has not yet been revealed what we shall be, but we know that when He is revealed, we shall be like Him."

1. Have you ever felt like you weren't growing as a Christian? Yes _____ No _____

2. If you confronted your friends as Janice did, how do you think they would respond?

_____

_____

3. Just as a plant needs nourishment to grow, so does our spiritual life to exhibit growth. What kind of nourishment fosters our growth as Christians?

_____

_____

• • • • • • • • •

John Mark is an example of personal growth. He served as the assistant of Paul and Barnabas on Paul's first missionary journey—at least as far as Perga in Asia Minor. At that point, John Mark deserted the missionary team and returned to Jerusalem (Acts 13:13).

We aren't given an explanation for John Mark's defection. Perhaps the young man suffered from culture shock, as they preached in strange Gentile lands. It may be that his duties—which probably involved making arrangements for travel, food, and lodging, as well as the instruction of new converts—became too burdensome for John Mark. Whatever the case, it appears that John Mark was simply not spiritually mature enough to handle the demands of the missionary trip. But did John Mark's failure permanently brand him as untrustworthy?

John Mark—"Useful for Ministry"

John Mark is a case study in second chances. Spurned by Paul because he had gone home to Jerusalem instead of continuing on a journey to Asia Minor (Acts 13:13; 15:38), John Mark was fortunate in that his cousin was the mentoring model, Barnabas (see 4:36–37). Just as he had done with Paul when no one else would come near him, Barnabas took John Mark home with him to Cyprus where he nurtured him personally and spiritually.

Thanks to Barnabas, John Mark turned out to be a special gift to the early church. He became a valued associate of Peter and probably traveled with him to Rome, where tradition holds that he composed his Gospel by writing down Peter's memories of Jesus' life and teaching.

Paul also finally recognized the value of John Mark. Late in life, he wrote to Timothy, urging him to "get Mark and bring him with you, for he is useful to me for ministry" (2 Tim. 4:11). Indeed he was. Early church tradition says that he was the first evangelist to Alexandria, Egypt, and the first bishop of that city. He won a great number of sincerely committed converts there.

 Acts 15:37–40

³⁷Now Barnabas was determined to take with them John called Mark. ³⁸But Paul insisted that they should not take with them the one who had departed from them in Pamphylia, and had not gone with them to the work. ³⁹Then the contention became so sharp that they parted from one another. And so Barnabas took Mark and sailed to Cyprus; ⁴⁰but Paul chose Silas and departed, being commended by the brethren to the grace of God.

1. If you had been a companion of Paul and Barnabas, whose side would you have taken regarding John Mark, and why?

2. Clearly, Paul revised his opinion of John Mark as indicated by his reference to John Mark as "my son" in 1 Peter 5:13. What encouragement can those who have suffered spiritual failures in the past draw from John Mark's life?

3a. We have all had moments when looking in a mirror that we wished we could change a physical characteristic. Suppose that mirror reflected your inner self. Which feature would you find least attractive (for example: my temper, my work habits, etc.)?

3b. Which feature of your character seems most attractive to you?

3c. Fortunately, God is at work within us even now to change the blemishes in our character. What is one way you can work with God to encourage change in the unattractive feature mentioned above?

_____

The Road Ahead

1. You are on your spiritual journey, from convert to Christlike. How far have you traveled?

_____

2. As you look down the spiritual highway, what road hazard do you see looming ahead (perhaps some change that God wants you to make but that you are resisting)?

_____

3. Is it possible to turn around and head in the wrong direction? If so, how?

_____

——◆ Changed for the Better ◆——

The Christian life is one of continual transformation, from the revolutionary change of our conversion to the daily renewal of our hearts and minds as we learn to live like Christ. We live in hopeful expectation of ultimate transformation, as well, when we shall be made perfect.

The world and its relationships have also undergone and continue to undergo transformation through the gospel message. It is a unifying message that tears down walls and heals divisions, not by force of arms, but through the power to change hearts and lives. A final transformation awaits this world, for God plans to create "a new heaven and a new earth" (Rev. 21:1). And we shall be its citizens.

But until that time, we must live in this imperfect world. Although we can look forward to our future perfection, it can be discouraging to have to deal with the flaws within us and others. The next chapter explores how we can overcome discouraging circumstances that confront us in the here and now.

The Darkness of Despair, the Light of Hope

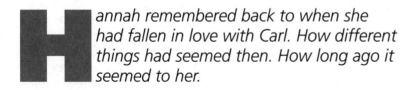

Hannah remembered back to when she had fallen in love with Carl. How different things had seemed then. How long ago it seemed to her.

Carl was the youth minister of their church, and Hannah had worked in the church office. When she and Carl had begun seeing each other, Hannah had become not only a part of Carl's life but also a part of his ministry. She had helped him work with the church's active youth group. Hannah had felt a special kind of fulfillment through her involvement in the ministry. Not only was she meaningfully involved in the life of the man she loved, she truly enjoyed being "big sister" to the teenagers.

When they got married, Hannah imagined that things would continue on as they had been. She hadn't anticipated that she would get pregnant— nor did she expect that her newborn son, Nathan, would have spina bifida. Two years later, Hannah couldn't help but look back on those happy days with bitterness. Of course, she loved her son. But she found all of her time was taken up in caring for his needs. She also ended up getting a part-time job at a dentist's office to help pay the additional medical

bills. On most nights when Carl was leading a youth activity, Hannah was at home taking care of Nathan.

At times it seemed to Hannah as though life had played a cruel joke on her. In her mind, marriage had always represented a life of sharing and togetherness, but for her it had come to mean separation, loneliness and sacrifice. The weight of her additional duties left her tired and dejected. Time and again, she would catch herself thinking back about how life had been during her engagement. In moments of despair, she would cry out to God, "Is this my life, Lord? Is this my marriage? How am I supposed to go on like this?"

◆ ◆ ◆ ◆ ◆ ◆ ◆ ◆ ◆

No one is immune to discouragement. It's part of our nature as emotional beings. Discouragement undermines our enthusiasm, weakens our resolution, and saps our strength. How do we overcome feelings of despair when our circumstances seem so hopeless? How do we persevere when discouraged?

1. Describe a situation that left you feeling deeply discouraged.

---

2. Did your discouragement end through a change of circumstances or a change of attitude?

Western culture not only encourages the "pursuit of happiness," it lures us into an expectation of happiness. The American Dream intimates that success and prosperity are ours for the taking. The miracles of modern medicine and technology promise health and contentment.

These myths of our modern world often lead believers into unrealistic expectations for their lives. And when life doesn't go according to plan, disappointment is sure to follow. Hannah entered her marriage with an image of what it would be like, but the reality didn't live up to her expectations. In fact, she came to feel burdened beyond her ability to cope.

Scripture imparts a different view of what the believer may expect in this life. Hardship will come, and the Christian can expect to face trials in life. But at the same time, we have one sure hope: God will always be with us. Paul speaks of this hope when he says, "Now hope does not disappoint, because the love of God has been poured out in our hearts by the Holy Spirit who was given to us" (Rom. 5:5). What Paul is saying is that our hopes for a great job, an ideal marriage and a trouble-free life may disappoint, but hope in God and His love for us never will.

Our hope in the Lord and His love provides the surest weapon against discouragement.

EUNICE—A MOTHER'S LEGACY

Eunice (2 Tim. 1:5) was Jewish, but apparently her father was not very orthodox: he violated one of the clear commands of the Law in arranging a match for his daughter with a Gentile (Acts 16:1). Later, when Timothy was born, he wasn't circumcised (16:3). So it seems that neither Eunice's father nor husband were observant of Judaism.

But Eunice was. Paul praised her for her "genuine faith," which she shared in common with Lois, her mother (2 Tim. 1:5). Eunice imparted that faith to her son, Timothy, and more than anyone else equipped him for a lifetime of usefulness for God.

Eunice is an encouragement for every woman faced with the daunting task of nurturing the spiritual life of her children, especially if she can't count on the help of a strong male. Eunice may have had no formal religious education and little encouragement from her family, except for Lois. But she had two crucial things going for her that offer hope for mothers today—the inherent power of being a mother and the dynamic power of a loving God.

For Eunice, her arranged marriage to a Gentile who did not share her Jewish faith must have been a great discouragement. Eunice later became a Christian, but it would appear her husband remained an unbeliever (Acts 16:1). We don't really know what her marriage was like, but it was clearly far from ideal. Yet through her faith, she persevered in what might have seemed a hopeless situation.

Her perseverance was rewarded, for God used her to instill the same faith in her son, Timothy. He would later become a traveling companion with Paul and an important leader in the early church. Although her husband may never have accepted the Lord as Savior, Eunice no doubt received great comfort and joy in her son's shared faith and love for the Lord.

1. Describe how each of the following can help us avoid unrealistic expectations for our lives.

   a. Reading about the lives of people in Scripture:

_____

   b. Placing our hopes and dreams for the future in God's hands:

_____

c. Taking a long-term view rather than banking on immediate fulfillment:

_____

d. Developing spiritual values rather than being motivated by selfish material interests:

_____

2. A woman who comes to Christ may find herself in the same situation as Eunice, married to an unbeliever. What encouragement might she find in Eunice's life?

_____

◆ The Fallen Find a Helping Hand ◆

"You've blown it again," Joe silently scolded himself. "What good are you?"

He walked along, hanging his head in remorse. There must be something in him that made him incapable of getting it right, thought Joe—some permanent character flaw, some genetic disposition to fail. He could almost hear the words his father used to say to him after a screwup.

"So you've done it again! You're going to be a failure all of your life, aren't you?"

I guess you were right, Dad. Looks like I'll never be the kind of person I ought to be, thought Joe.

"What does God want with a failure like me, anyway?" he muttered under his breath. ◆

◆ ◆ ◆ ◆ ◆ ◆ ◆ ◆ ◆

How many of us have had times when we felt as Joe did! Though we place our faith in a perfect Lord, we remain fallible human beings. Even when we actively strive to live according to God's will, there will be times when we succumb to temptation or fail due to our weakness.

And once we've fallen, we struggle to rise, discouraged by our shortcomings. Tragically, when repeated failures or serious sin brings us low, we may not even bother trying again. Yet when our confidence in ourselves is at an all-time low, God has the remedy. When we are powerless in our sins and failures, God's power will restore us. All we have to do is take His hand, and He will lift us to our feet again.

After swearing to follow Christ even unto death, Peter's three-time denial was a terrible failure. In Mark 16:7 the angel told the women who had gone to the tomb to tell "His disciples—and Peter" that Christ had been raised. Peter may have doubted whether he was still considered a disciple of Christ. That he had been singled out in the angel's message would have been burned into Peter's memory, for it was an encouraging sign of the forgiveness Peter would soon receive.

We too can take encouragement from Peter's reinstatement by Christ, for the forgiveness he received is also available to us each and every time we fall. And like Peter, God's grace will restore us to renewed relationship with Him (1 John 1:5–9).

Such limitless forgiveness is hard to imagine! It's pretty easy to forgive someone once or

continued

FORGIVENESS ABOUNDS

Do you ever feel hopeless regarding your faith? Do you doubt God's willingness to forgive you over and over again?

Peter (John 21:15) might easily have felt that way. He had risen to a position of leadership among Jesus' followers. He had even been given the "keys of the kingdom" (Matt. 16:19). And he had positioned himself as the defender of Christ when Roman soldiers came to arrest Him (John 18:10). But when he felt the heat of a national trial, conviction, and death, Peter denied three times that he even knew Christ (18:15–18, 25–27) and afterward disappeared. What Jesus had predicted about him came true (John 13:31–38).

So when Jesus engaged Peter in a conversation on the shore (John 21:15–23), Peter might easily have felt that he was already disqualified from further service for the Lord. After all, as we would say, three strikes and you're out. But Jesus reconnected with Peter and called him to genuine love and the continuation of His work.

Second and third chances are not often available in families, communities, or workplaces. All you have to do is fail once too often, and you're gone. But Christ offers tangible love and boundless forgiveness—to those who own up to their failures and repent (Luke 7:47). Can we offer anything less to our coworkers, families, and friends?

John 21:15–19

15So when they had eaten breakfast, Jesus said to Simon Peter, "Simon, *son* of Jonah, do you love Me more than these?"

He said to Him, "Yes, Lord; You know that I love You."

He said to him, "Feed My lambs."

16He said to him again a second time, "Simon, *son* of Jonah, do you love Me?"

He said to Him, "Yes, Lord; You know that I love You."

He said to him, "Tend My sheep."

17He said to him the third time, "Simon, *son* of Jonah, do you love Me?" Peter was grieved because He said to him the third time, "Do you love Me?"

And he said to Him, "Lord, You know all things; You know that I love You."

Jesus said to him, "Feed My sheep. 18Most assuredly, I say to you, when you were younger, you girded yourself and walked where you wished; but when you are old, you will stretch out your hands, and another will gird you and carry *you* where you do not wish." 19This He spoke, signifying by what death he would glorify God. And when He had spoken this, He said to him, "Follow Me."

continued

twice. But when another repeatedly fails us, we can develop a cynical attitude toward that person. That same cynicism may come to dominate our view of ourselves when we repeatedly fail. Like Joe, we may come to see ourselves as born failures.

Instead, we must accept the forgiveness that has been offered to us! Acceptance of God's forgiveness means changing our attitude toward ourselves and others. If God has forgiven us, we should not condemn ourselves. Once we confess our sins to God and take hold of His redeeming grace, the guilt and shame we feel will pass away (Heb. 9:12; 10:22). What a wonderful feeling to be washed clean of our past failures and be made new again! Each time we experience reconciliation with God, it is a reminder of our eternal redemption and rebirth through the sacrifice of Christ. And each time, we can begin anew to follow our Lord.

Stumbling After the Savior

1. Do you agree with the saying: "You learn more from your failures than your successes"?

_____

2. We are called to mirror the Lord's attitude toward failure in others. How can we offer forgiveness without letting others take advantage of us?

_____

Peter had failed, but not for all time. The forgiveness he received spurred him to new commitment to Christ. Before his denial, Peter had sworn that if necessary he would die for Christ's sake. After years of faithful service, Peter did indeed give his life for Christ.

The Lord's forgiveness is an endless reservoir; in its waters we can always find restoration and renewal. Our Father does not see us in our fallen state, but "holy, and blameless, and above reproach" (Col. 1:22). This is a great encouragement when we've fallen, but it's only the beginning! We have hope for the future as well. For just as God sees us in our perfection, He is continually at work within us to make us holy. This hope enables us to begin to live not as the sinner we were but as the person we are destined to become in Christ (1 John 3:3).

◆ ◆ ◆ ◆ ◆ ◆ ◆ ◆ ◆

Things had started out so well for the church at Ephesus. When Paul had begun his ministry there, the Ephesians had responded. In fact, the response was so great that Paul stayed and preached the word in the city for over two years! As a consequence, the gospel message spread throughout the entire province of Asia, the western portion of Asia Minor (Acts 19:10, 26).

It must have been an exciting time for Paul's missionary team—and for their new converts as well. The church swelled as friends and neighbors joined the ranks of the saved.

But in the midst of these tremendous successes, a terrible tumult broke out. Enemies among both the Jews and Gentiles stirred up the city into a frenzy. The repercussions of the uprising compelled Paul to leave Ephesus until things calmed down.

There is reason to believe that the wonderful freedom and rapid growth experienced by the Ephesian church was never the same again. The riot initiated a period of persecution for the young church, and the youthful enthusiasm of the Ephesian believers began to evaporate in the face of unexpected trouble. By the time Paul wrote his letter, it was to a church which had lost its early fire for the Lord in the face of increasing pressures. His words aimed to encourage the believers at Ephesus to put things in proper perspective, and view their present difficulties in the light of the spiritual realities that shaped their lives.

——◆ The View from Above ◆——

Acts 19:23–34

23And about that time there arose a great commotion about the Way. 24For a certain man named Demetrius, a silversmith, who made silver shrines of Diana, brought no small profit to the craftsmen. 25He called them together with the

continued

> *continued*
>
> workers of similar occupation, and said: "Men, you know that we have our prosperity by this trade. 26Moreover you see and hear that not only at Ephesus, but throughout almost all Asia, this Paul has persuaded and turned away many people, saying that they are not gods which are made with hands. 27So not only is this trade of ours in danger of falling into disrepute, but also the temple of the great goddess Diana may be despised and her magnificence destroyed, whom all Asia and the world worship."
>
> 28Now when they heard *this*, they were full of wrath and cried out, saying, "Great is Diana of the Ephesians!" 29So the whole city was filled with confusion, and rushed into the theater with one accord, having seized Gaius and Aristarchus, Macedonians, Paul's travel companions. 30And when Paul wanted to go in to the people, the disciples would not allow him. 31Then some of the officials of Asia, who were his friends, sent to him pleading that he would not venture into the theater. 32Some therefore cried one thing and some another, for the assembly was confused, and most of them did not know why they had come together. 33And they drew Alexander out of the multitude, the Jews putting him forward. And Alexander motioned with his hand, and wanted to make his defense to the people. 34But when they found out that he was a Jew, all with one voice cried out for about two hours, "Great is Diana of the Ephesians!"

This is a message that modern-day believers need to hear as well. It's all too easy to let the problems of our daily lives overwhelm us. When our current troubles loom large, they may become all we can see. At such times, we need to get some distance, and see our lives from a higher perspective. A greater reality lies behind the "real world" in which we live.

Paul reminds the Ephesians of the eternal truths of God's dominion over the world, His active power within their lives, and His infinite love for them (Eph. 3:15–19). When we see our lives through the lens of these spiritual truths, our disheartening problems won't seem so large after all. Then we will be able to see the world as it really is.

1. Do you find that you become consumed with your daily problems and lose sight of the bigger picture? Explain your answer.

_____

2. How does a recognition of the Lord's infinite power and love for you shield you from discouragement when problems arise in your life?

_____

3. Describe as best you can the depth of Christ's love for you.

_____

Paul was intimately familiar with the difficulties a Christian might face in life. Few can even hope to compare with the troubles he experienced (2 Cor. 11:21–29)! During his missionary travels, his life was in almost constant danger. The Jews pursued Paul wherever he went, raising opposition to his ministry. In fact, he wrote his letter to the Ephesians from prison! Yet Paul showed no sign of despondency, for he trusted in his Lord. Instead, he reached out to inspire others to have a new outlook on their lives—from God's vantage point.

By keeping in mind what God has done for us, and will do in the future, we too can find strength to deal with our present troubles. And when discouraged, we can turn in prayer as Paul does "to Him who is able to do exceedingly abundantly above all that we ask or think" (Eph. 3:20). Reliance on our loving and all-powerful Lord gives us the courage to press onward.

An Encouraging Word

A proper perspective on our lives isn't always enough to ward off feelings of discouragement. Though we may say all the right things to ourselves, we still feel down. We are emotional beings, and our emotional responses are not always subject to our control. In fact, they may undermine our ability to maintain our objectivity.

Paul's reliance on God is unquestionable, yet he too suffered emotional lows after disappointments. Paul's time in Athens was a period of disappointment for the missionary. The jaded Athenians gave little regard to the message of Christ's salvation. The good news failed to penetrate their intellectual cynicism. As a result, Paul failed to establish a church in Athens. It was one of the low points of his entire ministry.

However, Paul did not wallow in his misery. Instead, he turned for encouragement to his Christian brothers and sisters in Thessalonica. The report he received from Timothy proved to be just the emotional lift he needed.

1. How does Paul express his growing concern for the Thessalonians?

_____

2. Discouragements can change our whole outlook, and may give rise to irrational fears. Describe a time when a failure or disappointment darkened your perspective on life.

_____

ENCOURAGING THE BOSS

Separation from close friends can bring feelings of loneliness and loss, especially when one is facing disappointment or failure. Paul felt that way in Athens. Despite his strident efforts to present and defend the gospel, he met with only lackluster response from the Athenians (Acts 17:16–34). Not surprisingly, his thoughts turned toward the Thessalonians with whom he felt an unusually deep bond (1 Thess. 2:8; 2:17—3:1).

Anxious for news, Paul sent his valuable associate Timothy north for a visit (1 Thess. 3:2). The young man's report buoyed Paul up. Even as one city was resisting Christ, another was responding to Him in powerful and encouraging ways (3:6–10).

Paul's emotional honesty here is refreshing and instructive. Rather than deny or spiritualize his pain, he acknowledged it and took action. He needed the warm affection of the Thessalonians and especially the capable companionship of Timothy. Rather than live as a "Lone Ranger Christian," Paul stayed connected to other believers and relied on them for insight, encouragement, and support. In this way he honored a basic principle of Christian community (Heb. 10:24–25).

Does your supervisor need encouragement, affirmation, or help in keeping the big picture? Often when people are under great stress or feeling a sense of failure, the only thing they hear is what's wrong. Can you encourage yours with a word about what is *right*?

1 Thess. 3:1–10

Therefore, when we could no longer endure it, we thought it good to be left in Athens alone, ²and sent Timothy, our brother and minister of God, and our fellow laborer in the gospel of Christ, to establish you and encourage you concerning your faith, ³that no one should be shaken by these afflictions; for you yourselves know that we are appointed to this. ⁴For, in fact, we told you before when we were with you that we would suffer tribulation, just as it happened, and you know. ⁵For this reason, when I could no longer endure it, I sent to know your faith, lest by some means the tempter had tempted you, and our labor might be in vain.

⁶But now that Timothy has come to us from you, and brought us good news of your faith and love, and that you always have good remembrance of us, greatly desiring to see us, as we also *to see* you— ⁷therefore, brethren, in all our affliction and distress we were comforted concerning you by your faith. ⁸For now we live, if you stand fast in the Lord.

⁹For what thanks can we render to God for you, for all the joy with which we rejoice for your sake before our God, ¹⁰night and day praying exceedingly that we may see your face and perfect what is lacking in your faith?

3. How does knowing the importance of emotional support from others highlight the need for continued fellowship with other Christians?

◆ The Destination Makes the Journey Easier ◆

Jer. 20:14–18

14 Cursed *be* the day in which I was born!
Let the day not be blessed in which my
mother bore me!

15 Let the man *be* cursed
Who brought news to my father, saying,
"A male child has been born to you!"
Making him very glad.

16 And let that man be like the cities
Which the Lord overthrew, and did not
relent;
Let him hear the cry in the morning
And the shouting at noon,

17 Because he did not kill me from the
womb,
That my mother might have been my
grave,
And her womb always enlarged *with me*.

18 Why did I come forth from the womb to
see labor and sorrow,
That my days should be consumed with
shame?

Because of the despair conveyed in his writings, Jeremiah is often referred to as "the weeping prophet." He had reason for sorrow, for the life that God called Jeremiah to live was one of great hardship. God had determined to judge the nation of Judah. Jeremiah was given the onerous task of prophesying the doom of his own people and the destruction of his homeland.

How hard was his life? Let's take a look. As a young man, Jeremiah was instructed not to marry. His dark prophecies drew the hatred and scorn of his Jewish countrymen. In fact, Jeremiah's message was so unpopular that his enemies sought to kill him. Even his own family joined in the plot against his life! The intense isolation that he suffered caused Jeremiah to describe himself as "a man of strife and a man of contention to the whole earth" (Jer. 15:10). For over four decades, the people resolutely refused to respond to his prophetic ministry. Yet all the while, Jeremiah suffered endless anguish over the terrible fate that was to befall his nation. Little wonder that Jeremiah was overcome at times with intense sorrow.

Depression was a very real part of Jeremiah's life, but it did not stop him from faithfully

A PLACE CALLED HOPE

Hope is one of the most powerful motivators there is. People will struggle against enormous odds and wait out incredible adversity as long as they believe that things will eventually get better. When hope dies, human effort ceases and despair sets in.

The Bible is a book of hope. It offered hope to those for whom it was originally written, as well as to those who read it today.

The people to whom Jeremiah was writing had little hope for their immediate future. A long history of sin and rebellion against God had brought them to the brink of judgment. Their land was about to be overrun by invaders. Their cities would be destroyed, including the capital Jerusalem and its magnificent temple. They would become captives in a foreign land.

Yet even in the midst of such terrible times, Jeremiah promised that God would be with His people. They could take hope in the fact that the Lord Himself was orchestrating events, and that eventually He would bring them or their children back to their homeland (Jer. 29:4, 11–14; 31:16–17).

What keeps you going when things are not working out and life seems almost futile? What dreams will be fulfilled when your ship finally comes in? Scripture challenges us about where we put our hopes. It describes the lives of many groups and individuals in order to give us an overall perspective on life and its ultimate outcomes. In the Bible we find some horrifying incidents, as well as visions of a future that seems almost too good to be imagined. We find accounts of personal disasters, family chaos, war, death, destruction, and nations disappearing from the face of the earth, side by side with accounts of restored lives, reconciled families, renewal among nations, and promises of a blissful future for God's faithful people.

We keep hope alive by serving God wherever we are, no matter what our circumstances are or who the people around us are (Jer. 29:5–7; 1 Thess. 4:10–12). Hope means placing confidence in a sovereign God who will bring to pass His good purposes (2 Cor. 1:10; Heb. 6:19; 11:1)— ends that sometimes seem unreasonable to even expect (Rom. 4:18). Ultimately, Christians have hope because of Christ's resurrection from the dead (1 Pet. 1:21). He has promised us that eventually we will share in His glory (Eph. 1:18).

That hope gives us strength to make it through this troubled world, patiently enduring whatever we must, while we wait for the full realization of our faith (Heb. 13:14; 1 Pet. 1:6–16). Is this where your confidence is? ◆

serving God. The painful mission given to him by God caused Jeremiah much emotional tur-moil, yet his trust and dedication sustained him. Harsh though his life was, Jeremiah affirmed, "Blessed is the man who trusts in the Lord, and whose hope is in the Lord" (Jer. 17:7).

His final days may have been spent among the exiles in Babylon, where Jeremiah would have finally found peace and acceptance by his people. His prophecies to the exiles changed from words of doom to a promise of restoration. For seventy years they would suffer privation and isolation among a foreign people—much as Jeremiah had among his own people. Yet this promise he gave to them: "There is hope in your future, says the Lord, that your children shall come back to their own border" (Jer. 31:17). One day the people of Judah would return home.

Accepting Life's Restrictions

At first the exiles rejected Jeremiah's promise of restoration (Jer. 29:26–28). Only through surrender to God's will did they accept Jeremiah's prophecy with hope instead of despair.

Jeremiah also learned to overcome discouragement through submission to God. He was able to let go, and accept the portion God had given to him. By accepting what our Lord has given to us, we can come to terms with our own discouragements as well.

1. How does looking forward to heaven help you to remain steadfast through adversity?

_____

2. How does dedication to serving God help us to accept loss in our lives?

_____

◆ The Light That Shines in Darkness ◆

In the city of New York, there is a famous mission called God's Lighthouse. It is so-called because through its work, God offers the light of hope to those who are lost and in despair. The Lord is a beacon for believers as well, our source of hope when we feel helpless. He has given us many sources of encouragement that we can turn to when we are down: friends, family, our fellow believers, and church ministries. But when all else fails, we can find comfort and security in the presence of our God.

One source of discouragement we haven't looked at doesn't grow out of our circumstances, failures, or attitudes about the future. It is a hopelessness that grows out of a perception of our own insignificance. Low self-esteem can make us feel small and unimportant. We'll take a look at how to come to terms with challenges to our self-esteem. In the process, we shall see that there are no insignificant people in the kingdom of God! ◆

LITTLE PEOPLE WHO MADE
A BIG DIFFERENCE

Darryl hated family gatherings. They were a painful reminder of how he just didn't measure up to his parents' standards. They had hoped he would be a doctor, like his father and older brother. But he hadn't even made it to medical school. Instead, he had flunked out in his second year of college. Since then, he'd gone through three jobs in the span of five years. And now he was out of work.

Of his entire family, only Darryl had failed to achieve a level of success. His younger sister had just received an award of merit from her university. His sister-in-law was a successful journalist, and two of his cousins were lawyers. Table talk at dinner always centered around their accomplishments in their work—this operation, that legal brief. Darryl would just sit silently, feeling small and foolish among his siblings and cousins.

Worst of all, Darryl sensed that his family members treated him differently. The hint of condescension in their attitude toward him particularly stung. He could see in their eyes what they really thought of him. "Poor Darryl," their eyes seemed to say, "aren't you ever going to make something of yourself?" Darryl hated family gatherings!

♦ ♦ ♦ ♦ ♦ ♦ ♦ ♦ ♦

What does it take to really be somebody? In Darryl's family, a person's importance derived from job status and academic achievement. When Darryl measured himself by his family's standards, he just didn't measure up. As a consequence, Darryl's self-esteem suffered as he struggled with feelings of insignificance.

Darryl is not alone. By the world's standards of importance, most individuals are relatively insignificant. They don't possess great wealth or power. They will never become famous or gain renown for their accomplishments. They are the "little people" of the world. In all likelihood, you are one of them.

1.   Describe an occasion when you felt others were looking down on you.

2.   How did you feel as a consequence?

In life, each of us must struggle as Darryl did to establish a sense of significance. But if you are measuring yourself by the world's standards of importance, you're using the wrong yardstick! As is so often the case, the world's value system is upside down. Wealth and power are irrelevant in God's eyes. In His kingdom, significance is found through serving others.

ARE YOU CONFUSED ABOUT GREATNESS, TOO?

Significance is a tricky achievement. Too often it is built upon fame, money, marketing, power, position, or possessions.

The disciples were caught up in a value system based on these things, which caused them to compete with each other (Mark 9:34). In fact, the dispute over greatness resurfaced later (10:35–45). The quest for significance through power was an insidious problem.

Jesus noticed His followers' thinking and challenged it (9:35). He pointed out that true greatness is in serving others rather than out-

doing them. Later He suggested the same thing to a rich ruler (10:21).

To drive His point home, Jesus gathered a child in His arms and said that to welcome a child is to welcome both Christ and His Father (9:36–37). No wonder the apostle Paul, in writing to believers in Galatia, identified many childlike characteristics as highly valued works of the Spirit (Gal. 5:22–25). He contrasted those traits with some ugly ones that often accompany competition (Gal. 5:16–21).

Do you need to rework your value system? Are you addicted to fame and fortune? A good test is to ask yourself, *Where do children and the poor stand among my priorities?*

 Mark 9:33–37

³³Then He came to Capernaum. And when He was in the house He asked them, "What was it you disputed among yourselves on the road?" ³⁴But they kept silent, for on the road they had disputed among themselves who *would be the greatest.* ³⁵And He sat down, called the twelve, and said to them, "If anyone desires to be first, he shall be last of all and servant of all." ³⁶Then He took a little child and set him in the midst of them. And when He had taken him in His arms, He said to them, ³⁷"Whoever receives one of these little children in My name receives Me; and whoever receives Me, receives not Me but Him who sent Me."

One of the dangers of the quest for significance is that it becomes a competition to outdo others. The disciples fell into this trap when they argued who among them would be the greatest. But Christ had a shocking message for them: in God's kingdom, the greatest serve the least! He used a child as an example of this principle. Now, in both Jewish and Greek culture, a child had no status whatsoever, and was considered the least significant person in society. One can imagine the stunned silence as the disciples wondered at the meaning of Christ's words. How could one gain a sense of importance out of serving a child?

Christ answered their confusion. In God's view, service directed even to a little child is considered service to the Lord. Active service not only shows honor and respect to those served, but brings honor to the servant, whose significance comes from serving God.

Who's Who in God's Kingdom

People tend to derive their sense of significance from one or more of the following:

- skills or talents
- achievements
- fame
- wealth
- influence
- the love or esteem of others

1a. Darryl's sense of self-worth was undermined by his lack of status and achievements. Circle those items listed above that boost your sense of importance. Mark those that weaken your sense of importance.

1b. What do you rely on most for a sense of importance or value as a person? [Be honest!]

_____

_____

2a. What if Darryl took to heart Christ's words, "If anyone desires to be first, he shall be last of all and servant of all" (Mark 9:35). How would his evaluation of himself be changed?

_____

_____

2b. If Darryl's relatives viewed personal significance in this light, how might it change the way they perceive and treat Darryl?

_____

_____

——◆ Who, Me? ◆——

It's a great relief to be freed from the need to pursue self-importance. We can give up the rat race, and stop chasing after the piece of cheese—money, possessions, status. No longer do we have to live up to others' expectations—or even our own—to know that we count in God's eyes. And what God truly values is our service to others.

But service too presents a challenge. Many of us look at ourselves and wonder how we can be of great service to God. We may not see in ourselves the special gifts or talents we see in others. On the other hand, our limitations are usually all too apparent. So when an opportunity for service presents itself, feelings of inadequacy may rise up inside us. At such times, our personal shortcomings seem like such barriers that we often go out of our way to avoid the chance to serve.

Sometimes we are ill-equipped to serve in a particular way. Just because an opportunity to serve is there doesn't necessarily mean we should jump at it. If we are attentive to His voice, God will let us know how and where we can best serve Him.

The real test comes when God clearly communicates His will to us. If we see only our own weaknesses, we are likely to run from His call. But if we voice our self-doubts to God, He will have a ready answer for each of our insecurities. And though we may remain weak, He is strong.

"I'M TOO YOUNG!"

Young people can easily feel intimidated in the presence of older adults, especially if they must perform a solo activity or take a stand for a principle. When Jeremiah was called by God to serve as His prophet to Judah and the nations, he complained that he was too young (Jer. 1:6). Perhaps he was imagining how the stern faces of his elders would look when he announced that God was going to judge them for their sins.

Like Jeremiah, you may feel intimidated by older coworkers and superiors, members of your community, or relatives. Perhaps you are new on the job or have just graduated from school, or maybe you have just settled in a new community. As the young newcomer, you may be afraid to "make waves," especially if living according to biblical values goes against the prevailing culture. But consider these suggestions:

(1) Remember that you are God's representative—in your community, at school or on the job, and in your family. Ultimately, you are where you are to seek His glory, not your own power or prestige.

(2) Listen carefully for God's instructions to you. They normally come through prayer, reading and studying the Bible, and paying attention to the advice of seasoned believers who have walked the path before you.

(3) Place confidence in God's power and provision. The Lord will use your skills and abilities, but in His way, in His time, and for His glory. ◆

Jeremiah 1:4–10

⁴Then the word of the LORD came to me, saying:

5 "Before I formed you in the womb I knew you;
Before you were born I sanctified you;
I ordained you a prophet to the nations."

⁶Then said I:

"Ah, Lord GOD!
Behold, I cannot speak, for I *am* a youth."

⁷But the LORD said to me:

"Do not say, 'I *am* a youth,'
For you shall go to all to whom I send you,
And whatever I command you, you shall speak.

8 Do not be afraid of their faces,
For I *am* with you to deliver you," says the LORD.

⁹Then the LORD put forth His hand and touched my mouth, and the LORD said to me:

"Behold, I have put My words in your mouth.
10 See, I have this day set you over the nations and over the kingdoms,
To root out and to pull down,
To destroy and to throw down,
To build and to plant."

The mission God gave to Jeremiah probably sounded preposterous. A young man, probably around 20, Jeremiah was told he would be a prophet to the nations. God would set him "over the nations and over the kingdoms" (Jer. 1:10). The whole idea must have overwhelmed Jeremiah with a sense of his own inadequacy.

1a. When did God choose Jeremiah to serve as a prophet?

_____

1b. Although it may be hidden from us, clearly God chooses and prepares His servants with great care. What comfort can you draw from this when you feel inadequate?

_____

2. How did God respond to Jeremiah's excuse that he was too young and lacked eloquence?

_____

Many of the Lord's servants struggled with their weaknesses. Moses asked God, "Who am I that I should go to Pharaoh, and that I should bring the children of Israel out of Egypt?" (Ex. 3:11). Timothy's inexperience left him feeling inadequate to serve the church in Ephesus.

Even Paul knew feelings of weakness, such as the time he pleaded with God to remove his "thorn in the flesh" (2 Cor. 12:7). But God's reply to Paul was, "My grace is sufficient for you, for My strength is made perfect in weakness" (2 Cor. 12:9). As a consequence, Paul learned not only to accept but to boast of his shortcomings! For through his own weaknesses, he learned reliance on God's strength. What an astonishing truth! God can use our weaknesses to reveal His power through us. When we come to experience this truth in our own lives, Paul's paradoxical statement will make perfect sense: "When I am weak, then I am strong" (2 Cor. 12:10).

———◆ Those We Ignore God Adores ◆———

High school was its own little world. Students were divided up into cliques, often based on superficial characteristics such as clothing, attractiveness, athletic ability, or academic skills. If you were an athlete or a cheerleader, you might have been among the elite in high school. And those in a clique, as a rule, looked down on outsiders. The athletically gifted mocked the un-

coordinated, the smart kids looked down on the not-so-bright, and the popular kids usually couldn't be seen associating with the unpopular.

We like to think we have grown up since our high school days, but in many ways we continue to judge individuals on superficial grounds. When we walk into a room we start to size up the people we

see. The bright, gregarious, attractive, and successful—these are usually the ones who first attract our attention. We may also take special note of those that seem to be most like us, and share similar personalities or interests.

But what about the others? Often, our eyes begin to slide right over those that we judge to be of less interest. Not that we do so intentionally. After all, it's only natural for us to be drawn to certain kinds of individuals. But the kind of people we associate with may say something about our attitude toward others. Do we tend to see those that don't fit certain criteria as insignificant? In our view, are some people simply better than others? ◆

* * * * * * * * *

THE DEVOTED MARY

Scripture records only one sentence spoken by Mary of Bethany (John 11:32), and even that wasn't original; her sister Martha had already said the same thing (v. 21)! But what Mary may have lacked in outspokenness, she more than made up for in devotion to Jesus. All three portraits of her in the Gospels show her at the Lord's feet:

- During one of Jesus' visits to her home, Mary sat at His feet, listening (Luke 10:38–42).
- When Jesus came to Bethany after Lazarus' death, Mary fell at His feet, completely broken over the tragedy (John 11:32).
- During a Passover meal just before Jesus' death, Mary poured fragrant oil on His head and feet, and wiped His feet with her hair (Matt. 26:6–13; Mark 14:3–9; John 12:1–8).

On each of these occasions, this quiet woman was criticized by others. But apparently she didn't notice or didn't care. Mary seemed to be a woman who made choices based on a commitment to Jesus that went to the core of her being. In return, Jesus defended her actions, giving her freedom to be His disciple.

Mary is a model for anyone who lives in the shadow of a strong sibling or parent, or who prefers to listen rather than to speak. She demonstrates that preaching sermons or leading movements is not the only way to follow Jesus. One can also show devotion by listening to the Lord's voice and worshiping at His feet.

Mary seems to have been one of those quiet, shy individuals who just doesn't attract much attention. In contrast, her sister Martha was an industrious woman, quick to speak up or take charge. The difference in the personalities of these two sisters showed in their reactions. At the news that Jesus had arrived at Bethany after the death of Lazarus, Martha immediately rushed out to meet Him. Though in mourning, her words to Him were a forthright declaration of her faith in Christ as Messiah and the Resurrection to come. But Mary waited in the house until the Lord called for her. When she saw Him, Mary also expressed her faith in Christ, although with less eloquence than her sister. But when she threw herself at the feet of her Lord, her actions spoke of her devotion with an eloquence greater than words. The Lord was deeply moved by the sight of Mary weeping at His feet.

Mary did not stand out in a crowd or demand respect with her presence. Others showed little regard for her and were quick to criticize. But the Lord rejected their criticisms, for He could see what they could not. Christ saw Mary's heart, and knew the depth of her love for Him.

The incident described in John 12:1–8, when Mary anointed the feet of Christ, is one of the most beautiful examples of worship in the Bible. A more complete description of the event appears in the Gospel of Mark, in which Mary is unnamed.

Mark 14:3–9

³And being in Bethany at the house of Simon the leper, as He sat at the table, a woman came having an alabaster flask of very costly oil of spikenard. Then she broke the flask and poured *it* on His head. ⁴But there were some who were indignant among themselves, and said, "Why was this fragrant oil wasted? ⁵For it might have been sold for more than three hundred denarii and given to the poor." And they criticized her sharply.

⁶But Jesus said, "Let her alone. Why do you trouble her? She has done a good work for Me. ⁷For you have the poor with you always, and whenever you wish you may do them good; but Me you do not have always. ⁸She has done what she could. She has come beforehand to anoint My body for burial. ⁹Assuredly, I say to you, wherever this gospel is preached in the whole world, what this woman has done will also be told as a memorial to her."

At the Feet of Her Lord

1a. Why were the disciples so quick to criticize Mary's action?

_____

1b. If Peter had been the one to anoint the Lord with expensive oil, would he have likewise been criticized? Why or why not?

_____

2. The time Mary spent listening at the Lord's feet seems to have paid off, for her actions suggest an understanding that the disciples lacked. What did Mary's act foreshadow?

_____

3. Mary's was a great act of love, and in response the Lord promised that "wherever this gospel is preached in the whole world, what this woman has done will also be told as a memorial to her" (Mark 14:9). What is the significance of Christ's pronouncement for those of us who may not be respected teachers or leaders in the Church?

_____

_____

Mary's silent devotion is a testimony to all those who are tempted to overlook the inconspicuous and introverted among us. Though we often extend our praise and respect to those who serve in the spotlight, God is moved by what is in the hearts of His servants. No matter how we serve the Lord, if we do so out of love and commitment to Him, our service is worthy in His eyes, and we shall be rewarded for it.

◆ Reflected Glory ◆

Russell Bains looked away from the computer screen and rubbed his eyes. He didn't even know what time it was. Everyone else in the building had gone home long ago.

Get used to it, thought Russell angrily. He'd be working late for at least the next two weeks as he prepared a feasability study for Mr. Dodd, his department head. What really irritated Russell was that Dodd had dumped it in his lap at the last minute.

"Generating feasability studies isn't even my job," muttered Russell. But here he was anyway, while Mr. Dodd spent the week in Bimini. Was there any justice?

Russell jumped as the door swung open.

"Oops." Russell saw the face of an elderly man smiling through the door. Russell presumed he must be with the janitorial staff. "Excuse me. I didn't know anyone was still here. I'll take care of the other offices first."

"Why don't you just skip this office tonight? It's okay with me."

"I couldn't do that, Mr.— Bains," said the janitor, with a glance at the name on the desk.

"I'll tell you what," Russell said, "I need a break anyway. I'll go get something to drink, and let you do your job."

When Russell returned with his drink, he stood outside the office sipping his coffee. He was surprised to see how thorough and meticulous the old man was in performing his job. When he was finished, Russell returned to his desk.

"I'll see you tomorrow," said Russell with chagrin, as the janitor left his office.

Over the next few days, Russell saw the old janitor—whose name he learned was Jesse—every night. He continued to be impressed, even shamed, by the old man's diligence. Russell hoped to be retired by the time he reached that age, yet here was Jesse, working at what most would consider a menial job—and taking pride in it!

In exasperation, one night Russell finally said to him, "Personally, Jesse, I don't understand why you're so eager to knock yourself out over this job."

"I love my boss, Russell," said Jesse, with a sly wink. "Whereas I can tell you aren't too crazy about yours."

There was a knowing twinkle in Jesse's eyes. Apparently the canny old man had been observing his observer.

"I guess you got me there," Russell admitted. "But why should you?"

"Who are you working for, youngster?"

"Mr. Dodd, my department head."

"Well, that's pretty impressive, but not nearly as important as my boss."

"What?" Russell gave Jesse a quizzical look. "Just who do you think your boss is? The CEO?"

"God is my boss," Jesse flashed a smile. "Now it seems to me that the more important the boss, the more important the servant, don't you agree?"

At this, Jesse let out a wheezing laugh. Caught speechless at first, Russell couldn't help but join in with the old man's mirth.

As Russell worked to complete his report, he couldn't keep what Jesse had said out of his mind. And the more he thought about it, the more envious he became of this old janitor who worked hard for little money—and yet found satisfaction in it. Jesse obviously knew something—or someone—he didn't.

The night Russell finished the feasability study, he got an extra cup of coffee for Jesse and passed the time with some small talk as Jesse worked. After Jesse had finished and prepared to go, Russell thanked him for breaking the monotony of the last two weeks.

"You know, I've been thinking, Jesse," Russell paused, feeling somewhat foolish. "Well, seeing as I'm not too thrilled with my boss, maybe you could—um—introduce me to yours?"

"Son," replied the old janitor, "I thought you'd never ask." ◆

1. Jesse didn't estimate his importance based on his occupational status. In what did Jesse ground his sense of significance?

_____

2. How did this impact the way he performed his job?

_____

3. Who do you work for? How would it change the way you perform your job if God were your boss?

_____

You are working for God! As a Christian, you are responsible to Him in everything you do, including your work activities. As Scripture says, "Whatever you do, do it heartily, as to the Lord and not to men, knowing that from the Lord you will receive the reward of the inheritance" (Col. 3:23, 24). So when your human boss overworks you or fails to appreciate your service, remember that you are really working for a higher Boss. Our Lord never fails to notice our service on His behalf, and His rewards will last an eternity.

At the same time, the fact that we serve God first and foremost means adopting a new attitude toward our work. Our personal relationship with God is the real foundation for our significance in life. As the moon reflects the glory of the sun, we have reflected glory from God. This unmerited honor we have received brings a responsibility with it. We are God's representatives in the workplace and elsewhere. For this reason, the attitude with which we perform our jobs ultimately reflects on our eternal Boss and heavenly Father.

When you get down to it, our relative importance or unimportance in the eyes of others shouldn't even concern us. Like our worldly accomplishments, the praise of others is really of no consequence in the great scheme of things. When we think about importance, our attention needs to be focused not on bringing honor to ourselves but on bringing glory to our Master.

The highest praise we can ever hope to receive is our Lord's commendation: "Well done, good and faithful servant" (Matt. 25:21).

1a. Much of what we've been talking about in this chapter deals with personal identity. What does it mean to you to be a child of the Almighty God?

_____

1b. In the Kingdom of God, even masters are servants (Col. 4:1). Those who are in positions of authority ultimately serve a higher Authority. What does it mean to you to be God's servant?

_____

_____

A KINGDOM PERSPECTIVE ON SIGNIFICANCE

*J*esus wants His followers to evaluate turbulent times of change (Mark 13:33) not just from the perspective of history but even more from the perspective of His kingdom. As believers, we are citizens of eternity. Therefore, our confidence needs to be rooted in something far more important than our positions and achievements here and now. It's not that the here and now has no importance. But as we live our lives, God wants us to be loyal workers for His kingdom, serving the people He sends our way.

Is your significance tied too closely to achievements—building buildings, reaching business goals, acquiring material possessions, climbing career ladders? There's nothing inherently wrong with these. But if you lost them, would your confidence completely crumble? If your sense of worth depends on them, what happens when you reach the top of the ladder, only to discover that the ladder is leaning against the wrong wall?

The problem is that our world has a system of values that is upside down from the way God determines value. It lacks any sense of what Scripture describes as "calling," or what Christians later termed "vocation"—a perspective that God has called and equipped people to serve Him through their work in the world. Instead, our culture encourages us to climb a work/identity ladder that is ultimately self-serving, and often self-destructive.

Climbing that ladder can be very misleading. The higher one goes, the more one's identity, value, and security tend to depend on the nature of one's work. But what happens if we lose our position, titles, or high-level compensation? Perhaps this explains why severe emotional problems—drug and alcohol abuse, abuse of spouse and children, divorce, even suicide—often accompany job loss. If our significance relies on our job, then it dies with our job.

God calls us to a far more stable basis for significance. He wants us to establish our identity in the fact that we are His children, created by Him to carry out good works as responsible people in His kingdom (Eph. 2:10). This is our calling or vocation from God. According to Scripture, our calling:

- is irrevocable (Rom. 11:29).
- is from God; He wants to let us share in Christ's glory (2 Thess. 2:14).
- is a function of how God has designed us (Eph. 2:10).
- is an assurance that God will give us everything we need to serve Him, including the strength to remain faithful to Him (1 Cor. 1:7–9).
- is what we should be proclaiming as our true identity (1 Pet. 2:5, 9).
- carries us through suffering (1 Pet. 2:19–21).
- is rooted in peace, no matter what the circumstances in which we find ourselves (1 Cor. 7:15–24).
- is focused on eternal achievements, not merely temporal ones (Phil. 3:13—4:1).

Above all else, believers are called to character development, service to others, and loyalty to God. These can be accomplished wherever we live or work, whatever our occupational status or position in society. If we pursue these, we can enjoy great satisfaction and significance. No matter what happens on the job, we can join Paul in saying, "We know that all things work together for good to those who love God, to those who are called according to *His* purpose" (Rom. 8:28). ◆

2. What are some ways you can reflect God's glory through your life and work?

_____

_____

     God hasn't chosen His servants based on their power and importance in the world. Quite the opposite! For Scripture tells us that "God has chosen the weak things of the world to put to shame the things which are mighty" (1 Cor. 1:27).

     So let's stop worrying about how important we are. After all, we have infinite value to the only One who really counts! We are precious to Him beyond reckoning.

     Our real significance does not come from what we possess, what we have accomplished, or even who we are. It comes from Whom we serve.

     God can use the weak and feeble to accomplish great things in His name. But sometimes we are weakened by fear. Fear can cause us to hesitate instead of trusting in His strength. How do we conquer the fears that assault us as we seek to walk in faith? We'll look at this common problem in the next chapter.

MAKING OUR FOOTSTEPS FIRM

A Peruvian pastor recently reported an incident that occurred while in the guerrilla-controlled mountains of Peru. He had received a request to hold evangelistic meetings at a tiny church in a rural village. The village was in a region under the domination of Peruvian rebels with a reputation for violence and terrorist acivities. These communist rebels would be ill-disposed toward a pastor intent on converting a village in their territory. Once word of the planned meetings spread, the pastor suspected a trap would be set for him. And as the date for the first meeting approached, fear gripped him. He prayed and fasted for four days before leaving for the village.

As it turned out, the Peruvian pastor's fears were justified. The rebels had determined to kill this minister of the Lord. He would become another victim of their communist cause.

The rebel soldiers dressed as field workers and hid their weapons in the bushes, waiting for the pastor's arrival. But the pastor never showed up. Outraged, they returned to the village, intent on punishing the church leader for the failure of their plan.

What the guerrillas found when they arrived in the church leader's home stopped them in their tracks. There was the traveling pastor speaking with the church leader!

When the rebels demanded to know how the pastor had gotten to the village, he replied, "I walked down the only road that leads here."

"Why didn't we see you?" asked the soldiers in consternation. The pastor had no explanation for them. He said that he had seen them in the fields, but when they didn't greet him on the road, he just kept walking.

The guerrillas looked at each other in astonishment. They chose not to harm any of the brothers, and the meetings were held as planned.

A number of the guerrillas were at the special church services. Those fighting for liberation heard about true liberation found in Jesus Christ. Many of the terrorists were converted during the church meetings and left behind their violent past.

◆ ◆ ◆ ◆ ◆ ◆ ◆ ◆ ◆ ◆

The Peruvian pastor must have been terrified at the prospect of going to that little village in rebel territory, knowing the animosity the rebel leaders held for Christians. Knowing his life might very well be forfeited, he still found the courage to go serve God. As a consequence, God used the pastor to demonstrate the power of His supernatural protection to these guerrillas, the villagers, and the pastor himself.

In Western countries, Christians live their lives in relative peace and freedom from persecution. Few Western believers face the threat of death for their faith in Christ. But there remain countries where fear goes hand in hand with faith in Jesus Christ. In Iran, Iraq, Pakistan, and many other nations, believers are in danger of losing their property, freedoms—even their lives.

1. Whom did the Peruvian pastor turn to for courage and direction when afraid?

_____

2. Will the pastor find it easier or more difficult to go the next time he is called on to speak in a village under the control of rebels? Explain your answer.

_____

3. Suppose you had been in his shoes. What would it have felt like to walk up the mountain path to that village?

_____

Although by serving God our lives may not be at risk, fear can be a grave challenge to our faith as well. Fear is a natural reaction, but it springs from thoughts of what might happen. Just as the pastor from Peru must have imagined guerrillas falling upon him as he walked the path to the village, our fears grow out of the anticipation of evil consequences. We foresee impending pain or disaster, and fear takes root.

We are prone to make wrong choices when we are afraid. Though we seek to walk with the Lord, when a moment of fear seizes us, we often stumble and our footsteps falter. If we should hesitate, our fears gain the upper hand. Our courage dwindles until we no longer have the strength to resist. And instead of walking in faith, we find ourselves walking in fear.

Just because we are Christians doesn't mean we should never feel fear—far from it! The Peruvian pastor was a human being just like us, and he was very afraid! But he did not give in to his fears. He kept his footsteps firm as he followed the Lord. Those of us who struggle to overcome fears in our own lives may wonder where his bravery came from. How did he find the courage to walk that dangerous road? How can we find such courage when we are afraid?

THE SERVANT GIRL

Fear of the truth and its consequences can lead even the strongest among us to hide behind lies and half-truths. So it was for Peter, the stouthearted fisherman and leader among the apostles. No doubt fearing for his life as he sat in the courtyard of the high priest's house, Peter denied to a servant girl that he had any connection with Jesus (Luke 22:56–57).

Normally Peter would have paid little attention to the young woman, who was merely a doorkeeper in Caiaphas' household (John 18:15–17). But having watched his Master's arrest and perhaps having learned from John, who gained him access to the courtyard, about the events taking place inside, Peter told an outright lie. Apparently he

continued

continued

feared what the girl might say or do if he admitted to being one of Jesus' followers.

It's interesting to contrast this situation with Peter's later encounter with another doorkeeper, the servant girl Rhoda (Acts 12:1–17). On that occasion, it was not Peter who was afraid of the servant girl, but the servant girl who was astonished and overjoyed at seeing Peter, who had been miraculously delivered from jail. By that point, of course, Peter had repented of denying Jesus and had re-

ceived the Holy Spirit, who filled him with power and boldness to stand before not only the high priest (Acts 4:5–6, 18–21), but King Herod as well.

What place in your life is so vulnerable that you would tell an outright lie—even to someone that you would normally regard as inconsequential—rather than reveal the truth? Like Peter, are you afraid of the consequences of being identified with Jesus? If so, you need a dose of the Spirit's power to give you the courage to be honest (see Acts 1:8). ◆

 Luke 22:47–57

⁴⁷And while He was still speaking, behold, a multitude; and he who was called Judas, one of the twelve, went before them and drew near to Jesus to kiss Him. ⁴⁸But Jesus said to him, "Judas, are you betraying the Son of Man with a kiss?"

⁴⁹When those around Him saw what was going to happen, they said to Him, "Lord, shall we strike with the sword?" ⁵⁰And one of them struck the servant of the high priest and cut off his right ear.

⁵¹But Jesus answered and said, "Permit even this." And He touched his ear and healed him.

⁵²Then Jesus said to the chief priests, captains of the temple, and the elders who had come to

Him, "Have you come out, as against a robber, with swords and clubs? ⁵³When I was with you daily in the temple, you did not try to seize Me. But this is your hour, and the power of darkness."

⁵⁴Having arrested Him, they led *Him* and brought Him into the high priest's house. But Peter followed at a distance. ⁵⁵Now when they had kindled a fire in the midst of the courtyard and sat down together, Peter sat among them. ⁵⁶And a certain servant girl, seeing him as he sat by the fire, looked intently at him and said, "This man was also with Him."

⁵⁷But he denied Him, saying, "Woman, I do not know Him."

Peter illustrates the threat fear poses to our faith. Once we surrender to its influence, it becomes easier and easier to give in to fear. A pattern of avoidance develops. Prior to Jesus' arrest, Peter had sworn he was willing to give his life for Jesus (Luke 22:33). Indeed, it was Peter who had brashly attacked a member of the party that came to arrest Jesus. Yet here he was, mere hours later, frightened enough to lie about being a disciple of Christ to a servant girl!

When Footsteps Falter

1a. When Peter swore he would die for Christ, do you think Peter meant what he said?

1b. If he had thought more about the consequences of being Christ's disciple, would Peter have been better prepared to confront this frightening situation? Why or why not?

2. What happened to make Peter's customary boldness evaporate?

_____

Peter's first mistake was a failure to take Christ's advice. Jesus urged the disciples to "pray that you may not enter into temptation" (Luke 22:40). He even specifically warned Peter of the testing that would come, saying: "Satan has asked for you, that he may sift you as wheat" (v. 31). But Peter and the other disciples did not heed Jesus' advice. The result was that Peter denied Christ and fled with the rest of the disciples.

Fortifying the Fainthearted

Several things happened after the resurrection of Christ that helped to rob fear of its power over Peter. They are powerful resources for all believers who seek the resolve to do what is right when afraid. Explain how each can be a resource for the believer today.

• Peter came face to face with the resurrected Christ, a dramatic proof that his Master possessed power over life and death.

_____

• Out of love, the Lord forgave Peter for giving in to fear, and in response, Peter redevoted himself to serving Christ.

_____

• Peter was told he would one day lose his life for the Lord. In this way, Peter was set free from fear of evil consequences, for he learned to accept the price of serving God.

_____

• Peter received the Holy Spirit on Pentecost. The indwelling Spirit is a source of strength, and enables believers to avoid faltering as they "walk in the Spirit" (Gal. 5:25).

_____

——◆ A Harbor in the Storm ◆——

Don had always prided himself on his self-reliance. A successful professional, he had the confidence to tackle any problems that arose on his own. Naturally, stress and anxiety were a part of his life—but nothing he couldn't handle.

But on a routine visit to the doctor, Don learned that he had a malignant tumor. *The big C*, thought Don in horror. He had cancer. And he was afraid like never before.

Don's self-assurance crum-bled as a myriad of fears assailed him. Would he die? Would his three young children grow up without a father? Would he be impaired or overwhelmed by medical costs? He felt helpless. The shock was so great, it took a week before he could bring himself to tell his wife, Nancy.

After months of searching, it was by coincidence that Don learned of a new treatment for his cancer. He was surprised to meet a nurse at the facility who had been a client of his years earlier. As a Christian, Don took this as a sign of God's providence. Four years after his treatment, he is alive and cancer-free.

Don learned a great deal through his battle with cancer, and now speaks to groups about his experience. One thing he learned was just how vulnerable and helpless the cancer patient feels. And through the process of dealing with cancer himself, he learned of the peace that can be found through greater reliance on God. ◆

◆ ◆ ◆ ◆ ◆ ◆ ◆ ◆ ◆

Nothing in this world can provide us with a sense of complete security. To be alive is to be vulnerable.

In fact, our everyday lives are filled with sources of stress and anxiety. To overcome our insecurity, we may turn to forms of defense, or rely on the protection of others for safety. Often, like Don, we seek to become as self-sufficient as possible. In this way, we hope to become immune to the dangers that surround us.

But no matter what precautions we take, we will never find the inner peace we long for by building up our own defenses. Eventually, the chaos of the world will break through the barriers we have erected, and we will have no place left to hide.

All the defenses in the world can't provide real security. Only by turning to God and relying on His power can we find the surpassing peace that is a refuge in any storm. David gives expression to the inner peace that comes from trusting God in Psalm 56:3–4:

> Whenever I am afraid,
> I will trust in You.
> In God (I will praise His word),
> In God I have put my trust;
> I will not fear.
> What can flesh do to me?

◆ ◆ ◆ ◆ ◆ ◆ ◆ ◆ ◆

A FALSE SENSE OF SECURITY

It's a normal human tendency to flee from danger by running to places of safety. However, real peace and security do not come from gates, guards, or guns. Ultimately, they come from God.

The people of Jeremiah's day lived in an increasingly dangerous world. The Assyrian empire was in decline, creating political instability in the Middle East. Seizing the opportunity, the Egyptians began to stage offensive campaigns from the south. Meanwhile, Babylon was emerging as a new superpower.

Yet in the midst of these danger signs, false prophets in Judah comforted the Israelites with words of peace (Jer. 8:11). The citizens took comfort in their walled cities, assuming that these defenses would be a safe haven against hostile forces (Jer. 8:14). But they were merely denying

continued

continued

their true condition. The gravest danger the residents of Judah faced was one that they had created themselves, and one that they brought with them into their cities: they had turned their backs on God (Jer. 8:5, 8–12).

In our own day, many people have sought refuge from urban crime by moving to the suburbs. In fact, some new developments have taken a step back toward the days of walled cities by building gated communities. Such attempts to curb violent crime are understandable, but evil is not so easily excluded (Jer. 8:15). It cannot be controlled merely by controlling the environment. Ultimately, evil is a matter of dealing with sin, whether personal or institutional, and that means repentance and turning toward the Lord (Jer. 25:4–7; 35:15; Matt. 11:28).

What are you trusting in for peace and security? There's nothing wrong with wanting to protect yourself and your family from harm. But inner peace cannot come just from shutting out evils from the outside; it also takes rooting out evils from the inside. ◆

1a. How did God use cancer in Don's life?

1b. Why did God use the threat of invasion to frighten the inhabitants of Jerusalem?

2. Fear is our ally when it causes us to realize our vulnerability and develop greater dependence on God. But what does the example of Jerusalem indicate might happen for those who turn to a source of security other than God?

3. What is an area of insecurity in your life? How might God be using your insecurity to draw you to greater dependence on Him?

In the Midst of the Storm

 Mark 4:35–41

35On the same day, when evening had come, He said to them, "Let us cross over to the other side." 36Now when they had left the multitude, they took Him along in the boat as He was. And other little boats were also with Him. 37And a great windstorm arose, and the waves beat into the boat, so that it was already filling. 38But He was in the stern, asleep on a pillow. And they awoke Him and said to Him, "Teacher, do You not care that we are perishing?"

39Then He arose and rebuked the wind, and said to the sea, "Peace, be still!" And the wind ceased and there was a great calm. 40But He said to them, "Why are you so fearful? How is it that you have no faith?" 41And they feared exceedingly, and said to one another, "Who can this be, that even the wind and the sea obey Him!"

The violence of storms on the Sea of Galilee were notorious in Jesus' time as they are now. A deep depression surrounded by high hills, the Sea of Galilee is shaped like a bowl half-filled with water. Strong winds funnel into this bowl and clash with rising warm air, producing sudden furious squalls.

During such a storm, the sea itself would be whipped into a frenzy. Experienced fishermen, the disciples recognized the danger they were in as waves flooded the boat. They were in a panic when they came to Jesus and woke him. But with the words, "Peace, be still!" Jesus calmed the wind and sea (Mark 4:39).

1. What in the passage suggests that the disciples attempted to rely on their own skills and only turned to Jesus as a last resort?

_____

2a. Why did Jesus rebuke them for being afraid of the storm?

_____

2b. Jesus said to them, "How is it that you have no faith?" (Mark 4:40). How might the disciples have shown more faith?

_____

3. Who had more security?

    a. Someone who stood within the stone walls of Jerusalem in Jeremiah's time. _____

    b. One of the disciples on the storm-tossed Sea of Galilee. _____

The disciples didn't feel secure, but they were. For inside that boat was the Prince of Peace. He is our source of peace as well. The One who calmed the sea with a word certainly has the power to calm the storm of anxieties in us. We need only turn in faith to Him.

◆ Fighting Fire with Fire ◆

Rate your top three fears, in order from greatest to least.

1. _____ 2. _____ 3. _____

Which of these fears do you spend time worrying over the most? _____

Which of these fears has the greatest effect on your behavior? _____

Now you might think this is a strange question, but was God on your list of fears?

         Yes   *No*

If you answered "no," maybe He should have been! In fact, according to the Bible, God should have been #1 on your list of fears!

THE RIGHT KIND OF FEAR

Every culture seems to be afraid of someone. The Hebrews feared and hated the Romans because of the ruthless might of their occupation troops. Eventually those fears were realized as Rome viciously destroyed Jerusalem in A.D. 70 (see Luke 21:20). In recent years, the West feared destruction from Soviet nuclear missiles. Today there is growing alarm and outrage over drug- and gang-related violence in cities.

But in Luke 12:4–7 we see that Jesus redefines fear by rearranging our view so we look at things from God's perspective. He draws upon the Old Testament concept of the "fear of the Lord" (Prov. 1:7). This is not a fawning, cringing dread that keeps us wallowing in anxiety, but a respect for who God is—the One who holds ultimate power. When we have a balanced view of God, it puts our thinking in a proper framework. We view everybody and everything in relation to God's holiness, righteousness, and love. We can't ignore physical threats and violence, but we dare not ignore the One who holds sway over our eternal destiny.

Luke 12:4–7

4"And I say to you, My friends, do not be afraid of those who kill the body, and after that have no more that they can do. 5But I will show you whom you should fear: Fear Him who, after He has killed, has power to cast into hell; yes, I say to you, fear Him!

6"Are not five sparrows sold for two copper coins? And not one of them is forgotten before God. 7But the very hairs of your head are all numbered. Do not fear therefore; you are of more value than many sparrows.

---

1. How can a deep respect for God bring into perspective those things in life we fear most?

_____

2. We normally think of fear as a bad thing. What is an example from everyday life in which fear protects us from harm?

_____

3. What reason do believers have to fear God?

_____

4. Have you ever been afraid of God's judgment after doing something wrong?

             Yes   *No*

Sin may leave us fearful. Proverbs 28:1 tells us: "The wicked flee when no one pursues." But fleeing God will not bring relief from fear of judgment. Instead of running away from God, we should run to Him for mercy. When we repent of our sins, God will forgive us and soothe the fears that come from a guilty conscience (1 John 1:9).

DON'T WORRY

Of the texts in Scripture that discuss money and work, Matthew 6:19–34 are among the most frequently cited. Unfortunately, they are often used to imply that Jesus was against money and considered everyday work a distraction to things that "really" matter.

However, a careful reader will notice that Jesus condemned worry, not work (Matt. 6:25, 27–28, 31, 34). He never told us to stop working. Rather, He called us to correctly focus our faith on God, the ultimate supplier of our needs (v. 32).

God provides for people in many ways. The most common is through everyday work. He expects us to work diligently with whatever resources He gives us (2 Thess. 3:6–12). Of course, sometimes that normal means of provision fails for a variety of reasons: ill health, divorce from or death of a provider, loss of a job, natural disaster, changing markets, and other circumstances beyond our control.

It is precisely the fear of those possibilities that tempts us to worry so much and forget about trusting God. Why rely on Him, we figure, if He can't keep us from troubles like that? Why not just rely on ourselves and trust to our own devices? All the while we forget that God never promised that we wouldn't face hard times, and that He has many ways to help us through them when we do: family members, church communities, neighbors, charities, inheritances, even public agencies and nonprofit groups.

Certainly we need to pay attention to our physical and material needs. But Jesus urged us to stop worrying about things so that they dominate our lives and values. We can't do that and serve God at the same time (Matt. 6:24). Instead, we need to redirect our focus onto God's kingdom and righteousness (v. 33). That means adopting the values of the King and bringing Him into our work and lives. Jesus said that's what "really" matters. ◆

Matthew 6:19–34

¹⁹"Do not lay up for yourselves treasures on earth, where moth and rust destroy and where thieves break in and steal; ²⁰but lay up for yourselves treasures in heaven, where neither moth nor rust destroys and where thieves do not break in and steal. ²¹For where your treasure is, there your heart will be also.

²²"The lamp of the body is the eye. If therefore your eye is good, your whole body will be full of light. ²³But if your eye is bad, your whole body will be full of darkness. If therefore the light that is in you is darkness, how great is that darkness!

²⁴"No one can serve two masters; for either he

continued

continued

will hate the one and love the other, or else he will be loyal to the one and despise the other. You cannot serve God and mammon.

25"Therefore I say to you, do not worry about your life, what you will eat or what you will drink; nor about your body, what you will put on. Is not life more than food and the body more than clothing? 26Look at the birds of the air, for they neither sow nor reap nor gather into barns; yet your heavenly Father feeds them. Are you not of more value than they? 27Which of you by worrying can add one cubit to his stature?

28"So why do you worry about clothing? Consider the lilies of the field, how they grow: they neither toil nor spin; 29and yet I say to you that even Solomon in all his glory was not arrayed like one of these. 30Now if God so clothes the grass of the field, which today is, and tomorrow is thrown into the oven, *will He* not much more *clothe* you, O you of little faith?

31"Therefore do not worry, saying, 'What shall we eat?' or 'What shall we drink?' or 'What shall we wear?' 32For after all these things the Gentiles seek. For your heavenly Father knows that you need all these things. 33But seek first the kingdom of God and His righteousness, and all these things shall be added to you. 34Therefore do not worry about tomorrow, for tomorrow will worry about its own things. Sufficient for the day *is* its own trouble.

A Healthy Respect

1. How should reverence for God and His will for our lives change our pattern of living?

2. In what sense does fear of the Lord free us from the fears that plague those who do not know God?

———◆ The Courage of Conviction ◆———

In twenty-four hours, Bill Myers was scheduled to begin shooting the motion picture "Bamboo in Winter" on location near the Chinese border. As director, everyone looked to him in a crisis. The cast, the crew, the investors, all depended on him to get the job done.

And there was a crisis. On behalf of the cast and crew, the Chinese production manager told Bill that before filming he would be required to sacrifice a baby pig and burn incense to the local gods. If he didn't, the Chinese cast and crew would not work and thousands of dollars already spent would be lost.

It was a terrible moment for Bill Myers. As a Christian, he knew that a sacrifice to their gods was unacceptable. Second Kings 17:35 popped into his mind: "You shall not fear other gods, nor bow down to them nor serve them nor sacrifice to them."

He tried to talk his way out of it, to no avail. Then someone suggested a compromise. The assistant director could perform the sacrifice in his place. But Bill still felt this would violate his integrity as a Christian. He refused.

It became apparent that they had reached an impasse. Everyone prepared to leave. Though crestfallen, Bill silently sent a prayer to God to turn this defeat into victory.

Then an idea occurred to him. He knew that the Chinese accepted Jesus Christ as a god—one of the top 10 in their eyes. Why not lead the entire set in a prayer asking for Christ's protection from the other gods they feared?

When he suggested this solution, the Chinese crew and cast members excitedly agreed. The filming went on as scheduled, and was successfully completed. In addition, two of the cast members committed their lives to Jesus Christ. ◆

◆ ◆ ◆ ◆ ◆ ◆ ◆ ◆ ◆

Bill Myers encountered what appeared to be a hopeless situation. If he remained true to his faith in Jesus Christ, he would be letting a lot of people down. He would also be out of a job. Fear of failure could easily have driven him to compromise his moral principles. But Bill Myers' commitment to remain obedient to God would not permit compromise.

When we accepted Christ as our Savior, we committed our lives to Him. Fear challenges us to demonstrate our commitment to God. As long as we place something else before our desire to be obedient to the Lord, we run the risk that fear will overcome our commitment. Yet when our commitment is strong we can conquer our fears and obey.

ANANIAS—SCARED BUT OBEDIENT

Saul's reputation as a ruthless persecutor of Christians preceded him to Damascus (Acts 9:1, 10). Perhaps hearing that Saul was headed that way, Ananias mentally prepared himself to be hunted down, arrested, imprisoned, and ultimately martyred for following the new movement called the Way. In any case, he was no doubt stunned by the Lord's command to go and meet this dangerous enemy face-to-face! His words of protest indicate great fear.

But twice God commanded, "Go" (Acts 9:11, 15), and to his credit, Ananias—scared as he may have been—went obediently to lay hands on Saul that he might receive the Holy Spirit, and to baptize him. As a result, he witnessed the spiritual birth of early Christianity's greatest spokesperson. He also saw a dramatic demonstration of the truth that God's grace can overcome anyone's background.

Ananias' story challenges believers today to consider: Who might God want us to approach with the message of His grace? Who that we know is the least likely to respond to Christ—yet just might if only someone would reach out in faith and obedience?

 Acts 9:10–18

¹⁰Now there was a certain disciple at Damascus named Ananias; and to him the Lord said in a vision, "Ananias."

And he said, "Here I am, Lord."

¹¹So the Lord *said* to him, "Arise and go to the street called Straight, and inquire at the house of Judas for *one* called Saul of Tarsus, for behold, he is praying. ¹²And in a vision he has seen a man named Ananias coming in and putting *his* hand on him, so that he might receive his sight."

¹³Then Ananias answered, "Lord, I have heard

continued

> *continued*
> from many about this man, how much harm he has done to Your saints in Jerusalem. ¹⁴And here he has authority from the chief priests to bind all who call on Your name."
>
> ¹⁵But the Lord said to him, "Go, for he is a chosen vessel of Mine to bear My name before Gentiles, kings, and the children of Israel. ¹⁶For I will show him how many things he must suffer for My name's sake."
>
> ¹⁷And Ananias went his way and entered the house; and laying his hands on him he said, "Brother Saul, the Lord Jesus, who appeared to you on the road as you came, has sent me that you may receive your sight and be filled with the Holy Spirit." ¹⁸Immediately there fell from his eyes *something* like scales, and he received his sight at once; and he arose and was baptized.

1a. Did Ananias' protest concerning God's command indicate a lack of commitment to God?

_____

1b. Do you think Ananias' fears were justified? Explain your answer:

_____

2. Did Ananias prove that God came first in his life? If so, how?

_____

3. What is one thing in your life that competes for priority with your commitment to God?

_____

Fear's Mortal Enemy

Even though afraid, Ananias possessed the commitment to obey God's call. But do we? Where can we find the depth of commitment needed to give us victory against fear? And what is the source of this commitment? The answer is simple: love. Love for the Lord is the source of our commitment.

Consider Peter, whom we discussed earlier in this chapter. Peter was deeply ashamed of his cowardice when he denied Christ three times. He even wondered if he was to be considered an apostle anymore. Yet Jesus restored him with the words, "Do you love Me?" Three times Christ asked Peter this question, and three times Peter answered that he did. With this he was reinstated as an apostle whose duty to Christ was to "feed My sheep" (John 21:17).

Jesus illustrated a truth with His words, a truth that we can take advantage of when we are tempted to give in to fear. "Love casts out fear" (1 John 4:18). Each denial driven by fear was countered by a profession of love. When Peter confronted danger as a servant of the Lord in the future, he would not succumb to fear. His love for Christ was too great. As Christ promised, Peter did eventually give his life for Christ. Fear could not make Peter falter this time, for it was a sacrifice of love.

How else does love conquer fear? Answer the following to find out:

1. How does God's love calm the fears of the sinner who deserves judgment?

_____

2. How does love for others compel the believer to overcome the fear of rejection or ridicule?

_____

3. How does God's love for His children relieve the believer's daily fears and anxieties?

_____

◆ ◆ ◆ ◆ ◆ ◆ ◆ ◆ ◆

We are not alone when we are afraid. God is with us. He can give us the power to walk in faith. And should we falter as Peter did when he tried to walk upon the waves (Matt. 14:28–31), our Lord is there to reach out His hand and make our footsteps firm.

Yet we need motivation to resist our fears. That motivation comes from our love and respect for our heavenly Father. And what really stands in the way of commitment? For God has conquered even death on our behalf! The only thing left to fear is failing in our commitment, for then we risk missing out on the rich rewards the Lord has prepared for us.

But wait a minute! What are the rewards of following Christ? Should we expect the blessings of material wealth and worldly success? Or do all of our rewards await us in heaven? What is real prosperity, anyway? Let's find out!

THOSE WHO FOUND TRUE PROSPERITY

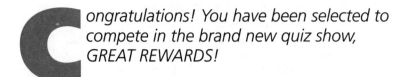ongratulations! You have been selected to
compete in the brand new quiz show,
GREAT REWARDS!

The rules of the game are simple. Answer each of the following statements with a True or False response. The category is: BUCKS AND THE BELIEVER.

Hands on your buzzers, contestants. Begin!

_____ Money is the root of all evil.

_____ Wealth is the result of God's blessing.

_____ Poverty is a virtue.

_____ Possessing great wealth is a sin.

_____ You should use money to make friends.

_____ Christian values are bound to "pay off" financially.

_____ Capitalism, which is based on making profit, is an evil economic system.

_____ God intends some to be successful and some not to be successful.

_____ Ten percent of every-thing we make belongs to God.

Okay. Buzzers down, contestants, and thanks for playing GREAT REWARDS!

Now, take a deep breath and relax, because this was only a practice run. The real contest comes later. We aren't going to make the correct answers available at this time, but if you really want to find out how well you performed, read on!

◆ ◆ ◆ ◆ ◆ ◆ ◆ ◆ ◆

PEOPLE, PROPERTY, AND PROFITABILITY

The gospel can produce radical changes as it affects people, property, and profitability. Consider three instructive examples from Acts:

Simon "the Great" (Acts 8:9–13, 18–24)
- A sorcerer with a large following.
- The gospel threatened his profitable business by demonstrating a greater power.
- Hoping to expand his repertoire, he offered to buy the apostles' power.
- Rebuked by the apostles, who called him to true repentance.

The Slave Girl at Philippi (Acts 16:16–40)
- Paul's gospel freed a fortune-teller from her occult bondage.
- Owned by a syndicate of investors, she had powers that earned them good money.

continued

continued

- Realizing their loss, they seized Paul and Silas and hauled them before the authorities.
- Punishment: beatings and jail.
- But lockup only led to further conversions.
- Morning brought embarrassment to the city as officials learned of the travelers' Roman citizenship.

The Silversmiths at Ephesus (Acts 19:1–41)

- Paul lectured daily in the school of Tyrannus, resulting in many conversions.
- Sales of silver statues of Diana (the Greek goddess of fertility) fell off, triggering an emergency "Chamber of Commerce" meeting.
- Artisans complained that Paul's gospel had reduced trade, ruined their reputations, and impugned their goddess.
- A riot was incited and Paul's associates were dragged before a lynch mob.
- The city clerk eventually restored peace and Paul quietly went on his way.

Good Ethics—Not Always Good Business

Christlike values do not necessarily produce financial gain in the marketplace. Sometimes they produce just the opposite. Scripture has no argument with making a profit except when it compromises people or the truth. At that point the gospel raises questions that any responsible believer must face. For example, a contract goes unsigned because a Christian refuses to offer money under the table. A sale is lost because a Christian refuses to lie to a customer. A promotion slips by because a Christian sets limits on the intrusion of work into his or her family and personal life.

Make no mistake, many people are receptive toward Christian principles at home and church, and even on the job—as long as such principles cost nothing. But the test of Christian commitment often lies in what one is willing to sacrifice.

What have your Christian convictions cost you? If nothing, are you making tradeoffs that you can't afford to make? Do you sometimes value possessions or power more than people? ◆

 Acts 16:19

[19]But when her masters saw that their hope of profit was gone, they seized Paul and Silas and dragged *them* into the marketplace to the authorities.

It's common to think of Christianity in terms of the spiritual impact it has on individuals and the world. But few of us think of our Christian values in terms of their economic impact. For most of us, the connection between the spiritual world and business world probably isn't all that apparent.

Why is that? After all, the Christian faith is a radical faith. Hearts and lives are radically changed through belief in Christ, so it shouldn't come as a surprise that the reverberations of change are felt in the working world as well.

Many of us may simply be confused about the relationship between our faith and our work. Like the statements in the "quiz show," we hear so many different viewpoints being expressed that we may not know what to believe. Is money a good thing or is it bad? Is it wrong to strive for prosperity? The ambiguity that exists in our minds when it comes to the subject of wealth may cause us to avoid the issue altogether. Some of us, though, may be avoiding the issue for another reason. Too much thought about how our beliefs should be affecting our work lives might prove to be both costly and inconvenient.

The fact is that believers cannot afford to ignore this issue. The Book of Acts clearly demonstrates the potential for conflict between Christianity and business interests. In fact, the only two times reported in Acts that Paul was threatened or harmed by Gentiles involved business losses (Acts 16:16–24; 18:23–30).

The possibility of conflict between faith and enterprise remains just as real today. For most adults, work occupies about half of their waking hours. If the believer's faith fails to impact his or her work, then how much effect can Christianity be having on that person's life? Certainly believers must work for a living, but when the responsibilities of occupation collide with responsibility to God, Christians need to be ready to make the tough choice—no matter what the price. ◆

1. When "business ethics" courses first started to appear in universities, some people joked that the term was an oxymoron. Now there are books on being a "successful Christian businessperson." Is this possible, or does being good at one necessarily mean you will be bad at the other?

2. Obviously there are some ways of making a living that a Christian should not even consider. But are some ordinary jobs simply wrong for a Christian? Put a checkmark next to those that you would not do as a matter of conscience.

> *Worker in a brewery*
> *A corporate lawyer involved in engineering hostile takeovers*
> *Secretary for a corrupt politician*
> *A soldier in the army*
> *A tobacco farmer*
> *A divorce attorney*

3. Just as some do today, Simon the sorcerer sought to wrongly profit from the gospel. When is it acceptable to make money from the gospel? Explain your answer.

4. When Paul cast the demon out of the slave girl, he ended her oppression both by the evil spirit and the syndicate who exploited her. When is the Christian duty-bound to likewise take a stand against injustice or exploitation in the workplace or society at large?

5. The silversmiths at Ephesus represent those who are opposed to Christianity because it threatens to impact their profits. What modern business or industry has become an enemy of Christ for financial gain (for example: the pornography industry)?

6. Have your Christian values ever come into conflict with your work duties? If so, describe the circumstances.

◆ Surrendering Status for Service ◆

Wy Plummer was a success. Like so many inner-city youths, he grew up in poverty and could only dream of one day being wealthy. But Wy had an inner determination that wouldn't succumb to the obstacles before him. Through years of struggle, he earned a degree in electrical engineering and secured a high-paying job with IBM. He moved to the suburbs and bought a house. He had made it.

Only one thing bothered him: he was miserable. Wy thought that satisfaction would come with prosperity, but it all seemed so meaningless. Was this the purpose of life?

One day an office manager invited Wy to a Bible study. Wy only scoffed—at first. But after three months of Bible study, he committed his life to the Lord. A few years later, he left his career at IBM behind and joined the church staff in his suburban community. When an offer came to work

for a church in the inner city, he scoffed at that as well. Then he accepted.

Wy's life has come full circle, and he has returned to the inner city world he once was so driven to escape. In his desire to serve, he has lost the wealth and status he once enjoyed. But he has found his life's purpose. As far as Wy is concerned, he is richer than ever. ◆

◆ ◆ ◆ ◆ ◆ ◆ ◆ ◆ ◆

1. Have you ever felt a conflict between gaining God's approval and achieving worldly success? Explain your answer.

2. Which has had a greater influence on your choice of vocation?

    a. religious beliefs
    b. prospects for financial gain
    c. desire to find a job that is challenging or enjoyable

CHRISTIANS AND MONEY

Paul ridicules the idea that God is in the business of dispensing material gain in exchange for spiritual cooperation (1 Tim. 6:5). That launches him into a discussion of money that modern believers do well to study carefully, given the emphasis on money in our culture. He speaks to three categories of people: those who want to get rich (vv. 6–10), those who want to honor God (vv. 11–16), and those who are rich and want to honor God (vv. 17–19).

continued

continued

Contentment versus Covetousness (6:6–10)

Paul warns us strongly against "the love of money" (v. 10). But let's be sure we interpret his words correctly. He does not say that money itself is evil (nor does any other Scripture). Neither does he say that money is *the* fundamental root of evil, or that money lies at the root of *every* evil. Rather, the *love* of money (something inside people, not money itself) can be *a* root (but not the only root) of all *kinds* of evil (but not of all evil).

But don't let those qualifications soften the blow: people who love money are vulnerable to all kinds of evil, the worst of which, Paul points out, is straying from the faith (see Col. 3:5).

Given that danger, believers should by all means avoid greed. Jesus gave a direct, unequivocal command to that effect. He didn't tell us to guard against it in others, but in ourselves (see Luke 12:15).

Paul offers the alternative to greed, or covetousness, as contentment (6:6–8). However, his description of contentment—food and clothing—sounds incredibly spartan in our own culture that extols self-made millionaires and entertains itself by paying video visits to those who live in opulent, even decadent lifestyles. Are believers required to take vows of poverty like Franciscan monks (see Matt. 10:7–10)?

No, but Paul does remind us in this passage what poverty really is: lack of food, clothing, and shelter adequate for survival where one lives. If we have these, we ought to be content. If not, then we are truly destitute and dependent on the charity of others for survival. The biblical concept of poverty is not merely having less than the average income, or some percentage of it, in one's society, as contemporary sociologists and economists tend to define it (see 2 Cor. 9:9–10).

Can Paul be serious? Is it really possible to be content, at least in our society, with merely the basics—food, clothing, and shelter? Paul should know. He experienced firsthand the wealth and privileges of prominence in the Jewish community and of Roman citizenship. Yet he also suffered extraordinary hardships in his work. Through it all he learned a secret that helped him maintain contentment. What was it? See Phil. 4:10–13.

A Charge to Timothy (6:11–16)

Paul's example was especially important to Timothy, his protégé in the faith. He challenges the young pastor to pursue a lifestyle that values character over cash (1 Tim. 6:11). The words are addressed to Timothy, but they apply to anyone who wants to honor God in life. Timothy needed to watch out for greed just like any other believer (see 1 Tim. 3:1; 3:3).

Paul was especially on the lookout for greed. Interestingly, one of his main strategies for avoiding it was to earn his own living as a tentmaker, rather than live off the generosity of others (see Acts 20:33–38).

Commands for Rich Christians (6:17–19)

Apparently there were wealthy believers in Timothy's church at Ephesus. The city was extraordinarily prosperous. In fact, its tourist trade brought in so much revenue that the town leaders opened the first world bank. Paul had penetrated this vibrant economic life with the gospel, winning many converts (see Acts 19:8–41). No doubt some of the rich Christians he addresses here brought their money with them into the faith—just like many in the modern church.

The question, then, especially in light of the teaching in 1 Tim. 6:6–10, is, what should people with money do if they want to honor God? Paul says they should start by examining their attitudes. Money has incredible power to create feelings of pride, superiority, and self-sufficiency (v. 17). So people of means have to learn to look beyond their money to God, the ultimate source of wealth.

But attitude is only half the battle. Sooner or later rich Christians need to take conscious, decisive action with their wealth. They need to put it into play serving God and others (6:18).

continued

continued

What About You?

What is your deepest desire? Is it to be rich rather than righteous? If so, beware! Longing for wealth leads to many dangers—even to death.

God wants you to grasp something far more permanent and satisfying—eternal life (6:12, 18). ◆

 1 Timothy 6:6–19

⁶Now godliness with contentment is great gain. ⁷For we brought nothing into *this* world, *and it is* certain we can carry nothing out. ⁸And having food and clothing, with these we shall be content. ⁹But those who desire to be rich fall into temptation and a snare, and *into* many foolish and harmful lusts which drown men in destruction and perdition. ¹⁰For the love of money is a root of all *kinds of* evil, for which some have strayed from the faith in their greediness, and pierced themselves through with many sorrows.

¹¹But you, O man of God, flee these things and pursue righteousness, godliness, faith, love, patience, gentleness. ¹²Fight the good fight of faith, lay hold on eternal life, to which you were also called and have confessed the good confession in the presence of many witnesses. ¹³I urge you in the sight of God who gives life to all things, and

before Christ Jesus who witnessed the good confession before Pontius Pilate, ¹⁴that you keep *this* commandment without spot, blameless until our Lord Jesus Christ's appearing, ¹⁵which He will manifest in His own time, *He who is* the blessed and only Potentate, the King of kings and Lord of lords, ¹⁶who alone has immortality, dwelling in unapproachable light, whom no man has seen or can see, to whom *be* honor and everlasting power. Amen.

¹⁷Command those who are rich in this present age not to be haughty, nor to trust in uncertain riches but in the living God, who gives us richly all things to enjoy. ¹⁸*Let them* do good, that they be rich in good works, ready to give, willing to share, ¹⁹storing up for themselves a good foundation for the time to come, that they may lay hold on eternal life.

1. How is Wy a good example of Paul's formula for success in 1 Timothy 6:6?

2. Paul tells believers that they should be content if they have food and clothing. Could you be satisfied earning a subsistence living? Why or why not?

3. Paul served as a model for Timothy in handling wealth. Who serves as a good model for you to emulate, and why?

4. "I don't love money. I just love what I can buy with it." Do you identify with this attitude? What costly possession do you have to guard against coveting?

5. Take a look at the things Paul advises us to pursue more than money in 1 Timothy 6:11. How do these "possessions" differ from those that you can buy?

_____

6a. Paul utters a warning and a suggestion in his word to the wealthy Ephesians (1 Tim. 6:17–19). Take a second look at what he said to them. What dangers come with wealth?

_____

6b. What can the rich person gain through the wise use of money?

_____

——◆ On Loan from God ◆——

 Luke 20:9–19

⁹Then He began to tell the people this parable: "A certain man planted a vineyard, leased it to vinedressers, and went into a far country for a long time. ¹⁰Now at vintage-time he sent a servant to the vinedressers, that they might give him some of the fruit of the vineyard. But the vinedressers beat him and sent *him* away empty-handed. ¹¹Again he sent another servant; and they beat him also, treated *him* shamefully, and sent *him* away empty-handed. ¹²And again he sent a third; and they wounded him also and cast *him* out.

¹³"Then the owner of the vineyard said, 'What shall I do? I will send my beloved son. Probably they will respect *him* when they see him.' ¹⁴But when the vinedressers saw him, they reasoned among themselves, saying, 'This is the heir. Come, let us kill him, that the inheritance may be ours.' ¹⁵So they cast him out of the vineyard and killed him. Therefore what will the owner of the vineyard do to them? ¹⁶He will come and destroy those vinedressers and give the vineyard to others."

And when they heard *it* they said, "Certainly not!"

¹⁷Then He looked at them and said, "What then is this that is written:

'The stone which the builders rejected
Has become the chief cornerstone' ?

¹⁸Whoever falls on that stone will be broken; but on whomever it falls, it will grind him to powder."

¹⁹And the chief priests and the scribes that very hour sought to lay hands on Him, but they feared the people—for they knew He had spoken this parable against them.

Jesus told this story to the throng of people in the temple. It was during the last week of His ministry, and He knew He must soon give up His life. Though the common people hung on the Lord's every word, they may not have understood its message. The vineyard was the nation of Israel and the tenants were the leaders of the people. God was the vineyard owner, and the son was Christ Himself.

The religious leaders also were in the crowd, and they understood the story all too well. Wealth, power, and prestige were all theirs. They would kill before they'd give it all away to some carpenter from Nazareth. And that is exactly what they did.

♦ ♦ ♦ ♦ ♦ ♦ ♦ ♦ ♦

Possessiveness doesn't seem to be all that bad a vice. After all, what's mine is mine, and what's yours is yours, right? If I don't want people borrowing my new car, that's my right. Sure, I've got a good job. So get your own. I hate it when people interrupt me while I'm relaxing after a hard day. This is my time. And don't even think of asking me for a loan. That's a sure way to kill a friendship.

But this isn't the kind of attitude that God desires from His children. Do you ever catch yourself thinking this way? If so, then beware! The same attitude of possessiveness drove the religious leaders to murder our Lord. The more you have, the tighter you hold on to it—until it becomes a stranglehold. Loosen up your grip, and remember: we don't own anything. It's all on loan from God.

WEALTH—HOLD IT LIGHTLY

Whether we own land, buildings, things, or cash, wealth is tricky to handle. How we hold these assets speaks volumes about our values. If we hold them too tightly, the results will likely be possessiveness, stinginess, manipulation, and elitism.

Barnabas converted some land that he owned into a cash gift for needy believers (Acts 4:36–37). Notice how he *let go* of the money, laying it at the apostles' feet to be administered by them. By contrast, Ananias and Sapphira practiced a similar transaction for the same need, but lied about it (5:1–2). Apparently they wanted to look good among the believers, but they also wanted to secretly hold onto some of their money from the sale.

God calls us as believers to hold our resources lightly. After all, everything that we have comes from Him. He gives it to us as a trust to be managed—not a treasure to be hoarded.

 Acts 4:37—5:11

³⁷having land, sold *it*, and brought the money and laid *it* at the apostles' feet.

But a certain man named Ananias, with Sapphira his wife, sold a possession. ²And he kept back *part* of the proceeds, his wife also being aware *of it*, and brought a certain part and laid *it* at the apostles' feet. ³But Peter said, "Ananias, why has Satan filled your heart to lie to the Holy Spirit and keep back *part* of the price of the land for yourself? ⁴While it remained, was it not your own? And after it was sold, was it not in your own control? Why have you conceived this thing in your heart? You have not lied to men but to God."

⁵Then Ananias, hearing these words, fell down and breathed his last. So great fear came upon all those who heard these things. ⁶And the young men arose and wrapped him up, carried *him* out, and buried *him*.

⁷Now it was about three hours later when his wife came in, not knowing what had happened. ⁸And Peter answered her, "Tell me whether you sold the land for so much?"

She said, "Yes, for so much."

⁹Then Peter said to her, "How is it that you have agreed together to test the Spirit of the Lord? Look, the feet of those who have buried your husband *are* at the door, and they will carry you out." ¹⁰Then immediately she fell down at his feet and breathed her last. And the young men came in and found her dead, and carrying *her* out, buried *her* by her husband. ¹¹So great fear came upon all the church and upon all who heard these things.

Barnabas had a gift for giving. He sold his land to feed the poor, and he gave his time and talents to mentor Paul in the faith. When the time came, he willingly gave over leadership of the missionary team to Paul (Acts 13:7, 13). With Paul, he refused to make a living from preaching the gospel (1 Cor. 9:6). In everything, Barnabas was committed to a spirit of generosity.

Ananias and Sapphira, like Barnabas, sold a possession and laid the money "at the apostles' feet." But they did not share Barnabas' inner spirit of charity. Ananias and Sapphira merely wished to appear generous, while still enjoying some of the profits of the sale. In essense, they sought to purchase "the praise of men" (John 12:43). They did not use their possessions for God's glory but for their own.

1. Suppose everything you have was borrowed from someone else. How would that change the way you view your possessions?

2. Jesus warned his disciples, "when you do a charitable deed, do not let your left hand know what your right hand is doing" (Matt. 6:3). How did Ananias and Sapphira violate this principle?

3. Why do you think Ananias and Sapphira were judged so harshly for their sin?

4. By giving generously we receive spiritual rewards in return (2 Cor. 9:6–8). But when we give little or grudgingly, our reward is also little. How does this spiritual principle apply to your own life?

◆ More Treasured Than Silver and Gold ◆

Prosperity is intended by God to be a blessing for those to whom it is given. In Old Testament times, the Israelites were promised prosperity if they remained obedient to God (Deut. 28). And although the New Testament promises spiritual wealth rather than material wealth will be given to the faithful, some still do receive material wealth as a blessing.

Affluence eases many of the burdens of life. There is no great virtue for the Christian in choosing a life of poverty—unless it is necessary to better serve the Lord. Paul makes clear that asceticism, the idea that one should renounce the goods of the world, should be rejected by the believer (Col. 2:18–23). The only true benefit of poverty is that it provides the believer with the opportunity to be "rich in faith" (James 2:5), for it produces a greater dependence on God.

But with the blessing of material wealth comes responsibility. We must resist the tendency to cling to or covet the world's goods. We are to be good stewards and use all that He *has put in our hands in ways that honor God. This applies not only to wealth but to our time, talents, and spiritual gifts as well (1 Pet. 4:10). If we are faithful servants, one day we will be amply rewarded for our wise management.*

JOSEPH—A MODEL FOR MARKETPLACE CHRISTIANS

f you work in today's marketplace, you may wonder at times how your faith applies in a tough business environment. If so, it helps to study the life of Joseph. He and Daniel, (see Gen. 39:1–5 and Dan. 2:46–49) are two of the best models in Scripture for how to honor God in a "secular" workplace.

Consider Joseph's circumstances. He was cut off from his family. He was part of a culture that worshiped pagan gods, and apparently he alone worshiped the true God. Thus he had no support system for his beliefs or values and no one to turn to for godly counsel as he made far-reaching decisions. His boss, Pharaoh, was considered a god by the Egyptians. Likewise Joseph's wife was an Egyptian and his father-in-law a priest of the sun-god.

How did Joseph maintain his faith in such an environment? Consider several ways:

(1) *He maintained his integrity.* Joseph steadfastly resisted the sexual advances of Potiphar's wife (Gen. 39:7–10). He realized that moral compromise would have been an offense not only against his master, but even worse, against God. He remained committed to what he knew was right, despite the consequences.

(2) *He kept doing his best even when the situation was the worst.* Unjustly thrown into prison, Joseph easily could have become bitter at God. He could have given up with the attitude, "What's the use?" Instead, he kept doing what God had designed Him to do—exercising authority, even in prison (Gen. 39:22–23).

(3) *He carried out the task he was given.* Promoted to Pharaoh's right hand, Joseph was faithful in the responsibility. He wisely planned for the coming famine and managed the Egyptian economy in a way that saved many lives (Gen. 41:46–49, 53–57). He recognized that the work itself was what God wanted him to do.

(4) *He used his power and influence compassionately.* Second-in-command under Pharaoh, Joseph could have used his position as an opportunity to "pay back" his enemies, such as his brothers, the slave traders, and Potiphar's wife. Instead, the record shows just the opposite: he used his power to bring reconciliation (Gen. 45:3–15; 50:20).

God used Joseph's faithfulness to preserve the children of Jacob (Israel) in order to fulfill His promise to Abraham (Gen. 45:5–8). In the same way, God intends to use believers today in positions great and small to accomplish His purposes. Therefore it is crucial that we honor God through our work. Like Joseph, we need to be people of whom there can be no doubt—we are those "in whom is the Spirit of God" (Gen. 41:38). ◆

Genesis 41:44–57

⁴⁴Pharaoh also said to Joseph, "I *am* Pharaoh, and without your consent no man may lift his hand or foot in all the land of Egypt." ⁴⁵And Pharaoh called Joseph's name Zaphnath-Paaneah. And he gave him as a wife Asenath, the daughter of Poti-Pherah priest of On. So Joseph went out over *all* the land of Egypt.

⁴⁶Joseph was thirty years old when he stood before Pharaoh king of Egypt. And Joseph went out from the presence of Pharaoh, and went throughout all the land of Egypt. ⁴⁷Now in the seven plentiful years the ground brought forth abundantly. ⁴⁸So he gathered up all the food of the seven years which were in the land of Egypt, and laid up the food in the cities; he laid up in every city the food of the fields which surrounded them. ⁴⁹Joseph gathered very much grain, as the sand of the sea, until he stopped counting, for *it was* immeasurable.

⁵⁰And to Joseph were born two sons before the years of famine came, whom Asenath, the daughter of Poti-Pherah priest of On, bore to him. ⁵¹Joseph called the name of the firstborn Manasseh: "For God has made me forget all my toil and all my father's house." ⁵²And the name of the second he called Ephraim: "For God has caused me to be fruitful in the land of my affliction."

⁵³Then the seven years of plenty which were in the land of Egypt ended, ⁵⁴and the seven years of famine began to come, as Joseph had said. The famine was in all lands, but in all the land of Egypt there was bread. ⁵⁵So when all the land of Egypt was famished, the people cried to Pharaoh for bread. Then Pharaoh said to all the Egyptians, "Go to Joseph; whatever he says to you, do." ⁵⁶The famine was over all the face of the earth, and Joseph opened all the storehouses and sold to the Egyptians. And the famine became severe in the land of Egypt. ⁵⁷So all countries came to Joseph in Egypt to buy *grain,* because the famine was severe in all lands.

1. Joseph's efforts to work and live responsibly never varied based on his circumstances. Is the same true of yourself? Why or why not?

_____

2. Which did integrity bring Joseph   a) prosperity, or   b) poverty _____?

3a. Integrity brought Joseph both poverty and prosperity at different times in his life. In fact, remaining faithful to his God and his master landed him in prison! And his labors in prison must not have seemed a sure road to prosperity to Joseph. The affluence he eventually achieved was actually a consequence of God's work rather than his own. What does Joseph's story say to those who believe the value of integrity is that it is profitable?

_____

3b. If prosperity wasn't the motive behind Joseph's faithful labor, what was?

_____

4a. Though Joseph's managerial work in prison may have seemed trivial, it helped to prepare Joseph to become ruler over all of Egypt, second only to Pharaoh! What significance does this have for those who are working in a position that is unfulfilling?

4b. How might God be using your present duties to prepare you for greater responsibility?

Using the Talents God Gave You

TRUE SUCCESS MEANS FAITHFULNESS

The story of the talents (Matt. 25:14–30) is about the kingdom of heaven (v. 14), but it offers an important lesson about success. God measures our success not by what we have, but by what we do with what we have—for all that we have is a gift from Him. We are really only managers to whom He has entrusted resources and responsibilities.

The key thing He looks for is *faithfulness* (Matt. 25:21, 23), doing what we can to obey and honor Him with whatever He has given us. We may or may not be "successful" as our culture measures success, in terms of wealth, prestige, power, or fame. In the long run that hardly matters. What counts is whether we have faithfully served God with what He has entrusted to us. By all means we must avoid wasting our lives, the way the third servant wasted his talents, by failing to carry out our Master's business.

 Matthew 25:14–30

¹⁴"For *the kingdom of heaven is* like a man traveling to a far country, *who* called his own servants and delivered his goods to them. ¹⁵And to one he gave five talents, to another two, and to another one, to each according to his own ability; and immediately he went on a journey. ¹⁶Then he who had received the five talents went and traded with them, and made another five talents. ¹⁷And likewise he who *had received* two gained two more also. ¹⁸But he who had received one went and dug in the ground, and hid his lord's money. ¹⁹After a long time the lord of those servants came and settled accounts with them.

²⁰"So he who had received five talents came and brought five other talents, saying, 'Lord, you delivered to me five talents; look, I have gained five more talents besides them.' ²¹His lord said to him, 'Well *done,* good and faithful servant; you were faithful over a few things, I will make you

ruler over many things. Enter into the joy of your lord.' ²²He also who had received two talents came and said, 'Lord, you delivered to me two talents; look, I have gained two more talents besides them.' ²³His lord said to him, 'Well *done,* good and faithful servant; you have been faithful over a few things, I will make you ruler over many things. Enter into the joy of your lord.'

²⁴"Then he who had received the one talent came and said, 'Lord, I knew you to be a hard man, reaping where you have not sown, and gathering where you have not scattered seed. ²⁵And I was afraid, and went and hid your talent in the ground. Look, *there* you have *what is* yours.'

²⁶"But his lord answered and said to him, 'You wicked and lazy servant, you knew that I reap where I have not sown, and gather where I have not scattered seed. ²⁷So you ought to have

continued

> *continued*
> deposited my money with the bankers, and at my coming I would have received back my own with interest. ²⁸So take the talent from him, and give *it* to him who has ten talents.
>
> ²⁹'For to everyone who has, more will be given, and he will have abundance; but from him who does not have, even what he has will be taken away. ³⁰And cast the unprofitable servant into the outer darkness. There will be weeping and gnashing of teeth.'

1. Why did the master in the parable give different amounts to the three servants?

_____

2. In another parable, Christ advised that we use money to "make friends" (Luke 16:9). By friends, Jesus meant converts. How can we follow His advice?

_____

3. Jesus told His disciples not to seek to accumulate earthly treasures, but to "lay up for yourselves treasures in heaven, where neither moth nor rust destroys" (Matt. 6:20). Christ's parable of the talents gives us a glimpse of the heavenly prosperity meant for those who are faithful with what they have been given. Describe something you have been given and how you could use it as an "investment" on God's behalf.

_____

The prosperity gained through faithfulness isn't just for the life to come. There is a prosperity of the soul that we can know right now (3 John 2). The Greek word for "prosper" used by John means "to travel well on a journey." We do not chase after this prosperity; it is something we enjoy through faithful service to God. Whatever our material circumstances, we can experience this spiritual well-being.

• • • • • • • • •

And now you know the way to true *prosperity, for it is spiritual not material. Use what you have wisely, for the reward you will receive one day will be beyond your wildest dreams (Rom. 8:18). And you only have the rest of your life ahead of you to earn it.*

All right, contestants. Are you ready to earn your great reward? Get ready. Begin!

• • • • • • • • •

We've examined the rewards of a Christian life, but what about its hardships? Is there a way we can avoid experiencing painful trials in this life? Do bad things just happen, or is there a reason for why we suffer? We will look at this difficult issue in the upcoming chapter.

TEMPORARY HARDSHIPS, LASTING REWARDS

Virginia couldn't understand what was happening to her. For some reason, migraine headaches had always troubled her. But only after the recent birth of her first child did they become a daily experience. When a headache came, it was nearly incapacitating.

Over the past three months she had gone to several specialists, but they could not identify the cause of her headaches. She had been given pain medication, a restricted diet, and received periodic follow-up exams. But still the dreadful migraines continued.

All of her adult life, Virginia had been a devoted Christian. She believed in God's love and His sovereignty over her life. But with the unceasing pain, doubt had taken root.

Since she was a teenager, she had kept a diary next to her bed, and almost every night, she would write a new entry. Just that morning she had seen another specialist, with no positive results. In the evening, a terrible headache had left her paralyzed with pain. As her agony finally drained away, though ex-

hausted, she picked up her diary and wrote:

January 23, 1987:

Today the doctor gave me the latest test results, which naturally showed that nothing was wrong with me. He even suggested that my headaches were psychosomatic. As though I'd wish this on myself!

Day after day after day, it's the same thing. I don't know how I'm supposed to go on like this. Why is God doing this to me? Doesn't He love me? Doesn't he care? Why should I believe in a God who lets me suffer like this for no reason? Why should I put my trust in a God that leaves me to helplessly endure such torment without an explanation?

◆ ◆ ◆ ◆ ◆ ◆ ◆ ◆ ◆

Suffering. There has never been a life that has not been touched by it. Nothing is more feared and despised. And as universal and hated as suffering is, it is often just as incomprehensible. Nothing else gives rise to so many heart-searching questions or so threatens the foundations of our faith in God.

"How could a loving God permit so much pain and suffering in the world," challenges an unbelieving world. And for a moment, our words catch in our throats. What do we say? Philosophers and theologians through the centuries have wrestled with the question. At one time or another, almost every one of us will be haunted by the question when pain and suffering make their unwelcome visit in our lives.

The people of the Bible suffered as we suffer, and as a consequence many experienced deep nagging doubts about God. Job is the archetypical example of inexplicable suffering. He was a righteous man, but his ten children, his worldly possessions, and his health were all taken from him. Yet through all these calamities Job remained steadfast in his faith.

Still, is it realistic to expect most of us to respond to suffering like Job? How well would another have stood up under such torment? The question isn't entirely hypothetical, for there was another who suffered the very same things as Job himself—his wife.

JOB'S FORGOTTEN WIFE

Because the Book of Job focuses on the person of Job himself, it is easy to overlook Job's wife. In fact, we are not even given her name. Yet this woman was Job's partner in all of the tragedies that struck him and his family, and for that reason alone she merits our attention.

Only one statement of Job's wife is recorded in the book, and it comes while she and Job are struggling with the overwhelming hopelessness of their situation. In agony and despair she cries out to her husband, "Do you still hold fast to your integrity? Curse God and die!" (Job 2:9).

Many condemn her for this outburst. But is that fair? If we were in her place, might we not say more or less the same thing? In fact, the comment of Job's wife challenges us to consider: How would we express our deepest grief and pain? How would we respond to the brutal loss of everything dear and precious to us?

The pain of Job is known through his many speeches, but the pain of Job's wife remains unknown. We can only imagine how great it was, and how incomprehensible her situation must have seemed. All ten of her children were dead, killed in a tragic windstorm (Job 1:18–19). Not one escaped. The loss of one child can be devastating to a mother; but how much can a mother's heart bear if she loses *all* of her children.

Then, while she was trying to cope with the shock of this catastrophe, she began to see her husband's body develop painful boils (Job 2:7). It was too much to bear. In the midst of all her other losses, she at least still had her husband. But now it appeared that he, too, was about to be taken away from her. This made her situation seem hopeless. Where was God? Why was He allowing this to happen? Why was He not doing something?

These were not abstract, theoretical questions for Job's wife. Her children were dead. Her husband was dying. *How could a God who allowed this to happen be trusted?* she must have wondered. Concluding that He could not, she chided her husband for hanging onto his faith (Job 2:9).

This heartrending cry of utter helplessness is understandable. It may be easier to deal with one's own pain than to see a loved one hurting and be powerless to stop it.

Job responded to his grieving, bitter wife with what seems to be a rather harsh reply, calling her a foolish woman (Job 2:10). But maybe this was the only way to break through her tears. Whatever the case, Job's remarkable statement pointed to the fact that no one is exempt from the realities of living in a broken world where sin and evil often have their way.

Centuries after these events, Jesus offered a similar perspective: "In the world you will have tribulation" (John 16:33). Some people say that when we trust in Jesus as Savior and Lord, He will take away all of our troubles. But clearly, He has not promised that. Instead, He has promised to be there with us in the midst of our trials: "*I will never leave you nor forsake you*" (Heb. 13:5). The Lord will walk with us through the realities of life.

Scripture does not tell us what happened to the faith of Job's wife. Perhaps she reflected on her husband's words and developed more trust in the Lord, despite severe tragedy; perhaps she never recovered from the deep wounds of loss.

If you were facing the kinds of circumstances that confronted Job's wife, what would be the quality of your faith? When troubles come your way, are you able to see past the pain to the Lord, who is always with you? Can you pray to Him with honesty, expressing everything that is in your heart? ◆

Job 2:9–10

⁹Then his wife said to him, "Do you still hold fast to your integrity? Curse God and die!"

¹⁰But he said to her, "You speak as one of the foolish women speaks. Shall we indeed accept good from God, and shall we not accept adversity?" In all this Job did not sin with his lips.

1. Who are you more like in your response to suffering   a. Job, or   b. Job's wife? _____

2. Have you ever experienced a period of intense suffering, whether physical or emotional? If so, describe it.

_____

3. Which is a greater test to your faith?
        a. your own suffering   b. the suffering of someone close to you

4. Describe the impact that suffering has had on the quality of your faith. Has it shaken your trust or led to a deeper faith in God?

_____

    Look at Job's reply to his wife. He doesn't give an explanation for suffering, but he does show an acceptance of pain as a part of life. His faith is sufficient to encompass sufferings from the hand of a loving God.

    Christ made it clear that we would suffer in this life. Undoubtedly, He was trying to warn us against developing a faith too shallow for the harsh realities of life. Too often, we imagine that God's love means pain-free living. When painful experiences come we need to enlarge our vision of God. This is what Job sought to do as he struggled to make sense of his suffering.

◆ The Search for an Answer ◆

November 1, 1988:

    Last week was my sweet little Andy's first birthday—and also the "anniversary" of my affliction. I guess you have to take the good with the bad. It's hard to believe I've lived like this for so long. I've even learned how to cope with the headaches, arrange my schedule, get done what I can manage through the pain. A year ago, I wouldn't have believed I could have endured it. I guess that's some encouragement anyway.

    Jack has been so supportive through everything. I know it's been a terrible ordeal for him as well. Last night he just held me while I cried myself to sleep—again. I just can't help wondering why I have to go through this.

    Is God punishing me for something? Am I supposed to learn something through all this? My sister says I just need to have more faith and I'll be healed. Well, I've prayed and prayed, but I'm still waiting to hear an answer. Are you listening, God? ◆

WHY?

Faced with sudden tragedy, such as the loss of health, wealth, or a loved one, the natural question to ask is: *Why?* Why did this happen? Why did it happen to me? Why now?

Job struggled with questions of "why" as he tried to make sense of his sufferings (Job 7:20–21). So did Jesus' disciples when they came upon a man who had been born blind. "Who sinned," they asked Jesus, "this man or his parents?" (John 9:1–2). They were asking why in the sense of *causality:* What was the reason for his blindness? They assumed that somehow sin must have been involved.

Yet on another level, the disciples were asking why in the sense of *purpose:* What was the significance for the man's blindness? In reply, Jesus borrowed an answer from Job. He assured His disciples that through the man's blindness, the glorious works of God would be made evident (Job 9:3–5). Then He fulfilled that claim by healing the man on both a physical and spiritual level.

Job, too, eventually realized the awesome glory and grace of God as a result of his sufferings (Job 42:1–6). That should offer some comfort to those of us today who face seemingly senseless tragedy.

The pain is real and must not be denied. But someday we will see the glory of God, even in the things that we suffer. We have the assurance of Job and Jesus on that.

Job 7:20–21

20 Have I sinned?
What have I done to You, O watcher of
men?
Why have You set me as Your target,
So that I am a burden to myself?
21 Why then do You not pardon my
transgression,

And take away my iniquity?
For now I will lie down in the dust,
And You will seek me diligently,
But I *will* no longer *be.*"

Job's faith would not allow him to reject God. But he did earnestly seek an explanation for his distress. Job longed for his suffering to end, but if he had to suffer, he wanted to know what purpose was being served by his pain.

In the time of Job, it was assumed that suffering was God's punishment for sins. Suffering humbled the proud and made sinners aware of their need for repentance, as it does today. Still, Job was convinced that he had done nothing to deserve the terrible afflictions he had received. Furthermore, he saw evil individuals prospering even while he lived in agony. How could a just God bring suffering on the innocent while the evil thrived? Because Job would not let go of his belief in a good God, he desperately yearned to understand God's reasons.

God eventually did reply to Job, but He never gave Job an explanation for why he had to suffer. Instead, God questioned Job! And in doing so, God made clear that Job could never hope to understand the Lord's purposes in all He does. Job needed only to trust in God, and know that He was just, merciful, and in control of all that happened.

In his anguish, he had demanded an explanation from God. Reassured by God's words, Job repented of his lack of humility. He had come to a new awareness of the majesty of God—and his own limitations.

1a. How does Job's experience of suffering without cause give comfort to someone who feels that he or she is being inexplicably punished?

_____

1b. Believers today may give misguided advice like Job's friends. "You must have done something wrong," some will say, or "you should pray harder for healing." They blame the sufferer for the suffering. If you were Virginia, how would you answer her sister's comment?

_____

2. How does God's reply to Job indicate that He desires believers to show faith and humility in the face of suffering?

_____

3a. The beggar's blindness was used by Christ to bring glory to God. How did Job's sufferings and later restoration bring glory to God?

_____

3b. How can the believer bring glory to God through his or her suffering?

_____

4. Describe what Job gained through suffering.

_____

Waiting for God

Before his encounter with God, Job felt a dreadful separation from God. "Where is God?" cried Job, as he lay in a pile of ashes, his body covered with sores (see Job 23:3, 8–9). Like Job, we may feel most alienated from God when we most desperately need Him. We seek His presence, but instead find only a terrible emptiness inside.

Although not all Christians experience this sense of separation from God, it seems to be a pattern in the suffering of believers. Perhaps God intends this feeling of abandonment to strengthen our faith and push us to anxiously seek Him. One thing is certain: if we search long and hard enough, we will find God. We will discover ourselves in the very presence of our Lord, and know comfort even in our pain.

But as we wait, we should not forget that Jesus Himself experienced the unutterable pain of separation from God as He hung upon the cross. In this and every other way, Christ shared our suffering. When pain makes us doubt if God really cares, we need only remember what God was like when He walked among the suffering in the form of a man. Jesus was no mere observer of the human condition—He reached out in love to heal the suffering. He had compassion on the needy. "In all their affliction He was afflicted," wrote Isaiah of the Messiah to come (Is. 63:9). Even in our darkest moments, we can find comfort in knowing our Lord truly cares when we hurt.

Virginia wanted to know why she had to suffer. But as Job's experiences show, there may not be a ready explanation. Put yourself in Virginia's place, and write a diary entry that describes what you know about God that would give you confidence in a time of suffering.

_____

_____

_____

_____

_____

_____

_____

_____

_____

◆ The Positive Side of Pain ◆

June 6, 1992:

I talked with a young woman today who has been suffering with severe back pain. Her name is Dotty, and her doctor hasn't been able to find any cause for the pain (not that that's any surprise to me!). She was very scared. When I told her about what I have been going through for the past four years, she started to cry.

She said she didn't know how she would make it, and so I told her about God and prayed with her. I took her number so I could call her and talk with her some more. It's really been amazing how many people God has brought into my life to minister to through my problem. I'm beginning to see what God is doing in my life.

I've changed, too. I don't know how many people have told me I'm an inspiration. Sometimes I don't feel like an inspiration! I remember how I used to be, though. I think God has used my suffering to strip away some of my own childishness. When I hear some of the dumb statements or empty phrases from people, I think, "Before I would have probably said the same thing!" Now I understand so much better what other people with pain are going through since I've been there myself.

I know I'm closer to God after going through this whole experience. With all the time I've spent on my knees, I ought to be! But if I hadn't spent so much time praying and looking for insight, would I have the deep communion with my Lord that I now have? I don't think so. Not to mention, I've learned to turn to God when something goes wrong. I'm still not pleased about the pain I've had to go through, but I thank God that it hasn't been for nothing. Sometimes I'm almost grateful.

◆ ◆ ◆ ◆ ◆ ◆ ◆ ◆ ◆

WELCOME TO STRESSFUL LIVING

For many people in the world today, tension, conflict, weariness, and suffering have become commonplace. Nevertheless, some offer the vain hope that life's troubles can be done away with, that we can somehow get to the point where things will always be great. They suggest that faith in Christ will deliver us into a state of serenity and ease and bring prosperity, health, and constant pleasure.

However, that was neither the experience nor the teaching of early Christians such as Paul, James, or Peter, and certainly not of their Lord Jesus. Paul described the life of a servant of God in terms of tribulation, distress, tumult, and sleeplessness (2 Cor. 6:4–5). But he also linked these stress producers with rich treasures that money cannot buy: purity, kindness, sincere love, honor, good report, joy, and the possession of all things (vv. 6–10).

So as long as we live as God's people on this earth, we can expect a connection between trouble and hope. That connection is never pleasant, but our troubles can bring about lasting benefits:

Jesus *told us that if we want to follow Him, we must deny ourselves and take up a cross.*

If we try to save our lives, we will only lose them. But if we lose our lives for His sake, we will find them (Matt. 16:24–25).

The writer to the Hebrews encouraged us that our troubles are often a sign that we are legitimate children of God, who lovingly disciplines us to train us in righteousness (Heb. 12:8–11).

James encouraged us to rejoice in our various trials, because as they test our faith, they produce patience, which ultimately makes us mature in Christ (James 1:2–4).

Peter *knew by personal experience the kind of pressure that can cause one's allegiance to Christ to waiver. He warned us that "fiery trials" are nothing strange, but that they actually allow us to experience something of Christ's sufferings so that we can ultimately experience something of His glory, too (1 Pet. 4:12–13).*

We can count on feeling stress if we're going to obey Christ. But we can take hope! That stress is preparing us for riches we will enjoy for eternity. ◆

---

 2 Corinthians 6:3–10

³We give no offense in anything, that our ministry may not be blamed. ⁴But in all *things* we commend ourselves as ministers of God: in much patience, in tribulations, in needs, in distresses, ⁵in stripes, in imprisonments, in tumults, in labors, in sleeplessness, in fastings; ⁶by purity, by knowledge, by longsuffering, by kindness, by the Holy Spirit, by sincere love, ⁷by the word of truth, by the power of God, by the armor of righteousness on the right hand and on the left, ⁸by honor and dishonor, by evil report and good report; as deceivers, and *yet* true; ⁹as unknown, and *yet* well known; as dying, and behold we live; as chastened, and *yet* not killed; ¹⁰as sorrowful, yet always rejoicing; as poor, yet making many rich; as having nothing, and *yet* possessing all things.

Job was given no reason for his suffering, but the same cannot be said for believers today. The New Testament explains several of the purposes for which God permits suffering. Suffering is part of the process by which the believer becomes more like Christ (Rom. 5:2–4). Our faith is tested and purified through suffering as precious metals are purified by fire (1 Pet. 1:7). Suffering makes us sensitive to the needs of others, so that we can provide the comfort we know in Christ to others in need (2 Cor. 1:3–7). And our pain opens up a pathway to a deeper, richer, and more meaningful relationship with the Lord (Phil. 3:10).

1a. Paul indicates in 2 Corinthians 6:4–5 that suffering is an authenticating mark of a servant of God. How does God use the suffering of His servants to demonstrate His power?

1b. According to vv. 6–7, what spiritual resources does God give to His servants to enable them to withstand suffering?

---

2. As Paul suggests in v. 10, such a life of suffering would be expected to produce sorrow. Yet at the same time, what did Paul's reliance on God bring him?

---

3. In this passage and elsewhere Paul points to the value of suffering in producing a Christlike character. For this reason, we should "glory in tribulations, knowing that tribulation produces perseverance; and perseverance, character; and character, hope" (Rom. 5:3–4). Describe the changes in character that have come about through pain and hardship in your own life:

Comfort from Above

2 Corinthians 1:3–7

³Blessed *be* the God and Father of our Lord Jesus Christ, the Father of mercies and God of all comfort, ⁴who comforts us in all our tribulation, that we may be able to comfort those who are in any trouble, with the comfort with which we ourselves are comforted by God. ⁵For as the sufferings of Christ abound in us, so our consolation also abounds through Christ. ⁶Now if we are afflicted, *it is* for your consolation and salvation, which is effective for enduring the same sufferings which we also suffer. Or if we are comforted, *it is* for your consolation and salvation. ⁷And our hope for you is steadfast, because we know that as you are partakers of the sufferings, so also *you will partake* of the consolation.

1. How might the comfort believers receive while suffering be used to comfort others in pain, as Paul suggests in 2 Corinthians 1:4?

_____

2. What are some ways a believer can bring comfort to one who is suffering?

_____

3. Describe a situation in which you were comforted while in pain. Was the comfort directly from God or through another person?

_____

◆ Sharing the Wounds of Christ ◆

March 19, 1994:

Today I had my first migraine in over a week. It was awful. I must already be forgetting what it was like when they came every day. Still, it keeps me aware of the blessings of health and well-being. I treasure every day that I live without pain.

Thank God that those days are becoming more common all the time.

During my headache, I turned out the lights and lay down. While I was lying there, I remembered that strange calm dream I had when I imagined I was in my glorified body floating effort-

lessly through the air. Just thinking about it seemed to help soothe my headache a little.

Nice to know it won't always be a dream. Someday I will be free of pain, forever. That's good enough for me. ◆

◆ ◆ ◆ ◆ ◆ ◆ ◆ ◆ ◆

SUFFERING OUTWEIGHS COMFORT

Comfort and ease were never intended for sinners. We can't handle them. As someone has well said, sin gives us the terrible ability to misuse any good thing. We are deluded if we think we can rise above this less-than-perfect condition without outside help.

Christ's intervention highlights the seriousness of our situation. It took suffering and death for Him to break the bondage that holds all of God's creation in its vicious grip. That made it possible for us to enter into new life. Now His work continues in us and with

us throughout our lives, and He gives us an opportunity to cooperate in our re-creation.

As believers, we inevitably find ourselves at war with our old ways, so we should not be surprised at pain and suffering in the walk of faith (1 Pet. 4:1). It is all part of the gift of believing (Phil. 1:29). It is the path to strength and steadiness (1 Pet. 5:10). It is the process of being completed (James 1:2–3).

Do you desire to arrive at a place of peace, joy, and serenity? Someday you will. That is not a false hope. But it is a *hope*: we won't enjoy those until we reach full maturity in Christ in the world to come (Rev. 7:9–17; 21:1–5; 22:1–6).

1 Peter 4:12–19

¹²Beloved, do not think it strange concerning the fiery trial which is to try you, as though some strange thing happened to you; ¹³but rejoice to the extent that you partake of Christ's sufferings, that when His glory is revealed, you may also be glad with exceeding joy. ¹⁴If you are reproached for the name of Christ, blessed *are you*, for the Spirit of glory and of God rests upon you. On their part He is blasphemed, but on your part He is glorified. ¹⁵But let none of you suffer as a murderer, a thief, an evildoer, or as a busybody in other people's matters. ¹⁶Yet if *anyone suffers* as a Christian, let him not be ashamed, but let him glorify God in this matter.

¹⁷For the time *has come* for judgment to begin at the house of God; and if *it begins* with us first, what will *be* the end of those who do not obey the gospel of God? ¹⁸Now

"If the righteous one is scarcely saved,
Where will the ungodly and the sinner
appear?"

¹⁹Therefore let those who suffer according to the will of God commit their souls *to Him* in doing good, as to a faithful Creator.

The coming of Christ gave new dimension to suffering, for God became man to suffer and die for our sakes. As believers, we are called upon to follow Christ's example of suffering for others. Just as Christ suffered unjustly, we too may suffer in His name. But in suffering for Christ's sake, we glorify God and open the way for great acts of faith. And by our suffering, we participate, through Christ, in our own redemption and the redemption of others.

1. Peter warned believers not to be surprised should they be required to suffer trials "as though some strange thing happened to you" (1 Pet. 4:12). How can we mentally prepare ourselves so that we aren't caught off guard when hardships come?

_____

2. Peter tells us that it is a blessing to suffer for the sake of Christ. No doubt he had in mind Christ's own teaching: "Blessed are you when they revile and persecute you, and say all kinds of evil against you falsely for My sake" (Matt. 5:11). What do you think is the nature of this blessing?

_____

3. Read 1 Peter 4:19. Who are those that suffer "according to the will of God"?

_____

4a. In what ways do Christians suffer persecution today?

_____

4b. Have you ever suffered on Christ's behalf? If so, describe the occasion.

_____

5. If there was no suffering in the world, would anyone come to salvation? Explain your answer.

 Romans 8:18–25

¹⁸For I consider that the sufferings of this present time are not worthy *to be compared* with the glory which shall be revealed in us. ¹⁹For the earnest expectation of the creation eagerly waits for the revealing of the sons of God. ²⁰For the creation was subjected to futility, not willingly, but because of Him who subjected *it* in hope; ²¹because the creation itself also will be delivered from the bondage of corruption into the glorious liberty of the children of God. ²²For we know that the whole creation groans and labors with birth pangs together until now. ²³Not only *that,* but we also who have the firstfruits of the Spirit, even we ourselves groan within ourselves, eagerly waiting for the adoption, the redemption of our body. ²⁴For we were saved in this hope, but hope that is seen is not hope; for why does one still hope for what he sees? ²⁵But if we hope for what we do not see, we eagerly wait for *it* with perseverance.

No Pain, All Gain!

Today we suffer the pains of this world. But one day we will be set free from all suffering. The pains we now know are momentary and will pass away. The joy to come will be everlasting.

1. What source of pain do you look forward to being rid of the most?

---

2. Read Romans 8:18 again. What a marvelous promise this is for those who suffer today! How does knowing that the wonders of heaven will make our present sufferings seem insignificant help us to endure when we are hurting?

• • • • • • • • •

We truly are blessed as children of God. We know that God cares about our pain, and will ensure we do not suffer without reason. For now, though we must suffer a little while, we can look forward with joyful expectation to the eternal glory that is ours in Christ (1 Pet. 5:10).

The lost in the world do not understand the suffering they experience. And truly their sufferings are futile, unless they come to know the Lord. This makes it all the more important that we reach out to those who suffer in spiritual darkness—whatever the personal cost to us—to offer them the glorious hope that we possess.

How can we be effective witnesses to the unsaved? How do we reach out to a world that is not only indifferent but hostile to our message? In the next chapter, we'll examine how we can confront an unredeemed world for Christ, and make a positive difference.

AMBASSADORS OF GOD'S KINGDOM

Bridgette didn't want to go to school today. What was worse, she was the teacher.

Her sixth grade class was about to begin a three-week study of biology. That had never been a problem until this year. In discussing the subject of biology, the new curriculum the school district was using this year made many references to evolution.

Bridgette just didn't believe that all life came about through chance. She believed in a Creator. How could she in good conscience teach something that she believed was wrong? Could she at least present the other side?

Last week, Bridgette had discussed her concerns with the school principal, Teri Bailey. She hadn't been receptive.

"District policy states that the interjection of religious beliefs into the discussion of an academic subject is forbidden. That's district policy, and it's the policy of this school," Ms. Bailey had told Bridgette stiffly.

"But the book presents evolution as unchallenged fact," Bridgette had argued. "It doesn't even make clear that evolution is a theory. Don't you think the school should encourage alternative viewpoints? Isn't that what academic freedom is all about?"

Ms. Bailey had refused to budge. Course content was determined at district level, and holds sway over the judgment of any individual teacher. She had even suggested that teachers could be fired if they failed to observe administrative policy. Bridgette had turned cold at the ominous implications of that statement.

I love my job, thought Bridgette miserably. *Maybe I should just keep my beliefs to myself. After all, how much difference will what I say make anyway?*

◆ ◆ ◆ ◆ ◆ ◆ ◆ ◆ ◆

The problem that Bridgette faced is becoming more common all the time. As a teacher, Bridgette was required to promote a belief that was contrary to her convictions as a Christian. And many others, regardless of occupation, face the same dilemma: whether to stand up in what they believe in—or remain silent.

These days, we encounter a growing climate of hostility to public expressions of faith in God. Taking a stand on moral issues may bring ridicule or personal attacks by opponents of Christianity. And according to many, the secularization of society means that Christians (and only Christians!) should have no part in the public forum of ideas. Consequently, in recent years it has become an accepted practice to treat believers with the same intolerance with which some charge Christians.

The response of many Christians to this increasingly antagonistic social climate has been to withdraw. Afraid of criticism, they keep their faith private. They hide their light and surrender to the darkness in the world.

But this isn't what Christ intended for his followers. We are called to engage an unbelieving world for Christ.

CALLED INTO THE WORLD

Should followers of Christ withdraw from the world to set up their own exclusive communities or retreat from society into "Christian ghettos"? Not if they are to fulfill Christ's prayer in John 17:18. Engagement, not isolation, is His desire.

Some early Christians sought refuge in the catacombs of Rome. But that practice was only temporary, and they were forced there only by the most extreme persecutions. Normally, they could be found actively participating in the society.

Actually, Scripture recognizes a tension between separation and involvement. Passages like Romans 12:2 and 1 Peter 1:14–16 urge us to pursue a distinctive, holy lifestyle. Our commitments, character, and conduct should contrast vividly with those of people who do not know or follow God. On the other hand, Jesus calls us to live and work side by side with those very same people. He sends us *into the world* to make an impact (see Matt. 5:13–16; Mark 16:15).

Naturally, that can lead to conflict. If our loyalty is given to Christ, we can expect tension with others who follow a different course. Whether we undergo mild teasing and insults or open hostility and even violence, "normal" Christianity involves conflict with the world to which we are called (see 2 Tim. 3:12; 1 Pet. 4:12–14). Fortunately, the New Testament gives us plenty of examples to follow:

Jesus. The Lord Himself came into the world to offer a new relationship with God. He didn't have to. He could have remained in His heavenly position. Yet He voluntarily left it all to die for us, and to deliver to a rebellious humanity God's offer of forgiveness, love, and acceptance (Phil. 2:5–8).

When Christ came into the world, His listeners showed initial interest. Yet gradually most of them turned against Him. Knowing full well the fate that awaited Him, He entered Jerusalem, ready to face persecution, arrest, and even death. His followers tried to divert Him (Mark 8:31–33), but He was determined to follow God's call into the world. Isolation and safety were not options.

Paul. The church's greatest messenger started out hating anyone who followed Jesus. Yet Christ Himself stopped him in his vengeful tracks and redirected his life to become a globetrotting messenger of faith and forgiveness.

However, Paul's first days as a Christian were spent in an isolated "retreat" in Arabia. But this withdrawal lasted only for a time, and only so that Saul

could emerge as *Paul, the apostle.* He crisscrossed the empire, bringing the gospel to dozens of cities and towns. These encounters led to numerous misunderstandings, deportations, arrests, physical abuse, and attempts on his life. Probably Paul sometimes longed for the safer, quieter days of his Arabian retreat. But once he responded to God's call to engage the world, there was no turning back. He also challenged others to live, work, and witness among the lost (1 Cor. 4:16–20).

Peter. Peter struggled throughout his life to break out of the separatist mentality he had grown up with. He didn't like the prospect of suffering and rejection, and at times took steps to forestall it (see Mark 8:31–38; Luke 22:54–62; John 18:10–11). He liked even less the idea of sharing God's good news of salvation with Samaritans and Gentiles.

But Christ kept calling Peter back to re-engage the world (for example, see Acts 10). In the end, he learned the necessity and the value of suffering (1 Pet. 4:1–2) and called others to do likewise (2:11–12).

Barnabas. A respected landowner, Barnabas enjoyed a relatively "safe" calling as a leader of the infant church in Jerusalem. But he accepted an assignment to visit Antioch and investigate rumors of Gentile

continued

continued
converts to the predominantly Jewish movement. Sure enough, he found that God was bringing all nations into the fellowship. So he sought out Paul, an unknown, to help him establish the new converts in the faith (Acts 11:19–26). Later, they traveled to Jerusalem to defend and extend this new "worldly" thrust in the growing work of God (Acts 15). ◆

 John 17:14–18

¹⁴I have given them Your word; and the world has hated them because they are not of the world, just as I am not of the world. ¹⁵I do not pray that You should take them out of the world, but that You should keep them from the evil one. ¹⁶They are not of the world, just as I am not of the world. ¹⁷Sanctify them by Your truth. Your word is truth. ¹⁸As You sent Me into the world, I also have sent them into the world.

1. What do you think Bridgette should do and why?

_____

_____

2. Where should the believer draw the line between allegiance to an employer and to God?

_____

_____

3. What did Jesus mean when he said that His followers "are not of the world" in v. 16?

_____

_____

4. What is wrong with a Christian keeping his or her faith private and just blending in with the rest of society?

_____

_____

5. In engaging the world for Christ, should Christians seek to influence public policy by political means? Why or why not?

_____

_____

6. What are two ways you can serve as a representative of Christ in the world?

_____

_____

──◆ The Duties of Dual Citizenship ◆──

There is a kingdom on earth that possesses no government, no unique language or set of customs, and no national borders. It is God's kingdom, and we are its citizens. Though we should observe the laws of the land in which we live (Rom. 13:1–3), the King of kings is the true authority in our lives. But what does our dual citizenship in God's kingdom require of us?

For all the differences between God's kingdom and earthly kingdoms, one thing remains the same. Both need a working force to thrive. Whatever occupation we have in the world, we're also one of God's laborers. And we've got a job to do: promote God's purposes in the world. This includes caring for the needy in society, confronting social injustice, evangelizing the unsaved, and providing training and support for the converted. Eventually our goal is nothing less than the conquest of the world for Christ!

WORKERS FOR THE KINGDOM

Do you ever wonder what your life contributes to the work of God in the world? If you are in a "secular" occupation, you may conclude that the only way to further the kingdom is to pray for and contribute financially to those who are in "full-time" Christian work. But are those your only options?

Paul described Aristarchus, Mark, and Justus as "fellow workers for the kingdom" (Col. 4:11), indicating that they may have been vocational Christian workers. However, there is no way to say whether they were employed in that work as a full-time occupation. In fact, if they followed Paul's example, they probably had other jobs through which they made their living (see Acts 18:1–3).

The point is that drawing a paycheck for doing "ministry" is not the criterion by which to judge whether someone is a worker for God's kingdom. Kingdom work involves promoting the values, beliefs, and lifestyle of the kingdom. That may involve professional employment such as pastoring a church or serving on a mission field. But kingdom workers are also found among doctors, accountants, engineers, painters, salespeople, auto mechanics, and homemakers. Wherever believers are furthering the goals and objectives of Christ, they are working for His kingdom.

How does your life promote the purposes of God? Do you use your skills and abilities toward that end, whether or not pay is involved? Or have you given up and concluded that because you are not a vocational Christian worker, you aren't really serving the Lord with your life and career? If so, you'll want to reconsider what it means to be a worker for Christ's kingdom!

Colossians 4:10–11

> [10]Aristarchus my fellow prisoner greets you, with Mark the cousin of Barnabas (about whom you received instructions: if he comes to you, welcome him), [11]and Jesus who is called Justus. These *are my* only fellow workers for the kingdom of God who are of the circumcision; they have proved to be a comfort to me.

1a. As a worker for God, what are the advantages of a vocational occupation?

_____

_____

1b. What are the possible advantages to serving God in a non-vocational capacity?

_____

_____

2. In John 17:15, Jesus warned that His servants would also face persecution. Here we see that Paul and Aristarchus are in prison. In the early church we know that both leaders and lay people suffered persecution. If we never encounter any conflict as a consequence of our faith, does that mean we aren't doing our jobs? Explain your answer.

_____

_____

3. What secular job would you use to figuratively describe the work you are currently performing as a member of God's kingdom: farmer, soldier, teacher, or something else? Suppose it's tax time, and you are filing your kingdom tax returns, to give "to God the things that are God's" (Matt. 22:21). What occupation would you write at the top of the form?

_____

* * * * * * * * *

Unfortunately, many Christians might best be described as "on the public dole." Some churches are filled with people who go to receive God's grace but fail to dispense the grace they receive to others. That's a shame, because every believer has a spiritual gift with which to serve God. Spiritual gifts provide believers with divine enablement for a particular ministry. Failure to use these gifts is a terrible waste of spiritual resources. For this reason, Peter urged believers: "as each one has received a gift, minister it to one another, as good stewards of the manifold grace of God" (1 Pet. 4:10).

Spiritual gifts come in many different forms: among them, helping, encouraging, teaching, and leadership. Some have been specially equipped for evangelism (Eph. 4:11). Does that mean that the rest of us don't have to concern ourselves with witnessing to the unsaved? Not at all! Each of us, whether called specifically to the task of evangelism or not, should "always be ready to give a defense to everyone who asks you a reason for the hope that is in you" (1 Pet. 3:15).

Many of us cringe at the idea of speaking about Christ to an unbeliever. We hear the word "evangelism" and the image of a televangelist waving his Bible and shouting at his audience and the TV audience involuntarily pops into our minds. But evangelism may take place in a much quieter way, through a lifestyle that reflects Christ's values, or in a moment when a friend needs comfort or advice. Even then, witnessing can be a daunting task, but if we don't let others know about Christ, who will?

Fortunately, we don't have to bring others to Christ all on our own. We have the help of the world's greatest evangelist, the Holy Spirit.

WHOSE JOB IS EVANGELISM?

One thing is certain about evangelism: both non-Christians and Christians feel uncomfortable with it. Bring up the topic of religion (let alone the gospel) with your unbelieving workmates, and the atmosphere suddenly tenses up. It's as if spiritual matters are out of place in a professional setting.

Consequently, many Christians fold their hands and shut their mouths when it comes to evangelism. They've decided it's up to God to bring people to faith. But they're not going to participate in the process.

Of course, in a way it is up to God to bring about salvation, as John 16:8 shows. The Holy Spirit is *the* great evangelist. Yet other passages urge us as believers to work *with* the Spirit in influencing others with the gospel. To understand our role in this joint venture, we need to rediscover the evangelistic work of the Spirit. This involves:

Common grace. No matter how bad things get in the world—plagued as it is with war, poverty, famine, disease, crime, family chaos, and so on—things would be far worse if it weren't for God's Spirit. The Spirit moves throughout the world, restraining the full onslaught of evil and promoting whatever is good. The Spirit does this for believers and unbelievers alike; hence the name, "common grace."

Because of this gracious work, the unbeliever is in a position to accept God's offer of

continued

continued

salvation, and therefore benefits from divine grace whether salvation occurs or not (Ps. 104:24–30).

Spiritual awakening. Unaware that God restrains evil and promotes good, an unbeliever can be glib about life and unapproachable concerning spiritual issues. So the Spirit's job is to awaken the unbeliever to his or her true spiritual condition. The Spirit may use a disturbing conscience, a declining hope, or a gripping fear. Other instruments include the law, government, and human kindness (Is. 57:20–21; Joel 2:28–32; Rom. 2:1–6, 15–16).

Conviction of sin. When the Spirit pricks an unbeliever's conscience, there may be feelings of acute guilt and fear of God's judgment (John 16:8; Acts 5:1–11). Such a person can become quite hostile, and even attack nearby believers. This is important to know; rejection of the gospel does not necessarily reflect failure on our part as Christ's representatives (though anger is justifiable if we're insensitive in our approach).

Regeneration. This part of evangelism is one that Christians too often take credit for, even though it is the work of the Spirit. Regeneration involves the giving of new life to a lost sinner (John 3:5–8). Only the Spirit can do that. As believers, we can do nothing but help this birthing process along.

Sealing and equipping. Finally, the Spirit "seals" the new believer in Christ; that is, the Spirit confirms and guarantees the believer's place in God's family and provides assurance of salvation (2 Cor. 5:5; Eph. 1:13). Moreover, the Spirit equips the new Christian to live and act as Christ's follower by providing spiritual power and gifts, and bonding believers together. New appetites develop—a love for Scripture, a hatred of evil, and a desire to share the faith.

In light of these evangelistic efforts of God's Spirit, how can believers cooperate with God in evangelism? Here are four ways:

Identify with Christ. We can start by publicly (yet sensitively) acknowledging our life in Christ, declaring our spiritual commitments and convictions. We can also act with Christ-like love toward others and demonstrate integrity in our work and lifestyle. And we can identify with the people of God. That doesn't mean we have to endorse everything that other Christians do. But we accept and affirm that we are part of God's family (John 13:14–15; 17:14–19; Phil. 3:17).

Proclaim the gospel. Jesus preached repentance and the forgiveness of sins. Similarly, He asks us to verbally communicate the gospel message to our relatives, friends, and coworkers. Naturally, we must avoid preaching more than we practice. However, evangelism demands more than a "silent witness." As important as it is, our lives alone are not enough to guide people toward Christ's work for them. We must also provide information that presents Christ's message clearly and persuasively (Matt. 4:17; Col. 1:26–29).

Appeal for a decision. God gives people a choice to accept or reject His salvation offer. Therefore, as the Spirit gives us opportunity, we should present the gospel and then ask the person to decide what to do with Jesus (2 Cor. 5:18–20). For instance: "Is there any reason why you can't give yourself to Jesus Christ and accept the work that He has done for you?" We can act as Christ's ambassadors, appealing to others to accept His gift of new life.

In a way we're like midwives, carefully assisting in a new birth. Obviously, timing is crucial. To try to force premature delivery by high-pressure tactics and insistence on a decision only produces hostility, sometimes even rejection. It can create lasting wounds that close people's minds to the gospel.

Nurture and train new believers. We can continue to work with the Spirit to help new Christians get established in their faith. As a mother nurtures her newborn child, so we can

continued

continued

nurture a baby believer (1 Thess. 2:7–8; 2 Tim. 2:2). We can assist the person in resisting temptation, developing new values, building relationships with other Christians, and gaining insight into the Bible. We can invite the "newborn" to pray with us, discuss God's Word, and worship the Lord.

Evangelism, then, is a cooperative effort between the Holy Spirit and those of us who follow Christ. As we interact with our associates, we should consider: "How is the Spirit working in this person, and how can I contribute to the process?" We can act like farmers, sometimes sowing new seeds, other times watering what someone else has planted. Occasionally we must root out an offensive weed left by someone else. But always our objective should be to reap a harvest to the glory of God (see John 4:34–38; 1 Cor. 3:5–7). ◆

 John 16:7–8

⁷Nevertheless I tell you the truth. It is to your advantage that I go away; for if I do not go away, the Helper will not come to you; but if I depart, I will send Him to you. ⁸And when He has come, He will convict the world of sin, and of righteousness, and of judgment:

1. Describe a time when you witnessed to someone who did not know Christ.

_____

2a. Describe the circumstances when you accepted Christ as your Savior. Was there another particular person that led you to the Lord?

_____

2b. Describe your inner change of heart that occurred at that moment through the work of the Holy Spirit.

_____

3. How have you prepared to "give a defense" should an opportunity to witness present itself?

_____

——◆ A Church Divided Against Itself ◆——

"Jerome, could we talk to you for a moment?"

The youth minister escorted the young man into one of the church offices. The pastor was waiting in the room, sitting behind the desk.

"C'mon in, Jerome," said the pastor with a smile. "Have a seat. We just want to talk with you for a moment."

Jerome sat down nervously, absently putting a hand over the hole in his jeans.

The pastor looked at the youth uncertainly. Jerome had only attended the downtown church twice before, and this was the first time he had been to a youth activity. He was very quiet and most of the other teens seemed to shy away from him. It was understandable. Most of them were upper-middle-class kids from the suburbs, but Jerome was a poor kid from a public housing project near the church.

"We're glad you could come today, but we were told something that concerned us, and we wanted to talk with you about it. After the meeting, someone saw you pick up Lucy's purse. Now, she found it on a table later, and she says nothing was missing."

"Still, we'd like to encourage a trusting atmosphere here. So we want to make sure that everyone respects other people's property." The pastor gave Jerome a meaningful look.

"She left it under her chair," replied Jerome in a subdued voice. "I just picked it up and put it on the table so it wouldn't get lost."

"Okay, Jerome," said the pastor with a nod. "We're not accusing you of anything. We just wanted to make our position clear. All right?"

Jerome nodded silently.

The pastor hoped the problem was solved. What he didn't realize was how he had hurt the sensitive young man.

The pastor's hopes were answered though, for it was never an issue after that day. None of them ever saw Jerome again. ◆

◆ ◆ ◆ ◆ ◆ ◆ ◆ ◆ ◆

Just as each believer is a representative of Christ to the unsaved, so the church as a whole must present itself as the embodiment of Christ in the world today. To do so effectively, unity among Christians is essential. If prejudice, conflict, and division rages within the church, the unbelieving world will see only a reflection of itself. Instead, the church should possess a oneness of purpose and a bond of love that erases the distinctions between believers.

Yet so often this is not the case. There are many distinctions that exist among Christians: differences in social status, ethnic background, culture, values, and behavior. The natural tendency to evaluate others based on how they differ from us may create conflict and threaten to divide the body of Christ. To overcome such divisions, every believer has a duty to conquer the prejudices and distinctions in his or her own heart, and embrace fellow Christians in a unifying spirit of love.

WE ARE FAMILY!

In Galatians 3:28, Paul emphasizes that three major social distinctions no longer matter in Christ:

- *Ethnicity:* "neither Jew nor Greek."
- *Socioeconomic status:* "neither slave nor free."
- *Gender:* "neither male nor female."

First-century culture was deeply divided along these lines. So was the church. But Paul stressed, "You are all *one* in Christ Jesus" (italics added).

Christians have become children of God through faith, which means we are all in the same family. We are no longer divided by ethnicity, social status, or gender, but have become brothers and sisters in God's family.

One powerful symbol of that new unity is baptism (3:27). As part of the baptismal ceremony, a believer affirms the lordship of Christ and his or her commitment to a new way of life. Paul is possibly quoting from a first-century baptismal creed (v. 28) to remind us of our promise to "put on Christ," not in word but in deed.

In the early Christian communities that meant that both Gentiles and Jews could exercise their spiritual gifts. Both slaves and masters could pray or prophesy. Both women

continued

continued

and men could enjoy full membership in the body. "Christ [was] all and in all" (Col. 3:11). The breaking down of traditional barriers wasn't just a future hope. The early church worked to make it a reality.

Which brings us to the question: What

walls of ethnicity, status, or gender divide believers today? Are we willing to model reconciliation between different and even antagonistic groups? If not, then is our church truly a sign of God's kingdom, or merely a human institution?

Galatians 3:27–28

27For as many of you as were baptized into Christ have put on Christ. 28There is neither Jew nor Greek, there is neither slave nor free, there is

neither male nor female; for you are all one in Christ Jesus.

Do you recall how people reacted when the Berlin Wall came down? The unimaginable had happened: an impassable barrier that had existed for decades fell overnight, and the peoples of two nations were united as one people! Yet the early church effectively brought down walls of separation between peoples far more intractable than any physical wall. The divisions built into the very fabric of their societies rival any that exist in the world today. For those alive in Jesus' time, the idea that these barriers should fall was unthinkable.

Yet the gospel of Christ accomplished this and more. It replaced hatred with familial love and rewrote the laws that governed society. This love between the followers of Christ erased old wounds and inequalities, and brought unity of mind and purpose in its stead. What love accomplished puts mere political power to shame. How might we benefit from this power that the early church possessed? How can we exercise the same power in our lives today? Let's take a look.

LOVE NEVER FAILS

Are you ever in doubt about what you should do in a given situation? One rule of thumb that always applies is, Do unto others as you would have them do unto you *(Matt. 7:12).*

This "golden rule" is universally recognized. It summarizes the principle of love as an ethical cornerstone for life. In fact, Jesus taught that the greatest commandment was to love God with all of one's heart, soul, and mind, and the second greatest was to love one's neighbor as oneself *(Matt. 22:37–39).* Likewise, James called love the "royal law" *(James 2:8),* and Paul wrote that of

faith, hope, and love, love was the greatest; it never fails *(1 Cor. 13:8, 13).*

We also see this in Hebrews. Having summarized the vast changes brought about by the coming of Christ, the book's final chapter begins with a clear statement about one thing that has not changed, love. Love among believers must continue *(Heb. 13:1).* The writer goes on to list several ways in which that can happen:

- Hospitality toward strangers; in our day these might include immigrants, the homeless, and people of a different race than we are *(v. 2).*

continued

continued

- *Remembrance of prisoners; it would be just as easy to forget them, but the principle of love says we ought to treat them* as if chained with them *(v. 3).*
- *Faithfulness to our marriage; this goes beyond sexual fidelity to active enrichment and development of our partner (v. 4).*

- *Contentment regarding money and possessions; this is a severe challenge in modern culture (vv. 5–6; see Luke 12:15; Phil. 4:10–13).*

  Christlike love is very practical. It seeks expression toward a wide variety of people. Is that love "continuing" in your life? ◆

 Hebrews 13:1–6

Let brotherly love continue. ²Do not forget to entertain strangers, for by so *doing* some have unwittingly entertained angels. ³Remember the prisoners as if chained with them—those who are mistreated—since you yourselves are in the body also.

⁴Marriage *is* honorable among all, and the bed undefiled; but fornicators and adulterers God will judge.

⁵*Let your* conduct *be* without covetousness; *be* content with such things as you have. For He Himself has said, "I will never leave you nor forsake you." ⁶So we may boldly say:

> "The LORD *is* my helper;
> I will not fear.
> What can man do to me?"

——◆ The Power of Love ◆——

1. What does Paul refer to that violates the principle of love we are to live by?

_____

_____

2. What is a specific way that you can show love through hospitality, as the author of Hebrews suggests in 13:2?

_____

_____

3. Christians are supposed to show love first and foremost to fellow believers. But loving care is to be extended to others as well. Explain why this is an important duty for a believer.

_____

_____

The New Commandment

The disciples were gathered in an upper room eating supper. In the middle of the meal, Judas Iscariot, the group's treasurer, rose and left. The oil lamps flickered momentarily as he passed out the door into the darkness that had descended over Jerusalem.

The remaining disciples wondered absently where he might be going at this late hour. Perhaps, they thought to themselves, Judas had gone to buy food for the approaching Passover feast, or to give alms to the poor.

But Jesus knew better. Soon his betrayer would return with a detachment of soldiers to arrest Him. The time had come for Him to depart from the world and return to His Father.

Christ looked at the eleven remaining disciples. Gently, He explained to them that soon He would be leaving, and they would not be able to go with Him where He went. A look of concern crossed Simon Peter's face. Where was the Lord going? he wondered.

Jesus chose not to explain further. Instead, He said, "a new commandment I give to you" (John 13:34).

The disciples stopped eating when Jesus made this pronouncement, and turned their full attention on Him.

"Love one another; as I have loved you," Christ instructed them. "By this all will know that you are My disciples" (John 13:34–35).

✦ ✦ ✦ ✦ ✦ ✦ ✦ ✦

What was so new about this commandment? After all, the Old Testament commanded God's people to "love your neighbor as yourself" (Matt. 22:39).

The answer is that His disciples would use Christ's love as the model for how they should love one another. And Christ's love is sacrificial. They should love their fellow believers not as themselves but before themselves. By practicing Christlike love, the disciples would truly reflect Christ to the world.

The commandment that Christ gave to His disciples (John 13:34–35) extends to those who follow Him today. The love of Christ is to be the defining feature of every believer's lifestyle. How can we exhibit such a selfless love? Not by our power alone, for such a love is more than merely human; it is Christ's presence living within us.

Together, the church possesses a power that the world does not recognize as its own, something strange and wonderful—the visible power of Christ's love. Above all, this sets us apart as children of God. As Paul says: "though I speak with the tongues of men and of angels, but have not love, I have become sounding brass or a clanging cymbal" (1 Cor. 13:1). Rational arguments and bold declarations of faith in Christ will not alone move hearts to commit to Christ. But God's love possesses such power. And when we live by the power of this love, we demonstrate the reality of Jesus Christ for all to see.

Christ revealed the nature of perfect love in His life on earth. His example remains the best way for Christians to know the real meaning of love. However, no finer description of Christ's love exists than the definition of love Paul gave in his first letter to the Corinthians.

1 Corinthians 13:4–8

⁴Love suffers long *and* is kind; love does not envy; love does not parade itself, is not puffed up; ⁵does not behave rudely, does not seek its own, is not provoked, thinks no evil; ⁶does not rejoice in iniquity, but rejoices in the truth; ⁷bears all things, believes all things, hopes all things, endures all things.

⁸Love never fails. But whether *there are* prophecies, they will fail; whether *there are* tongues, they will cease; whether *there is* knowledge, it will vanish away.

1. List the virtues that Christlike love gives rise to in this passage (for example: "love suffers long" is the virtue of patience or perseverence).

_____

2. How does Christlike love differ from the concept of love that is prevalent in modern society?

_____

3. Although Paul's definition is an ideal of love, the love of Christ is above all practical. As Christians, it should be a recognizable part of our lives. What is one *specific* way that you can show Christlike love to another believer?

_____

4. What is one specific way you can show Christlike love to someone who is not a believer?

_____

IS THERE ENOUGH EVIDENCE TO CONVICT YOU?

Are you a "closet" Christian, an undercover follower of Christ, keeping your faith a secret? Would your friends or coworkers describe you as a loyal believer? Is there any evidence that could be used to convict you of practicing the faith?

The religious and political leaders of Israel wanted to rid themselves of Jesus. They tried every means possible to convict Him of a crime. They paid an informant from among Jesus' own followers—but he returned their money and declared the Lord to be innocent (Matt. 27:3–5; Mark 14:43–46). They orchestrated an armed mob to intimidate Him—but He kept His cool and

continued

continued

restrained His followers (Matt. 26:51–54). The leaders even presented witnesses to testify against Him in court—but the witnesses either perjured themselves or contradicted each other (Mark 14:55–56).

People tried to convict Jesus of a crime—something bad—for which they lacked even a shred of evidence. Suppose you were on trial instead of Jesus. What would be some of the best evidence against you, that you were "guilty" of following Christ—something good, and something for which there should be evidence? Would there be anything conclusive? Here is a checklist to consider:

EVIDENCE OF FOLLOWING JESUS

____ Displays the "beautiful attitudes" described by Jesus in His Sermon on the Mount (Matt. 5:3–16).

____ Thinks with a transformed mind, expresses a spirit of genuine love, and shows respect for authority (Rom. 12:1–2; 13:1–7).

____ Reflects the "lifestyle of love" (1 Cor. 13).

____ Displays the fruits of the Spirit described by Paul (Gal. 5:22–26).

____ Looks out for the interests of others in the humility of Christ (Phil. 2:1–4).

____ Rejoices always, prays without ceasing, and in everything gives thanks (1 Thess. 5:16–18).

____ Carries out works of faith and compassion (James 2:14–17), controls the tongue (3:1–11), and is known for wisdom (3:13).

____ Holds to the truth about Jesus (2 John 4, 3 John 3–4) and defends it (Jude 3).

Is there enough evidence to convict you of faith in Christ? ◆

——◆ Representing Christ to the World ◆——

Living as Christ's representative on earth is a challenge. It may mean persecution; it may require sacrifice. But this is what each of us has been called to do as a follower of Christ. That's why we are here.

Yet as we remain on this earth, we should never forget that we belong to a spiritual kingdom. We are just passing through. But while we are here, how can we live a truly spiritual life? In the next chapter, we will uncover the secrets to living a spiritual life in our material world.

SPIRITUAL LIVING IN A MATERIAL WORLD

Lee became a Christian a year ago. He'd been through the six-week course on what it meant to be a Christian at his new church. He'd attended Sunday service every week. Each morning when he got up, he devoted twenty minutes to Scripture reading and prayer.

But Lee was confused. The pastor had said in his last sermon that the Bible challenges every believer to exhibit a spiritual lifestyle as they live in the world. Lee wanted to be spiritual, but he wasn't sure he knew what exactly it required.

What is spirituality? he wondered silently. Is it talking or behaving a certain way when you are with fellow Christians? Does being spiritual mean withdrawing from the world and devoting yourself to spiritual disciplines? Such a monastic lifestyle didn't really appeal to Lee. But if that was what was necessary . . .

Finally, Lee broke down and went to the pastor.

"Pastor Green, I've got kind of an ordinary life, but I'd like to have a spiritual life," he said. "If I knew what a spiritual life was."

"Well, Lee," replied the pastor, "a spiritual life isn't any particular kind of life. Anyone can have a spiritual life if their life is centered on Christ and His values."

◆ ◆ ◆ ◆ ◆ ◆ ◆ ◆ ◆

It's an exciting time, that period that immediately follows a person's acceptance of Christ as Lord and Savior. Everything seems so new! The reality of being a child of God is just beginning to dawn within the mind of the recent convert. A new life has begun!

New believers are like treasure hunters who find a beautiful and intricate device. They turn it over and over in their hands, marveling at the workmanship. But eventually they stop and wonder to themselves, "How exactly do I use this thing?"

After the initial thrill of new life in Christ, the believer is faced with a perplexing question: now that I am a new creation in Christ, how am I supposed to live? I can see that this new spiritual reality I possess is a wonderful thing, but how do I make it work in my everyday life?

There really is no mystery. Spirituality is simply living by spiritual values rather than being controlled by materialistic attitudes and concerns. When we put our relationship with the Lord at the center of our lives, Christ's values will find expression in our daily lives.

The struggle is allowing spiritual values to direct our lives when the momentary difficulties and demands of life threaten to consume our attention. How do we maintain perspective and put God first, yet still deal with the concerns of daily living?

Peter wrote his second epistle with the expectation that he would soon die. He recognized the dangers of being drawn away from spiritual living by involvement in worldly affairs. Peter had a piece of advice for the early Christians to help them maintain a balanced perspective necessary to spiritual living. One day the world will pass away. And for now, we should live with an eye to those things that will endure.

KEEPING THE BIG PICTURE

Where were you ten years ago? Does it seem like a distant memory, or as if it were only yesterday? Does the here and now totally consume you, dominating your perspective? Where do you expect to be ten years from now?

As Peter neared the end of his life, he wrote a letter in which he offers some insight into the nature of time and eternity. He beckons us to view time in both thousand-year units and as mere days (2 Pet. 3:8), recalling the beginnings of creation (vv. 4–6). He also projects into the future, when judgment will be rendered and new heavens and earth will be home to those who fear God (vv. 10–13). Peter reminds us that God values a day as much as a thousand years, affirming the importance of the here and now (v. 8). But he also affirms God's activity long before we came on the scene (v. 9).

Peter's perspective challenges us to live with a view toward eternity and values that last—purity, holiness, and righteousness (vv. 11, 14). We need to avoid getting caught up in the here and now and losing sight of our eternal destiny. Neither the joys of today nor the problems of this week can quite compare with what God has prepared for us in eternity. Peter urges us to stick with the basics of the faith and resist the fleeting enticements offered in this present moment (vv. 17–18).

 2 Peter 3:8–14

8But, beloved, do not forget this one thing, that with the Lord one day *is* as a thousand years, and a thousand years as one day. 9The Lord is not slack concerning *His* promise, as some count slackness, but is longsuffering toward us, not willing that any should perish but that all should come to repentance.

10But the day of the Lord will come as a thief in the night, in which the heavens will pass away with a great noise, and the elements will melt with fervent heat; both the earth and the works that are in it will be burned up. 11Therefore, since all these things will be dissolved, what manner *of persons* ought you to be in holy conduct and godliness, 12looking for and hastening the coming of the day of God, because of which the heavens will be dissolved, being on fire, and the elements will melt with fervent heat? 13Nevertheless we, according to His promise, look for new heavens and a new earth in which righteousness dwells.

14Therefore, beloved, looking forward to these things, be diligent to be found by Him in peace, without spot and blameless;

Notice what Peter is saying. He isn't suggesting we ignore what is going on around us and spend our time staring up into the sky as we wait for Christ's return! He is trying to remind us that this world and everything in it is temporary. Don't cling to the world and its goods. Instead of living for the moment, live for eternity.

1. From an eternal standpoint a thousand years is like a day. In other words, the world is transitory. How does this perspective help us to avoid getting caught up in the momentary concerns of life?

2. At the same time, to God a day is like a thousand years. In other words, what happens now has eternal significance. How does this encourage the believer to use wisely the time he or she has been given on earth?

_____

3. In recognition of Christ's eventual return, we should be motivated to live holy and godly lives. "Holy" means literally "set apart" or "separate" from the world. Since Peter was talking about the believer's conduct, it is clear he didn't expect them to literally withdraw from the world. What did he mean?

_____

——◆ Straight to God's Ear ◆——

When Christ returns, He will set things right. No longer will we struggle to live spiritual lives in a fallen world. Fortunately, we don't have to wait for Christ's return to receive the practical results of our spiritual relationship with God. We have a "hotline" to God right here and now through prayer.

Prayer is an important resource for spiritual living. Prayer allows us to experience closeness with God and recognize His presence in our lives. Prayer is a demonstration of our reliance on God. And prayer is practical, for in prayer we can communicate our daily needs and desires directly to our Lord and know that He will respond.

ELIJAH

What sort of person does it take to pray effectively? James offers Elijah as a model (James 5:17–18).

In a way, Elijah seems an unlikely choice to be a model for ordinary people. After all, he was one of Israel's greatest prophets. He took on the evil Ahab and Jezebel, brought a punishment of drought on the land, called down fire from heaven, and was translated to heaven in a whirlwind accompanied by fiery chariots (1 Kin. 17–22, 2 Kin. 1–2). How much do we have in common with such a man? How could our prayers possibly emulate his?

Yet James insists that "Elijah was a man with a nature like ours." So apparently he did not pray because he was a great man; perhaps he became a great man because he prayed.

James shows some reasons why Elijah's prayer life was so effective:

- He prayed; one cannot be effective in prayer unless one prays in the first place.
- He prayed fervently; he was aware of what he was praying, and kept praying with diligence and discipline.
- He prayed an "effective" prayer (v. 16); that is, he expected results.
- He was a righteous man (v. 16); he did not allow sin to cloud his conversation with God.
- He prayed specifically, first for a drought, then for rain, in accordance with God's Word (see Deut. 28:12, 24); he prayed according to Scripture.

Elijah was a great prophet granted extraordinary results by God. Nevertheless, there is no reason why any believer today cannot pray using the same principles as he did. Imagine what God might do in our world if Christians began praying like Elijah!

James 5:16–18

¹⁶Confess *your* trespasses to one another, and pray for one another, that you may be healed. The effective, fervent prayer of a righteous man avails much. ¹⁷Elijah was a man with a nature like ours, and he prayed earnestly that it would not rain; and it did not rain on the land for three years and six months. ¹⁸And he prayed again, and the heaven gave rain, and the earth produced its fruit.

1. Prayer should be undertaken in faith—not the certainty that we will get what we pray for, but the assurance that God will hear and respond. We should pray often (1 Thess. 5:17), and concerning everything, no matter how unimportant it may seem (Phil. 4:6).

    a. Do you approach God with uncertainty or with trust in your own prayer life?

_____

    b. With diligence or with impatience? _____

    c. Regularly or infrequently? _____

    d. Only about big things or concerning everything? _____

2. How can you exercise more effective prayer like Elijah?

_____

3. Prayer is not a magic power for achieving our ends, but God does want us to pray so that He can show mercy to us. Describe an instance when your prayers were mercifully answered by God.

_____

4. How does prayer help you to live spiritually?

_____

Our Daily Bread

    Prayer was an important part of Jesus' life while He was on earth. It was His only means of communicating with His Father. On many occasions, He withdrew to a place of solitude in which to pray (Matt. 14:23; Mark 1:35; Luke 6:12).

    Jesus presented a model prayer for His disciples to follow, now known as the Lord's prayer (Matt. 6:5–13). It is a prayer of enablement for spiritual living that every believer today would be wise to emulate.

Matthew 6:5–13

5"And when you pray, you shall not be like the hypocrites. For they love to pray standing in the synagogues and on the corners of the streets, that they may be seen by men. Assuredly, I say to you, they have their reward. 6But you, when you pray, go into your room, and when you have shut your door, pray to your Father who *is* in the secret *place*; and your Father who sees in secret will reward you openly. 7And when you pray, do not use vain repetitions as the heathen *do*. For they think that they will be heard for their many words.

8"Therefore do not be like them. For your Father knows the things you have need of before you ask Him. 9In this manner, therefore, pray:

Our Father in heaven,
Hallowed be Your name.
10 Your kingdom come.
Your will be done
On earth as *it is* in heaven.
11 Give us this day our daily bread.
12 And forgive us our debts,
As we forgive our debtors.
13 And do not lead us into temptation,
But deliver us from the evil one.
For Yours is the kingdom and the power
and the glory forever. Amen.

1. Jesus stresses in His prayer that His Father's "will be done," (Matt. 6:10). Similarly, John tells us that the Lord will hear and respond when we ask for anything "according to His will" (1 John 5:14). How does this directive indicate we are to approach prayer?

2a. Christ asked His Father to provide for physical needs—but only for today. Why do you suppose He limited His request to that day?

2b. How does the reliance on God's provision through prayer free the believer from becoming absorbed in material concerns to the detriment of his or her spiritual life?

3. What in the Lord's prayer indicates that if we ask Him, God will provide for our spiritual needs as well?

4. How does the Lord's prayer reveal Jesus' faith in the dominion of the spiritual realm over the physical world around Him?

◆ Setting Priorities ◆

Lee Pendleton is an insurance salesman. He travels most of the week around his home state, selling group policies to businesses. He has a cellular phone and a pad of paper with a list of contacts and their phone numbers. Lee spends sixty to seventy hours a week working and although he has a wife and two kids, he is afraid to cut back on his hours for fear of losing customers. The competition is fierce, and there are plenty of rival salespeople who would love to steal his business out from under his nose. A member of his own church beat him out on a prospective client, which led to angry words. The two do not speak when they see each other in church.

Lee has written enough group policies to qualify for the trip to Hawaii five years in a row. He makes a lot of money, but there's a price to pay as well. Last week, he missed his seven-year-old son's birthday party. At least half the time, he sleeps in a hotel room in some town on his sales route.

Lee, who became a Christian two years ago, does his best to make it to church every week. He says a short prayer in the morning, and after that, it's work time. If you asked him if he thought he was living a spiritual life, he would probably say no. Not that he wouldn't like to—if he had the time. ◆

◆ ◆ ◆ ◆ ◆ ◆ ◆ ◆ ◆

Spiritual living requires setting priorities in our lives. What is really important to us? Is it spending time with our family or buying a new luxury automobile? Does our job encourage harmonious relationships with others or does it foster backstabbing and power-grabbing? Do we have time to respond to others' needs, or are we too busy trying to supply our own?

Our habits and routines may be in tune with or conflict with the spiritual values we hold. And if we think about it, we can usually recognize those patterns of behavior that war against our desire to be spiritual. In light of this, it is important that we choose occupations, activities, and patterns of behavior that promote rather than interfere with a spiritual lifestyle.

QUIET LIVING IN A HECTIC WORLD

If any one word characterizes life in the modern world, it may be the word hectic. *The rat race. The grind. The fast lane. The laser lane. Things seem to move faster and faster, and anyone who can't keep up is in danger of being left behind.*

For that reason, Paul's exhortation to "lead a quiet life" (1 Thess. 4:11) seems out of step with contemporary culture. How can one lead a quiet life when technology accelerates change and increases complexity? When television and other media bring the world into our homes and broadcast private lives to the world? When a global economy makes everybody's business our business?

The challenge to lead a quiet life in a hectic world is considerable, but as believers we can take decisive steps that will benefit us personally and spiritually. Actually, Paul gives us an important first step in the exhortation to "work with [our] own hands." The focus is not on "hands" but on

continued

continued

"your own": it was not manual labor that Paul insisted on, but self-support (see 2 Thess. 3:6–12).

As far as quiet living, Paul was probably not objecting to noise and sound as such, but to needless distraction. One way that most people could bring a little more peace and quiet into their homes would be to cut their television viewing in half. Imagine the time left for family members and neighbors, personal reflection, and prayer!

However, the real thrust of this passage is not so much for believers to lower the noise level around them as to live peaceably with others,

without disturbance or conflict (compare Rom. 12:18; Heb. 12:14). Minding our own business and working for ourselves are both means to that end, the end of "[walking] properly toward those who are outside [the faith]" (1 Thess. 4:12).

How can we live peaceably? By avoiding quarrels and complaints (Col. 3:13); by refusing to take offense when others hurt us (Matt. 5:7–12); by not getting entangled in the affairs of others (Prov. 6:1); and by humbly accepting the circumstances that God sends us for our good, rather than grumbling (Rom. 8:28; Phil. 4:11–12). ◆

1 Thessalonians 4:9–12

9But concerning brotherly love you have no need that I should write to you, for you yourselves are taught by God to love one another; 10and indeed you do so toward all the brethren who are in all Macedonia. But we urge you, brethren, that you increase more and more; 11that you also aspire to lead a quiet life, to mind your own business, and to work with your own hands, as we commanded you, 12that you may walk properly toward those who are outside, and *that* you may lack nothing.

1. How does a hectic schedule undermine spiritual living?

_____

_____

2. Describe one distraction to spiritual living that you can eliminate or reduce in your own life.

_____

_____

3. In referring to the aspirations we should have, Paul is not only describing guidelines for living, he is also describing an attitude toward daily life. Describe the attitude that Paul desires Christians to possess.

_____

_____

Paul's message was not a suggestion that believers should strive for a stress-free lifestyle. Even if it were desirable, such a goal is unattainable. Nor could Paul's own life be described as free from stress or devoid of complications! But in his own case, Paul had "learned in whatever state I am, to be content" (Phil. 4:11). He had attained the spirituality to live life free of worldly concerns, through complete dependence on "Christ who strengthens me" (4:13). Because he longed for his fellow Christians to share the freedom of spiritual living, he wanted to make the road as easy as possible.

Paul's advice in this passage is reminiscent of Jeremiah's advice to the exiles in Babylon. Jeremiah told the Israelites carried into exile to "build houses and dwell in them; plant gardens and eat their fruit." In addition, they should "seek the peace of the city," and "pray to the Lord for it" (Jer. 29:5, 7). Jeremiah knew the exiles would be there for a while, and they would need to learn to live in this foreign land. He encouraged them to choose a lifestyle that nourished their spiritual well-being until the time came that they could return home.

Until Christ comes, we are living as exiles in this world. Although we don't belong here, we have to do our best to live spiritual lives in the midst of a world flawed by sin.

——◆ All Work Is Worthy ◆——

As we look to live spiritual lives, we will naturally want to choose a spiritual occupation. After all, other than our families, our work is the biggest single factor in our lives. But does that mean that every believer should choose a job in the ministry? Perhaps a job that serves others in a vital way, like a doctor or social worker, would be a spiritual occupation. But what about someone who works on a production line or as a data entry operator—or a thousand other jobs that lack apparent spirituality? Is someone in an ordinary secular occupation simply stuck doing work that lacks spiritual value?

Fortunately, no. All work can be spiritual!

Remember Joseph? Seventh son of a wealthy livestock owner in Canaan, he had a prophetic dream that he would be in a position of authority over his older brothers. But he had no idea what career changes he would have to go through to reach that position! His brothers, angered by his claim, sold Joseph into slavery. Eventually, he ended up as a household servant in Egypt.

Joseph must have been struck by the irony of his situation. He had dreamed of being master, but had ended up a slave! However, Joseph worked so diligently and honorably that his master, Potiphar, made him the manager of his household.

Then it happened again! Unjustly accused of sexual assault by Potiphar's wife, Joseph was thrown into prison. Yet even there Joseph's character shined through, for he soon became the warden's assistant in the prison. In fact, they trusted his honesty and faithfulness so implicitly that they did not even bother to check up on his handling of prison security!

Joseph eventually ended up in command of all Egypt, second only to Pharaoh! In that capacity, he showed the same character that he had in all his work. Joseph's work was spiritual, for wherever he served, Joseph used his work to honor God.

Like Joseph, in whatever we do, our spiritual values can find expression as we endeavor to honor God in our work.

THE SPIRITUALITY OF EVERYDAY WORK

What do Colossians 3:1–2 imply about everyday work? Is it possible to hold a "secular" job and still "seek those things which are above" rather than "things on the earth"? Or would it be better to quit one's job and go into the ministry?

The issue here is *spirituality*, the capacity to know, experience, and respond to God. How is it possible to bring spirituality into "secular" work? Consider:

If Christ is Lord over all of life, then He must be Lord over work, too. Colossians 3 does not distinguish between the sacred and the secular, but between the life that Christ offers, (the "things above") and its alternative—spiritual death apart from Him (the "things on the earth"). This is clear from the preceding context (Col. 2:20) and the rest of chapter 3: "earthly" things include fornication, uncleanness, passion, etc. (vv. 5, 8); the "things above" include tender mercies, kindness, humility, etc. (vv. 12–15). Spirituality has to do with conduct and character, not just vocation.

It also has to do with the lordship of Christ. Christ is Lord over all of creation (Col. 1:15–18). Therefore, He is Lord over work. Whatever we do for work, we should do it "in the name of the Lord Jesus" (Col. 3:17), that is, with a concern for His approval and in a manner that honors Him. In fact, Paul specifically addresses two categories of workers—slaves (vv. 22–25) and masters (4:1)—in this manner.

The Spirit empowers us to live and work with Christlikeness. Spirituality has to do with character and conduct, regardless of where we work. Christ gives the Holy Spirit to help us live in a way that pleases Him (Gal. 5:16–25.) That has enormous implications for how we do our jobs, our "workstyle" (Titus 2:9–10).

Furthermore, Scripture calls us "temples" of the Holy Spirit (1 Cor. 6:19). An intriguing image: In Exodus 31 and 35, the Spirit enabled Hebrew workers to use their skills in stone-cutting, carpentry, lapidary arts, and so on to construct a beautiful, functional house of worship. In an even greater way, we can expect the Spirit to enable us to use our God-given skills and abilities to bring glory to God.

God values our work even when the product has no eternal value. A common measure of the significance of a job is its perceived value from the eternal perspective. Will the work "last"? Will it "really count" for eternity? The assumption is that God values work for eternity, but not work for the here and now.

By this measure, the work of ministers and missionaries has eternal value because it deals with the spiritual, eternal needs of people. By contrast, the work of the shoe salesman, bank teller, or typist has only limited value, because it meets only earthly needs. Implication: that kind of work doesn't really "count" to God.

But this way of thinking overlooks several important truths:

(1) God Himself has created a world which is time-bound and temporary (2 Pet. 3:10–11). Yet He values His work, declaring it to be "very good," good by its very nature (Gen. 1:31; Ps. 119:68; Acts 14:17).

(2) God promises rewards to people in everyday jobs, based on their attitude and conduct (Eph. 6:7–9; Col. 3:23—4:1).

continued

continued

(3) God cares about the everyday needs of people as well as their spiritual needs. He cares whether people have food, clothing, shelter, and so forth.

(4) God cares about people, who will enter eternity. To the extent that a job serves the needs of people, He values it because He values people. ◆

 Colossians 3:1–17

If then you were raised with Christ, seek those things which are above, where Christ is, sitting at the right hand of God. ²Set your mind on things above, not on things on the earth. ³For you died, and your life is hidden with Christ in God. ⁴When Christ *who is* our life appears, then you also will appear with Him in glory.

⁵Therefore put to death your members which are on the earth: fornication, uncleanness, passion, evil desire, and covetousness, which is idolatry. ⁶Because of these things the wrath of God is coming upon the sons of disobedience, ⁷in which you yourselves once walked when you lived in them.

⁸But now you yourselves are to put off all these: anger, wrath, malice, blasphemy, filthy language out of your mouth. ⁹Do not lie to one another, since you have put off the old man with his deeds, ¹⁰and have put on the new *man* who is renewed in knowledge according to the image of Him who created him, ¹¹where there is neither Greek nor Jew, circumcised nor uncircumcised, barbarian, Scythian, slave *nor* free, but Christ *is* all and in all.

¹²Therefore, as *the* elect of God, holy and beloved, put on tender mercies, kindness, humility, meekness, longsuffering; ¹³bearing with one another, and forgiving one another, if anyone has a complaint against another; even as Christ forgave you, so you also *must do*. ¹⁴But above all these things put on love, which is the bond of perfection. ¹⁵And let the peace of God rule in your hearts, to which also you were called in one body; and be thankful. ¹⁶Let the word of Christ dwell in you richly in all wisdom, teaching and admonishing one another in psalms and hymns and spiritual songs, singing with grace in your hearts to the Lord. ¹⁷And *whatever* you do in word or deed, *do* all in the name of the Lord Jesus, giving thanks to God the Father through Him.

1. How did Joseph "seek those things that are above" (Col. 3:1)?

_____

2. If Joseph had your job, how would he perform differently than you?

_____

3. What are two specific ways that you can express spiritual values in your work?

   a) _____

   b) _____

◆ Living Victoriously ◆

ALL THINGS FOR GOOD?

Romans 8:28 is easy to quote to someone else. But what about when it's *your* turn to suffer? Is there comfort in this passage? Notice two important things as you consider Paul's words here:

(1) All things work together *for* good but not all things *are* good. The loss of a job, a tyrannical boss, physical illness, or family troubles are not good *per se*. In fact, often they are the direct result of evil. That's important to observe. Believers are never promised immunity from the problems and pains of the world. Every day we must put up with much that is not good.

(2) Nevertheless, good can come out of bad! This verse promises that God uses all the circumstances of our lives—both the good and the bad—to shape outcomes that accomplish His purposes for us. And His purposes can only be good, because He is good by definition (James 1:17).

So how can you make this verse work for you as you face tough, troubling times?

• Affirm your trust in God's presence.
• Align your goals with God's purposes.
• Accept the reliability of God's promises.

Romans 8:28

²⁸And we know that all things work together for good to those who love God, to those who are the called according to *His* purpose.

We will be victorious! All the pain, the heartaches, the trials and disappointments to which we are subject in this life will be worth it. Even now He is at work bringing us to perfection, making us fit citizens for the perfect world He is preparing for us.

And as we look forward to a future free from the sin and suffering that mars this world, we can begin living victoriously today. By living spiritual lives now—in our work, our relationships with others, and in close fellowship with our heavenly Father—we will be living in harmony with the glory that will one day be ours. And as we remain in God's will, our hearts testify to our future bliss, and the certainty "that all things work together for good to those who love God, to those who are the called according to His purpose" (Rom. 8:28).

So Great a Cloud of Witnesses

In the last twelve chapters, we have learned a great deal about the men and women who lived in Bible times. As we've examined the lives and experiences of these people, what have we seen? We've seen ourselves! Reflected in their lives are all the challenges we encounter in living a life of faith. We have seen the struggles, the failures, the temptations to which we are all prone. And we have also seen the blessings, the accomplishments, and the power that can be ours through faith in Christ.

Now it is time to take a look back, and see what we have gained from their lives, and what we can incorporate into our own lives. You will be invited to consider how you have identified with the believers of past generations. Hopefully, a look through their eyes has allowed you to see how you can live a more effective and satisfying Christian life.

They stand as portraits for all time of ordinary lives transformed by the presence and power of Jesus Christ. Now it's your turn. As you live your life for Christ, remember that you are being cheered on by "so great a cloud of witnesses" (Heb. 12:1). If you live your life faithfully, one day you will take your place among them.

♦ ♦ ♦ ♦ ♦ ♦ ♦ ♦ ♦ ♦

——♦ Heroes with Human Faces ♦——

Those "heroes of the faith" recorded in the Bible seem larger than life—until we take a closer look. When we do, we find that they are fallible human beings just as we are. But these ordinary individuals accomplished great things through faith and submission to God.

In chapter one, we learned that our Lord does not expect perfection from us. Nor can we hope to achieve righteousness through our own powers, for to God "all our righteousnesses are like filthy rags" (Is. 64:6). Instead, in response to our simple faith, God confers righteousness upon us and has accepted us as His beloved children.

Like the heroes of old, we too can transcend our limitations through reliance on God's power, and obtain "a good testimony" (Heb. 11:2). Our Lord asks only that we trust and obey. He will do the rest.

♦ ♦ ♦ ♦ ♦ ♦ ♦ ♦ ♦ ♦

1. How has the knowledge that the "heroes of the faith" were ordinary people like yourself encouraged you to live a more heroic life for Christ?

2. How have you put to use in your own life the power of faith exhibited by the great men and women of the Bible?

—◆ The Troubled Path of the Prodigal ◆—

It all began with Adam and Eve in the garden. That fateful decision—a single fruit plucked from a forbidden tree—was a declaration of rebellion against God. In Adam we all fell, and that rebellious spirit is now part of our very nature. It is the root of sin and separation from God. And although Christ has set us free from enslavement to our sinful nature, like the prodigal son, we can choose to turn away from God to follow its direction.

In chapter 2, we saw the painful price believers pay in turning away from their God. Rebelliousness promises freedom but leads to enslavement to sin. We can avoid the temptation to rebel by not allowing selfish pride to take root in our hearts. An attitude of humility and submission before God will protect us from falling away and allow us to experience true freedom in living for God.

Yet even if we should turn from God, He will actively work to draw us back to Him. When we do return with penitent hearts, He will be waiting with open arms to graciously receive us. There is no limit to God's boundless forgiveness.

◆ ◆ ◆ ◆ ◆ ◆ ◆ ◆ ◆

1. How has a deeper understanding of the nature and cost of rebellion against God influenced you to root out rebellious tendencies in your own heart?

_____

_____

2. How has the knowledge that God is always willing to forgive you when you turn to Him in repentance given you greater security in your relationship with the Lord?

_____

_____

—◆ Keeping in Step with God ◆—

In chapter three, we explored the dangers of running ahead of God. When we try to take matters into our own hands, and fail to take care to remain in God's will, we court disaster.

God never rewards unethical means to achieve good ends. Like Jacob, we suffer needlessly when we resort to sin rather than rely on God. And like Abraham, we may stray from God's will when we fail to trust God to accomplish His ends in our lives. The impulsiveness of Peter and the spiritual pride of Josiah led both to act without seeking guidance from God.

One way we can make an effort to keep in step with our Lord is by careful examination of our motives before we take action. Are we responding to His will or our own? By developing an attitude of patience, and actively seeking His guidance, we will learn how to stay in His will and not stray from it.

◆ ◆ ◆ ◆ ◆ ◆ ◆ ◆ ◆

1. How have you gained a greater awareness of your need to seek God's guidance in your life through studying the lives of those who strayed from God's will?

_____

_____

2. As a consequence, what steps have you taken to "keep in step" with God?

_____

_____

◆ Encounters with the Living God ◆

Biblical history is the story of God revealing Himself to humankind. Several specially chosen individuals experienced dramatic encounters with God, with life-changing consequences. In many cases, these personal experiences with God awakened a new knowledge and vital faith in the recipients.

The longing to experience God exists in every human heart. Just as the ancients did, we too desire to know God in a personal way. And we can! In fact, modern Christians are blessed with many avenues for experiencing God's presence in our lives. Through prayer we commune with the Almighty. In His Word, we encounter God's direct communication with us. And as believers, God is never far from us, for He lives within our hearts. At special moments, He reaches out to fill us with the wonder of His presence.

In addition, we serve as living conduits for others to encounter God today. For His Spirit lives and works through our lives to accomplish God's ends. By reflecting God's love in our relationships with others, we draw others to relationship with the Lord we have come to know.

◆ ◆ ◆ ◆ ◆ ◆ ◆ ◆ ◆ ◆

1. Describe how you experience God's presence in your life:

_____

2. How have you sought to cultivate greater intimacy with the Lord?

_____

_____

3. How has your appreciation for the way in which God manifests Himself in your life grown?

_____

_____

───◆ The Healer's Transforming Touch ◆───

Chapter 5 explored God's power to transform minds and lives, vividly portrayed in the life stories of men and women in the Bible. Some changes came about suddenly, such as the transformation that Matthew underwent when he was saved, or the life change that Mary Magdalene experienced after her miraculous healing by God. In the spiritual growth of Paul and John Mark, we saw that change can take place gradually, even imperceptibly, as the Lord works within our hearts.

God's power is not limited to transforming the lives of individuals. In the Bible, we witness the amazing power of the gospel to transform the world and its relationships. The wall of hatred between Jews and Gentiles crumbled before the power of God's Word. The cultural divisions between the rich and poor and between men and women also underwent transformation as the gospel established a new spiritual equality for all before God.

His transforming touch extends to each of us. As believers, we have all been made "new creations" in Christ. And the believer's life is an unfolding process of transformation as God works within us. In the future, we can look forward to the ultimate transformation, as we are made perfect in every way.

1. How do you see God working to change you now?

_____

_____

2. What change in your character would you like the Lord to make, and how are you actively seeking to promote that change in yourself?

_____

───◆ The Darkness of Despair, the Light of Hope ◆───

We all know how discouraging life can be at times. Life's troubles, missed opportunities, and creeping doubts can lead to feelings of despair. People who lived in biblical times were no more immune to discouragement than we are. But they found resources to help them overcome discouragement in their lives.

What are these resources? Friends, family, fellow Christians and the church are among the sources of encouragement that we can turn to for an emotional lift. And when we struggle with despair, we can find comfort in the Lord.

In addition, we can prevent discouragement from taking hold by avoiding unrealistic expectations, trusting in God's forgiveness and restoration when we fall, and recognizing that our sovereign God is at work behind the scenes. Finally, the best weapon we possess against discouragement is the hope we have in the Lord, who loves us beyond measure. No matter how hopeless the situation appears, it isn't beyond God's power to remedy.

◆ ◆ ◆ ◆ ◆ ◆ ◆ ◆ ◆

1. What resources do you commonly turn to when discouraged?

_____

_____

2. Hope is a willing reliance on God's unfailing love, regardless of circumstances. Has your hope in God grown stronger or weaker in the last year? How has that effected your level of discouragement in trying circumstances?

_____

_____

──◆ Little People Who Made a Big Difference ◆──

Throughout history, the poor and lowly swelled the ranks of God's servants. Christ surrounded Himself with little people, those considered insignificant or undesirable by the cultural standards of His day. In the early church, Paul testified that there were "not many mighty" (1 Cor. 1:26).

Scripture reveals God's contempt for worldly standards of greatness. God's standards of significance are the opposite of the world's: greatness is found through serving others. For that reason, "God has chosen the weak things of the world to put to shame the things which are mighty" (1 Cor. 1:27).

Sometimes we are tempted to think we are too small and weak to make a difference for God. Biblical believers also struggled with feelings of inadequacy, such as Jeremiah, Moses, Timothy, and even Paul. They learned that it was not their strength and abilities that were needed, but God's strength.

By adopting the Lord's perspective, we will be able to see past the superficial features by which people evaluate others to the intrinsic value that all individuals possess in God's eyes. And when we turn our eyes on ourselves, we will not judge our importance based on our accomplishments, status, or possessions. We will see ourselves as servants of the Almighty and beloved children of God.

◆ ◆ ◆ ◆ ◆ ◆ ◆ ◆ ◆

1. How has your sense of significance changed through an understanding of God's perspective on greatness?

_____

_____

2. How has this changed your approach to achieving success?

_____

_____

◆ Making Our Footsteps Firm ◆

In chapter 8, we looked at fear—a significant stumbling block for many Christians in their walk with God. The Bible recounts many instances when fear hindered individuals in choosing to remain faithful to God. Yet many stood firm in their faith and overcame fear.

We will never be immune to fear, but we can defeat it. When fears grip us, we can find peace through reliance on God. There is no greater source of security than our Lord. He has given us the Holy Spirit as a source of strength when we are afraid. Finally, fear must be broken by something stronger than itself. Our commitment to God, though tested by fear, can remain steadfast if it is founded in an abiding love for the Lord.

It's important to remember that there is one kind of fear we should always surrender to—fear of the Lord! A healthy respect and reverence for the One whose power is supreme in the universe will help to put into perspective the lesser powers of this world. After all, when we have God on our side, what enemy need we fear?

◆ ◆ ◆ ◆ ◆ ◆ ◆ ◆ ◆

1. How has fear posed a challenge to your faith?

_____

_____

2. This chapter suggested that "fear of the Lord" should be at the top of your list of fears! How are you doing at putting fear of the Lord first?

_____

_____

◆ Those Who Found True Prosperity ◆

What is true prosperity? Scripture presents a view of prosperity radically different from the perspective adopted by the world in which we live. For the believer, wealth is not an end in itself, but both a blessing and responsibility.

Wealth also poses a threat for the Christian. A recognition that all we have is given to us by God, and that we are to manage it wisely, enables us to hold our wealth lightly.

Though the world prizes wealth and material possessions above all else, the successful figures of the Bible portray the nature of true prosperity. These individuals reveal that there are greater values than the value of a dollar. Like them, the believer needs to be prepared to choose responsibility to God before the drive to get ahead. Sometimes that may require risking our jobs when integrity demands it; other times it may mean surrendering money and status to more effectively serve God.

Ultimately, the goods of the world will pass away. Treasures that endure come from faithful service to our Lord.

◆ ◆ ◆ ◆ ◆ ◆ ◆ ◆ ◆

1. What does prosperity mean to you? Do you possess prosperity?

_____

_____

2. How are you taking Christ's advice to "lay up for yourselves treasures in heaven" (Matt. 6:20)?

_____

_____

◆ Temporary Hardships, Lasting Rewards ◆

From earliest times, suffering has been one of the chief challenges to faith. How do we make sense of suffering in our lives and in the world, and yet hold on to our belief in a powerful and loving God?

There are no easy answers, but believers in ancient times who confronted the problem of suffering show us that even in distress, we can hold firm to our trust in God with the full knowledge that our sufferings will come to an end, but our rewards will be everlasting.

In the meantime, we may never know exactly why we suffer. Yet there is purpose in our pain. Suffering has value in producing a Christlike character in us, and makes us more sensitive to the needs of others. In addition, suffering tests our faith and opens the way to deeper relationship with the Lord.

The Lord is not unaware of our suffering. He cares—enough to suffer pain and death Himself on our behalf. The pains we undergo today give us an opportunity to share Christ's sufferings, just as we will one day share His glory.

◆ ◆ ◆ ◆ ◆ ◆ ◆ ◆ ◆

1. How has a greater understanding of the purpose of suffering helped you to endure pain without bitterness toward God?

_____

_____

2. Christ suffered greatly for our sakes. How much are you willing to suffer for Christ?

_____

_____

◆ Ambassadors of God's Kingdom ◆

As believers, we are commanded to go forth into the world with the good news of Christ's saving sacrifice. In doing so, we soon learn that the world is not only indifferent but hostile to our message. In chapter 11, God's "ambassadors" showed us how we too can confront an unredeemed world for Christ and make a positive difference.

In living as ambassadors of God's kingdom, we may suffer persecution. Yet our duty to our King is to promote His purposes in the world, through care for those in need, confronting social injustice, and evangelism. We aren't alone in this task: we have the assistance of the Holy Spirit. Only the Spirit truly possesses the power to change hearts and minds.

Our witness to the world is centered in the unity that exists in the community of believers and the Christlike love that we extend to others. Such love is sacrificial. By exhibiting Christ's love in the world, we give testimony to the reality of Jesus Christ for all to see.

◆ ◆ ◆ ◆ ◆ ◆ ◆ ◆ ◆

1. How are you living as an ambassador of God's kingdom?

_____

_____

2. How have you committed yourself to show Christlike love to others?

_____

_____

◆ Spiritual Living in a Material World ◆

The gospel challenges us as believers to live spiritual lives, yet we continue to exist in a fallen world. The lives of believers in Bible times reveal both the difficulties of and solutions for living as citizens of the kingdom of God while remaining in a world that is flawed and chaotic.

To live a spiritual life means to be guided by spiritual values rather than controlled by material attitudes and desires. When we put our relationship with the Lord at the center of our lives, Christ's values will be evident in all that we do. For this reason, no matter what position in life we find ourselves, we can experience the rewards of spiritual living.

How do we resist falling prey to worldly concerns? By keeping in mind the transitory nature of this world, we can avoid the tendency to cling to the things of the world. In addition, we can promote spiritual living through careful attention to our priorities in life and by cultivating closeness with the Lord through prayer.

◆ ◆ ◆ ◆ ◆ ◆ ◆ ◆ ◆

1. What "things on the earth" (Col. 3:2) still threaten to draw you away from God?

_____

_____

2. Since becoming a Christian, how have you progressed toward living a spiritual life?

_____

_____

——◆ Living By Example ◆——

We've learned so much by looking at the real-life experiences of the men and women of Bible times! And we share so much in common with them as well.

Now the challenge is to put into practice all we have learned from them—to follow in their footsteps, and "run with endurance the race that is set before us" (Heb. 12:1)! By following their examples, we too can live victorious lives in Christ.

And when we reach our final destination, they will be waiting for us at the finish line. Are you ready? Get set! Go!

LEADER'S GUIDE TO REAL LIFE, REAL PEOPLE

This workbook has been prepared primarily for individual study. Nevertheless, it lends itself to group study and discussion. Each member of a group should have a workbook and complete each chapter in preparation for a group meeting.

Forming and Leading a Study Group

1. There are many settings for study and sharing our faith—Sunday school, a small group in the home, a few co-workers meeting over lunch. All that's really required is a desire to grow in our faith, and to support and be supported as we each seek to go on with Christ.

2. Group sizes differ. The smallest, and often most significant group, has just two or three people. Usually ten or twelve people is as large as this kind of group should grow. Many think about eight is ideal.

3. Everyone should make preparations for group meetings. This means reading thoughtfully through a chapter or section of a chapter you agree on beforehand, and filling in the blanks honestly. It's not necessary to share everything you write down when the group meets. But do be ready to share whatever you feel free to communicate.

4. The leader in a sharing and study group is not the "answer person." Instead the leader encourages sharing, sets the tone by his or her own sharing, and takes the lead in expressing appreciation for what each person contributes.

5. When the group meets one or two may pray, and then move to sharing what God has been saying to each one through the Scriptures and this workbook. The group study plans are intended to help your group begin exploring issues raised in each chapter, and are purposefully "open." The Holy Spirit will lead each study group into specific issues.

Chapter 1: Heroes with Human Faces

Life is full of difficult choices. And as fallible human beings, we're often faced with the need to make painful decisions. Men and women whose experiences are recorded in Scripture give us insights that help when we face hard choices today. Mary, the mother of Jesus, displays the importance of a simple, obedient faith. Abraham reminds us that God knows the future and has our best interests at heart. David, Israel's greatest king, reminds us that faith provides the courage we need to dare great things.

The fact is that Scripture is filled with stories of men and women who were enabled by faith to meet life's challenges successfully—and triumphantly. Like us, they were ordinary people. What made the difference in their lives was a firm faith in God. The very thing that can make us heroes, too!

Lesson Objectives

1. To review how difficult choices and tough decisions can test your faith.
2. To learn to rely on the Lord's strength to accomplish great things.
3. To assure us that God knows the future.

Launching Activity

Go around the group and share one "heroic" thing you did as a child.

Discuss

1. Whose kind of faith do you need most for a challenge you face in your life right now? Mary's? Abraham's? David's?
2. How has your faith changed your approach to difficult decisions in the past?
3. What is there about the results of Mary's, Abraham's, or David's faith that gives you courage to do the right thing today?

Prayer

Praise God for being the kind of Person you can trust completely, mentioning at least one specific quality of His that gives you confidence.

Chapter 2: The Troubled Path of the Prodigal

The Bible traces the troubled path of God's people as they frequently rebelled against Him. It also records stories of individuals who turned away from God. Through it all, God's grace shines clear, as He continues to love and express willingness to restore these people.

Hosea's experience with his unfaithful wife reminds us how deeply our own unfaithfulness hurts the Lord. The experience of Lot and his wife warn us against the dangers of wanting worldly wealth and prestige. Jonah's story underlines the fact that even though we fight against God, He will accomplish His purposes—and give us a second chance to have our part in fulfilling His plan. Perhaps most wonderfully, the familiar story of the prodigal son portrays God's eagerness that we return to Him, and His delight when we do.

Lesson Objectives

1. To show that God brings judgment on those who repeatedly turn from Him.
2. To examine modern-day idolatries as they affect our spiritual growth.
3. To reassure us of God's promise of restoration and return to His enfolding care.

Launching Activity

Tell about a time when you ran away as a child and how your parents reacted.

Discuss

1. How many different words can we come up with that describe how God might feel about those who rebel or turn away from Him?
From the passages studied, which of these words accurately describe His feelings?
2. How might the story of Jonah help a person who feels he or she can't be used by God because of some past, terrible sin?
3. If we were to map the prodigal son's spiritual journey, what would the major turning points be? Right now, where are you along the prodigal's road?

Prayer

Ask God to help each of you to see Him as the welcoming Father, so that you will never hesitate to turn to Him after you have sinned.

Chapter 3: Keeping in Step with God

Waiting is never easy. Especially when we feel pressured to make a decision. Some argue that we figure out what the loving thing to do is—and simply do it. But is it safe or right to act without a sense of acting in God's will? Abraham couldn't wait for God to keep His promise of a son, and the result is the Arab/Israeli hostility that even today tears the Holy Land apart. Jacob chose to lie to obtain a blessing already promised him, and spent years separated from his family. The impetuous Peter was often rebuked by the Lord for his hasty actions. Even godly people like Peter and King Josiah can and do run ahead of God. How important that we learn to rely on the Lord, and wait prayerfully and confidently for His time.

Lesson Objectives

1. To compare choices of right or wrong from both ethical and moral models.
2. To examine how our manipulation of events can distract from God's promise to us.
3. To emphasize the need to have a life plan that corresponds to God's plan.

Launching Activity

Describe one decision you made too hastily, and regretted later.

Discuss

1. Why is it hard to wait for God's timing? What is the hardest thing you are waiting for right now?
2. Which person are you most like: Jacob and Rebekah, who used wrong means to achieve God's purpose? Abraham and Sarah, who tried to achieve God's purpose in their own

strength? Peter, who often acted impulsively? Josiah, whose spiritual pride caused him to fall out of step with God.

3. Did any one verse of Scripture mentioned in this chapter stand out as especially meaningful to you? Which one, and why?

Prayer

Thank God for His wisdom not only in planning good for you, but in knowing just when and how to bring that good to pass.

Chapter 4: Encounters with the Living God

No one can understand the true nature of Christian faith without understanding it as the divinely revealed pathway to personal encounter and restored relationship with God. Doctrinal beliefs are important. But personal relationship with God is central.

Job felt the need for a personal encounter with the Lord as he was plunged into intense suffering. A woman with a chronic hemorrhage struggled through the press of a crowd to merely touch Jesus' clothing, hoping for healing. When we feel as these two must have, it's good to remember that God has revealed Himself to us in Scripture. We aren't likely to hear His spoken word or touch Him physically today, but we can know Him intimately as we explore His revelation of His character, His values, His plans, and His matchless love for us in Jesus.

Lesson Objectives

1. *To examine personal encounters of biblical persons with God.*
2. *To show how God encounters us when we are in need.*
3. *To learn how to witness to Christians and unbelievers.*

Launching Activity

When did you first experience God in a personal, intimate way?

Discuss

1. Did you have a need like that of Job or the woman with the hemorrhage that made you seek a personal relationship with God?
2. What person was most instrumental in helping you come to know God personally? What about that person seems "Christlike" to you?
3. Can you share one Bible passage that gives you a sense of who God is and has shaped your sense of relationship with Him?

Prayer

Praise God for seeking a personal relationship with human beings, and for taking every step necessary for us to encounter Him.

Chapter 5: The Healer's Transforming Touch

The New Testament is rich in stories of Christ's ability to heal physical diseases and deformities. Often overlooked is an even more significant exercise of His power: the power to transform individuals and correct our spiritual deformity. We see it in Scripture in the transformation of money-driven outcasts, Matthew and Zacchaeus, the tax collectors. We see it in the transformation of the demon-possessed Mary of Magdala. We see the same kind of transforming power at work in society as Christ affirms the significance of women as persons with a worth and value unrecognized in that era. We see Christ's transforming power in the breaking down of the ethnic and social barriers that separated races and classes, bonding all together as brothers and sisters in His body, the Church. Even a person so set in his ways as Saul was transformed to become the apostle Paul. Transformation typically does not happen overnight. But God invites us to go with Him on a lifelong journey—a journey which we know brings us, and His Church, closer and closer to Christlikeness.

Lesson Objectives

1. *To review the transforming power of Christ in today's society.*
2. *To confirm our task to go and tell the "Good News" of the resurrection.*
3. *To remind us of God's inclusion of all persons, not just the Jews.*

Launching Activity

Share one way in which you are different now than when you first became a Christian. How quickly or slowly did the change come?

Discuss

1. How do we explain the transformation of Levi [Matthew] and Zacchaeus, and the failure of the Pharisees to be transformed by Christ?
2. What kinds of transformation does Jesus seek to effect in individuals and the Church? For instance, Zacchaeus was transformed FROM selfishness TO generosity, FROM dishonesty TO honesty. What are other FROM/TO transformations highlighted in the Bible?
3. Are you satisfied with the pace of transformation in your own life? What FROM/TO changes do you believe God wants to work in your life?

Prayer

Praise God for Jesus' power to transform, and express your own commitment to open your heart to His transforming work.

Chapter 6: The Darkness of Despair, the Light of Hope

Our faith doesn't insulate us from times of despair. That's something many Christians don't seem to understand. So many of us hide our real feelings, fearful of what others will think, and ashamed of what we ourselves may see as spiritual weakness. Yet even King David cried, "Why are you cast down, O my soul? And why are you disquieted within me?" (Ps. 42:5).

When we are disquieted, we can look to God as David did for the gift of hope. Eunice, the mother of Timothy, had a less than ideal marriage. Yet she shared her faith with her son, and saw him grow to become a leader in Christ's Church. Peter was crushed by awareness of his own weakness. Yet Christ's gift of forgiveness restored both his position as chief of the apostles and his hope. Paul constantly experienced hostility in his ministries. Yet again and again, God acted to protect him and to build the church. Through all this, the indomitable apostle remained committed to His mission, and found encouragement in news that His converts remained committed to the Lord. However discouraged we may become, we need to remember that God is in charge, and hope confidently for Him to bring good out of the circumstances that otherwise would breed despair.

Lesson Objectives

1. *To learn ways of getting beyond discouragement.*
2. *To develop realistic expectations for our lives.*
3. *To show that forgiveness is available whenever we fall from grace.*

Launching Activity

Share how you normally handle times of depression or despair?

Discuss

1. Who do you think had the most reason to be discouraged?
  - a. Eunice, in an unhappy marriage?
  - b. Peter, who failed God and himself?
  - c. Paul, who experienced constant opposition?

2. What gave each of these three Bible persons hope?
 What do you think would give you hope and bring you out of despair?
3. How important is encouragement from other persons when you feel discouraged?
 Who are the people to whom you feel most free to share your "down" times?
 How do they help you?

Prayer

Pray that your group might learn to encourage one another.

Chapter 7: Little People Who Made a Big Difference

Very few of us are "significant" in the world's sense. Some of us may even feel insignificant within our own families. Isn't it great that we're each significant in God's family! And what's more, that each of us can become great!

In God's value system greatness is rooted in service. And we are equipped by God to serve. Jeremiah felt inadequate when called to become a prophet. Yet we see him now as an Old Testament giant. Moses was deeply aware of his inadequacies when God called him to deliver Israel from Egypt. Their greatness grew out of their response to God's call.

It's the same for us today. Whatever work we do, whatever relationships we have, if we see them as opportunities to serve God and do the best we can, our lives and work will truly be significant in His eyes.

Lesson Objectives

1. To confirm that we are very important in God's sight.
2. To realize that God chooses and prepares us to fulfill His mission today.
3. To show that our importance to God is not based upon our occupation.

Launching Activity

Who that you know sees you as a "somebody?" Why does that person see you as important to him or her?

Discuss

1. What criteria does the world use to determine whether or not a person is important? List, then evaluate. Which have some validity?
2. Which of these three Bible personalities teaches us the most about being a significant person: Jeremiah, Moses, or Mary? What does this person's life teach?
3. What steps do you intend to take this coming week to act as one of God's "great ones"? How will what you plan to do glorify God?

Prayer

Praise God that He permits us to serve Him and others, and that He equips us with all we need to do so.

Chapter 8: Making Our Footsteps Firm

Fear poses a threat to every Christian. Believers today need not fear losing their lives or homes if they take a stand for Christ. Yet the fear of ridicule, fear of what others might think, does drain the resolve of far too many believers. The threat fear poses is nothing new. Peter knew it when he denied Christ three times the night before His crucifixion. But later a transforming experience with Jesus gave Peter the courage to speak out boldly for His Lord. Christ, who stilled a storm on the Sea of Galilee, can quiet our hearts, and remind us that He Himself is our security.

In a very real sense the issue we face is: Which "fear" will dominate in our lives? The fear of others? Or fear of the Lord—a fear which has no hint of terror but rather exists as an awed awareness that Christ is real, and in charge of every circumstance of our lives? When we maintain this fear, as did God's messenger to Saul, Ananias, we will have the courage we need to obey God, and overcome all lesser fears.

Lesson Objectives

1. *To look at fear as it impacts our daily decisions.*
2. *To explore the consequences of being a disciple of Christ.*
3. *To learn to rely on God's power for our inner peace.*

Launching Activity

Looking back, what fears have hindered you as you've tried to follow Christ?

Discuss

1. How do true stories like that of the Peruvian pastor encourage us to follow Christ more faithfully? Do you have a story to tell that might encourage others in your group?
2. What resurrection resources that changed Peter's life have made a difference in your life, giving you more courage to obey?
3. What lessons can we apply from the Acts 9:10–18 story of Ananias, who feared going to see Saul, but subsequently obeyed God?

Prayer

Meditate silently on Christ's stilling of the storm on the Sea of Galilee. Visualize Him with you as He was with the disciples. Then thank Christ for His presence and His control of the circumstance when we feel fearful.

Chapter 9: Those Who Found True Prosperity

Christian faith often contributes to material success. At the same time, there may well be conflicts between our spiritual commitments and economic goals. For instance, some occupations seem to be in direct conflict with Christian values. At other times an employer may ask us to do things that violate our convictions. Advertisers may create desires for possessions that we might not otherwise experience.

In view of such conflicts, it's important that we develop a biblical view of wealth and prosperity, and of Christian values that will guide us in resolving inner conflicts. Barnabas, whose sensitivity to others is a model of generosity, exemplifies one basic Christian value. Joseph, who worked faithfully even when his efforts were not appreciated, models an attitude toward work that we should nurture apart from consideration of financial rewards. And Jesus' story of the talents reminds us that using the gifts God has given us is of greater value than any material rewards.

Lesson Objectives

1. *To review how we can deal with conflicts between our spiritual commitments and economic goals.*
2. *To emphasize that the gifts God gives us are of greater value than our material wealth.*
3. *To encourage believers who are feeling pressure to work in occupations that are against their beliefs.*

Launching Activities

Take the quiz at the beginning of chapter nine. If group members have different answers to any questions, discuss to discover why.

Discuss

1. What impact has your Christian commitment had on your economic situation? Do you think that being a Christian has made you better off or worse off financially? Why?
2. Have you ever been pressured at work to do something that would violate your Christian commitment? What happened? How did you resolve the conflict?
3. What biblical principles explored in this chapter did you find most significant for developing your own attitude toward money and wealth?

Praise God for His commitment to supply all our needs according to His riches in glory.

Chapter 10: Temporary Hardships, Lasting Rewards

We've touched on it before. Now we take a more personal look at suffering. Like Virginia, featured in this chapter, each of us will face suffering and disappointment. The issue is not whether we will have to suffer, but how we will respond when suffering comes.

Suffering may shake our trust in God—or lead to a deeper faith. Despite Job's many torments, and the insensitivity of his friends, the experience ultimately brought Job closer to the Lord. He did not learn the "why" of his suffering. Instead Job learned to trust God completely.

The New Testament does reveal a number of ways in which God uses suffering in our lives, and it gives us insights into the deeper spiritual meaning of suffering as well. Whatever happens, we learn through Christ's sufferings that God does bring good from pain and are encouraged to trust that He will use our pain in a redemptive, loving way.

Lesson Objectives

1. *To explore how God can allow pain and suffering into the lives of believers.*
2. *To learn how to find purpose in our lives when nothing seems to go right.*
3. *To explore how believers can comfort their friends who are suffering.*

Launching Activity

What have you learned through times that you have suffered? What do you think you might have learned if you had approached suffering with greater trust?

Discuss

1. Do you think that ultimately Job benefited from his suffering or was harmed by it?
2. Share your answers from the section on "The Positive Side of Pain" and from the sections following. What new insights did you gain from the passages studied?
3. Do you agree or disagree with this statement: "If Christ suffered, why should we expect to live without pain?" Why?

Prayer

Praise God that Christ was willing to suffer for us, and that even now He suffers with us when we are in pain.

Chapter 11: Ambassadors of God's Kingdom

Though the temptation is strong to withdraw from the unbelieving world into exclusive Christian communities, that is not how Christ lived, nor what He intended for us. Rather, we have been commissioned by the Lord to "go into all the world and preach the gospel" (Mark 16:15).

The apostles did just that. Against much opposition, individuals like Paul and Peter spread the good news throughout Palestine, and out into the Roman world. Nor was the work of spreading the Word limited to the apostles of God. As a citizen of God's Kingdom on earth, every believer is responsible to be a worker for God. This responsibility will require certain sacrifices, and may at times lead to persecution. Yet God has equipped each believer for service in the world, and additionally provides powerful aid in accomplishing our duties through the working of the Holy Spirit. Consequently, believers are really coworkers with God.

Not only is every believer enlisted as witnesses for the Lord, the Church as a whole is a witness to the reality of Christ in an unbelieving world. The love and unity modeled by the believing community strongly testifies to the Lordship of Christ in the lives of His followers. Christlike love should characterize not only the relationships among Christians, but also the believer's relationships with the unsaved.

Christ's love for us was such that He gave His own life that we might be saved. Our lives are to be a reflection of His love, so that others may likewise be moved to commit their lives to the Lord and gain salvation in Christ.

Lesson Objectives

1. *To explore ways Christians can be "in the world" but not "of the world."*
2. *To encourage believers to witness in an unfriendly world.*
3. *To learn ways in which Christian love can be experienced in daily life.*

Launching Activity

Share a witnessing experience in which you were involved. Consider the different forms witnessing took in the group members' stories.

Discuss

1. How has the growing tendency to regard personal faith as a private matter impacted the witness of present-day Christians?
2. What about speaking about your faith makes you feel uncomfortable? What circumstances for witnessing do you feel most comfortable with?
3. How is the modern church an effective witness for Christ? How is it less than effective?
4. What are instances of sacrificial love that you have been the recipient of? What is an occasion that you have shown Christlike love to another?

Prayer

Praise God for the love that He has shown you through Christ's saving sacrifice. Pray that He will give you the wisdom, courage, and opportunity to be an effective witness of His love in your life.

Chapter 12: Spiritual Living in a Material World

Salvation isn't the conclusion of the Christian experience; it is the beginning of a new life characterized by spirituality rather than the earthly attitudes and concerns. As we live our lives in a fallen world, we are constantly challenged to live by spiritual values rather than falling back into a futile lifestyle patterned by the world.

Peter knew the challenge of spiritual living—his early behavior as a follower of Christ was often less than spiritual! He also saw the threat that worldliness posed for the early church, and counseled believers to remember that the world and its hollow values were passing away. Similarly, Paul advised converts to set priorities in their lives that would encourage spiritual living. A life conducive to spirituality is characterized by productive work, freedom from unnecessary distractions, and peaceful relations with others in our community. This will establish a firm foundation for living according to godly values.

Cultivating a close relationship with the Lord through a vital prayer life is key to overcoming the pull of earthly desires. As we walk closely with the Lord, our lives will blossom with the fruit of spiritual living: kindness, humility, meekness, longsuffering, forgiveness, and above all, love. And these qualities will be reflected in all we do.

Lesson Objectives

1. *To discover how to live a spiritual life seven days a week.*
2. *To recognize when we are reverting to our worldly values.*
3. *To develop a strong prayer life that will give us the fruits of the Spirit.*

Launching Activity

What does it mean to you to live a spiritual life? How does the world undermine our efforts to live by spiritual values?

Discuss

1. How do Paul's guidelines for our personal priorities encourage spiritual living? Are you living in tune with these priorities? If not, why not?
2. Do you find your work spiritually rewarding? What spiritual values are you expressing through your work?
3. How have you cultivated a close relationship with the Lord? How has this "hidden" relationship fostered spiritual values in your life?

Prayer

Thank the Lord for the perfect world He has prepared for you in eternity. Ask for His aid in living a life in harmony with the glory that will one day be yours.

Chapter 13: So Great a Cloud of Witnesses

This last chapter is intended to be a review of what members of the group study have learned as they've explored the lives of biblical men and women. The chapter also allows participants an opportunity to examine how to incorporate into their own lives the life lessons portrayed in Scripture.

It may be difficult to get through the entire review chapter in one group session. As a consequence, you may decide to break the chapter into two group studies, the first a review of chapters 1–6 and the second for chapters 7–12. Alternatively, to save time, you might wish to use only one or two questions from each chapter section for group discussion.

As you progress through the chapter reviews, encourage group members to reflect on which Bible persons have special relevance for them, and share with the group whose life experiences they identify with the most. Their lives are enduring examples for us to learn from and to live by.